The Post-War Experimental Novel

The Post-War Experimental Novel

British and French Fiction, 1945–75

Andrew Hodgson

BLOOMSBURY ACADEMIC
LONDON • NEW YORK • OXFORD • NEW DELHI • SYDNEY

BLOOMSBURY ACADEMIC
Bloomsbury Publishing Plc
50 Bedford Square, London, WC1B 3DP, UK
1385 Broadway, New York, NY 10018, USA
29 Earlsfort Terrace, Dublin 2, Ireland

BLOOMSBURY, BLOOMSBURY ACADEMIC and the Diana logo are trademarks of
Bloomsbury Publishing Plc

First published in Great Britain 2020
Paperback edition published 2021

Copyright © Andrew Hodgson, 2020

Andrew Hodgson has asserted his right under the Copyright,
Designs and Patents Act, 1988, to be identified as Author of this work.

Cover design: Eleanor Rose
Cover image © Getty Images

All rights reserved. No part of this publication may be reproduced or transmitted in any form or by any means, electronic or mechanical, including photocopying, recording, or any information storage or retrieval system, without prior permission in writing from the publishers.

Bloomsbury Publishing Plc does not have any control over, or responsibility for, any third-party websites referred to or in this book. All internet addresses given in this book were correct at the time of going to press. The author and publisher regret any inconvenience caused if addresses have changed or sites have ceased to exist, but can accept no responsibility for any such changes.

A catalogue record for this book is available from the British Library.

Library of Congress Cataloging-in-Publication Data
Names: Hodgson, Andrew, author.
Title: The Post-War Experimental Novel : British and French Fiction,
1945–1975 / Andrew Hodgson.
Description: London, UK ; New York, NY : Bloomsbury Academic, 2020. |
Includes bibliographical references.
Identifiers: LCCN 2019010098 | ISBN 9781350076846 (hb) |
ISBN 9781350076860 (epub) | ISBN 9781350076853 (epdf)
Subjects: LCSH: Experimental fiction, English—20th century—History and criticism. |
Experimental fiction, French—20th century—History and criticism.
Classification: LCC PR888.E982 H63 2020 | DDC 823/.91409—dc23
LC record available at https://lccn.loc.gov/2019010098

ISBN: HB: 978-1-3500-7684-6
PB: 978-1-3502-2623-4
ePDF: 978-1-3500-7685-3
eBook: 978-1-3500-7686-0

Typeset by RefineCatch Limited, Bungay, Suffolk

To find out more about our authors and books visit www.bloomsbury.com
and sign up for our newsletters.

For Alan Robert Hodgson

Contents

Preface	ix
Partition One – Motive: The Sense Something is Missing	1
1.1 A critical moment – opening a space of discourse	1
Critical climate – historic	1
A wound in cultural history	5
Critical climate – current	8
Attempting to access a point in the past as a synchronic, 'lived-in' space	11
1.2 On the literature of this study	14
Nationality, experience and social relation	14
On the post-war experimental novel as an 'avant-garde realism'	18
Social engagement and the experimental novel	21
To plot this further in the post-war	26
1.3 Conflicts in cultural production	30
Contemporaneous cultural climate	30
Dominant literature as societal 'normalizer'	34
'Reactionary' Vrance	38
Case in point	41
The predicament of cultural refusal	43
1.4 Historical contexts	46
Writing out of the 1945 event	46
The new 'new'	53
1968 as performative re-adhesion	54
The old new veneer	59
Era as here presented	61
Partition Two – Diagnoses: The Confused Narrative of the Post-War Human	65
2.1 The sense something is missing	65

	A mimesis of violent stupefaction	66
	Impossible confrontations	74
	The act of forgetting	79
	Sorge and the continuity human	84
	Cycling violence	89
2.2	Communal supplication, individual terraforming	98
	Depictions of communal, quotidian life	99
	Characterization of an immersive object space	99
	The peripherals assert themselves	105
	The representative unstable self	116
	To follow the thread of an insane norm	120

Partition Three – Treatment: Breaking Down Within the Horizon of the Real — 125

3.1	Creating space in text	125
	Za – Um	127
	Ergodic engagement	130
	Spatial multiplicity	133
	Open signifiers	135
3.2	Babel, babble, xenoglossia and private language	138
	Glossolalia	139
	Écrits bruts and the experimental novel	141
	Qonestsans	143
	Language as structural reality referent	147
	Slang, idiom, argotique	149
	Synchronicities in the published/unpublished work	151
3.3	Cut, shuffle, re-align, re-define	154
	No lie junk	155
	Liberating the page	157
	Hysterical mimesis	160
	The response-ible reader	162
	Shuffle	163

Notes	173
Index	205

Preface

The study that follows constitutes an attempt to re-read the experimental novel of post-Second World War Britain and France as a critical socio-cultural entity; in doing so it raises a corpus of (what is generally termed) 'innovative writing' buried from current narratives of literary history. Since its period of emergence, the experimental novel has undergone an imposed process of occultation; its artefacts rejected and maligned, appropriated and marginalized. As traditionally omitted or fringed cultural artefacts, they therefore offer a critical window into the societal conditions of their generation and initial reception that too is occulted by this process. And as such, these are novel-objects that, when re-included in cultural discourse, fundamentally recast established coding and cognition of spaces from which they have been largely severed: 'Literature', 'the avant-garde', societal relation; culture itself.

Researched and written between 2012 and 2015, subsequently edited in 2018, the project of reading the experimental novel as an entity integrally engaged in these spheres took on a sense of attempting to square the circle. The perspectives raised within the experimental novel, and established dominant coding of these fields did not, do not easily align; neither in agreement nor opposition. If this dissonance between critical structure and literary object, as will be seen, has been taken by some to demonstrate that the experimental novel does not belong, as it were, in these fields, I have regarded the glitching effect created by drawing the two together as a short-circuiting that demonstrates it does. However, if this short-circuiting has traditionally been perceived to glitch the literary artefact, to *de-literature* the experimental novel, it is more my understanding that it is dominant cultural and critical structure that appears *de-structured* in this confrontation. It is this understanding that it is not the circle that has to be squared that forms my base of approach to the matter of this study; to the topographical interrogative observation of the post-war experimental novel and its interactions with these fields that I herein carry out.

It is in this sense of confrontations, and destabilizations we appear to find the experimental novel's socio-functionality. As cultural artefacts of reflexive (reflex/bonded reflection) societal critique they appear designed to carry out such a short-circuiting process as a mode of critical engagement. As perhaps seen in the three progressions of social praxis the structure of this book follows, and that were ascribed as internal processes to the experimental novel itself by Émile Zola when first conceptualizing such an entity in *Le Roman expérimental* (1880). Progressions which he directly lifted from Claude Bernard's treatise on experimental medicine, *Introduction à l'étude de la médecine expérimentale* (1865) (hence the medical terms and terminology that follows): (1) the perception of a social sickness, (2) the diagnosis of a social sickness, (3) the treatment of a social sickness.[1] As such, this book cycles through three partitions: (1) 'Motive: the sense something is missing', in which the issues of living experience of the Second World War and the processes of social normalization in its aftermath are observed. (2) 'Diagnoses: the confused narrative of the post-war human', in which impossibilities in human recall and perception are met, and followed to portrayals of human-in-society as read through depictions of human-in-text-space; protagonist-in-milieu. (3) 'Treatment: breaking down within the horizon of the real', in which radical treatment of language and textual form in the experimental novel is read as an attempted answer to the problematics observed in the previous two partitions. Here, a critical image is evoked of the experimental novel depicting socio-cultural delusion and amnesia – it, and its contents, being equally locked in this collective 'sickness' – paired with radical attempts to meet these human and societal dysfunctions, maybe even in some sense, escape them. And as such, my critical project here perhaps mimes that of the experimental novel to some degree. In forming a space by which its mechanics and interactions might be more clearly observed, that space itself takes on something of which it is designed to 'contain'.[2] A project perhaps most succinctly put by Conroy Maddox:

> I seek only the gestures of a lonely ruthless quest.
> To resurrect if only for a day the marvellous
> dressed corpse of my desire.

Larvae, moths, necrophors.
To perpetuate the cemetery, to plaster you with sea-weed,
To open up a gap and produce a breakdown.[3]

I begin.

ARH
Paris, 2012–15; 2018

PARTITION ONE

Motive: The Sense Something is Missing

1.1 A critical moment – opening a space of discourse

To attempt to critically approach the experimental novel that emerged in post-war Britain and France is to meet with a series of obstacles and blockages. Cultural screens that occlude and warp clear observation and cognition of both the texts that describe such a presence in literature, and the historical conditions in which this presence was generated and initially received. Screens that have for decades interceded between the critic and reader who might attempt to engage with the experimental novel of the era, and the texts and writers that would people such an entity. This first partition negotiates this series of occlusions, and in doing so aims to arrive at a clearer view of what the experimental novel of that time potentially was, what it was potentially attempting to do and how it was attempting to do it. This might in turn contribute towards a clearer understanding of the post-war as a spatio-temporal paradigm in literature, culture and societal experience.

Critical climate – historic

The first of these occluding screens is the historic treatment of these texts, and their moment of appearance, in critique itself. The period following the Second World War, a post-war era that can be roughly delimited as spanning the years 1945–75 for the contexts of this study, inhabits a space of dysfunction in Anglo-American critical coding of modern literary history. In dominant critical practice it has for decades been treated as a field of intermediaries, a space populated by figures and texts of aesthetic break, pivot or transition; entities to be selected and deselected; appropriated and omitted to fit the shifting -ism designations that underpin established understandings of the 'literary modern'.[1] It is a space where critics plot the historical continuity and discontinuity, aesthetic opposition and collapse of a vast binary system: 'modernism', and its apparent later reflex, '*post*modernism'. As such, the post-war era appears the 'liminal ground' where these two entities fitfully fail to align; a 'no-man's-land' of dates,[2] events, figures and texts claimed and refused, and with which two trenches are dug and re-dug.

The dysfunction of the modernism-postmodernism construct has been addressed before and, as endnotes here suggest, in studies dedicated to revealing its wider effects far beyond the scope of our own. And so, for our purposes and for point of illustration, I shall give a clipped rendition of its historicizing (mal)praxis in motion. According to Brian W. Shaffer, modernism 'persisted until 1945'.[3] This would perhaps neatly suit the parameters of this study; as an 'innovative' presence in literature, we might claim the experimental novel simply picks up where that earlier 'innovative' entity left off, on a linear timeline of *the* modern literary tradition. However, 'Faulkner pegs the dates of modernism in England at 1910–1930',[4] pushing the slide-rule back and producing a temporal liminality that would problematize any sense of generational continuity we might draw. These 'bookends of 1910 and 1930 [...] are widened in other versions to anywhere between 1880 and 1950',[5] and indeed far beyond the borders of England. 'Some critics would give priority to the pre-war years, others to the post-war period; some again favour one year, 1922, as the "*annus mirabilis*."'[6] For Fredric Jameson, modernism as a specific 'cultural movement and moment has been retrospective since the 1950s'.[7] Writing in 1968, Frank Kermode states, 'everybody knows what is meant by modern literature, modern art, modern music. The words suggest [...] the experiments of two or more generations back.'[8] Kermode assumedly indicating writers of the 1920s, *at latest*, as the subject matter for his classification.[9] And yet, for Brian McHale, modernism not only continued to the 1950s, but the writing of Alain Robbe-Grillet and Samuel Beckett in that decade represents a point of 'transition' from an 'epistemological modernism', to an 'ontological postmodernism'.[10] As for this second sorting structure, counter to McHale, Arnold Toynbee 'detected its [postmodernism] beginning in the 1870s', and 'Charles Jencks [wrote of it] as beginning on 15 July 1972 at 3:32 pm'.[11] David Harvey similarly notes 'a sea-change in cultural as well as in political-economic practices since around 1972',[12] and though he says 'I cannot remember exactly when I first encountered the term postmodernism,[13] Harvey opts to peg 'a historical marker' in 1974.[14] This, he argues, is when an old 'Baudelairean' universalizing modernism 'conjoining of the ephemeral and the fleeting with the eternal and the immutable',[15] shifted to a postmodernism of 'fragmentation, indeterminacy, and intense distrust of all universal or "totalising" discourses'.[16] Attempting to bring clarity to these vague assignations of observable difference between modernism and postmodernism, Ihab Hassan detailed a table of his own contrasting principles of the two in 1985:

Modernism	Postmodernism
Romanticism/Symbolism	Pataphysics/Dadaism
Form (conjunctive, closed)	Antiform (disjunctive, open)
Purpose	Play
Design	Chance
Hierarchy	Anarchy...[17]

This gives image to the wider positions of opposition, break and transition raised above; the very postures adopted to classify a modernism and a postmodernism demonstrate a 'binary analysis which a poststructuralist postmodernism should have made obsolete'.[18] In attempting to clarify, quantify; to define the modernism-postmodernism paradigm, its discourse relies on the exact binary oppositional structures the emergence of modernism and postmodernism in the (nineteenth and/or) twentieth century had, they argue, progressively, and/or ultimately, 'freed' culture, literature from. Considering the totalizing oppositions constructed in their name, these classifications would seem somewhat self-defeating in this respect, and counter to what Kermode states, it would appear nobody is particularly sure what is meant by either.

As can perhaps be here observed, the search for transition, 'break or opposition between "modernism" and "postmodernism"' appears a largely arbitrary critical project, and further, is 'a somewhat parochial topic in Anglo-American culture'.[19] As will become apparent in this study, in France, as indeed in the wider non-anglophone world, this compulsive search for abstracted dialectical opposition and reconciliation in twentieth-century literary history has not occurred to this extent of apparent dysfunction. As Gérard Genette describes postmodernism for a French audience in *Palimpsestes* in 1982, with reference to John Barth's *The Literature of Replenishment* (1980): 'the pertinence of this concept is not particularly clear, and the frontier that Barth tries to trace between the modern and postmodern literatures seems very fragile'.[20] This would appear to be a fair description of the wider sorting process. A fragile sorting and re-sorting that is now widely regarded itself a discontinued critical project: according to Harvey postmodernism, and with it this reflexive binary system, was pronounced to have ended in 1990.[21] Yet its centrality to our understandings of what modern literature is, and how that entity interacts with wider cultural, societal and historical conditions has had profound effect both within and beyond 'Anglo-American culture': our conceptions of a literary history of the modern epoch still appear dominated by the interactions of these two highly selective definitional presences. As Jago Morrison writes as late as 2003, 'for several decades after the end of the Second World War, the novel appeared to be dead. As a vehicle for literary experimentation [...] book fiction could not hope to survive', until a miraculous Lazarus-like revival in a 'postmodernist' 1980s.[22] On this understanding, it would appear that between James Joyce (1882–1941) and Barth's frontiersmanship with *The Literature of Replenishment*, the novel as an artistic genre had ceased to be. The canonized flashpoints of modernism and postmodernism passed back and forth continue to occlude the wider body of epochal modern literature omitted by that process, beyond that process's end.

With the apparent exception of the fetish of Robbe-Grillet, whose '*nouveaux romans*' were regarded by his French contemporaries as fairly middling if not fundamentally undermining of wider innovation in French literature,[23] the experimental novel that emerged in Britain and France in the period 1945 to 1975 would appear, by design or by-product, one casualty of this critical practice. If included at all in narrations of modern literary history, it is relegated to a pale afterlife of the earlier construct, or a contingent archaeology of the latter. Its artefacts are literary outliers or 'experiments' 'aberrant' to dominant classifications of the wider 'literary modern'.[24] As a presence in literature, the experimental novel appears fundamentally undermined by a critical drive that would take the undermining Robbe-Grillet as a prime exemplary. As B.S. Johnson mis-paraphrases Nathalie Sarraute to diagnose the era,[25] in 1973: 'Sarraute once described literature as a relay race, the baton of innovation passing from one generation to another. The vast majority of British novelists has dropped the baton, stood still, turned back, or not even realized that there is a race.'[26] The critical status of the post-war would then appear reliant on the redundancy of the 'vast majority' of literary artefacts of the post-war era to the baton-passing generational continuity of tradition progression; a redundancy to which those like Johnson are too assigned. A status that has seemingly concretized the 'naïve' perception that – as Genette writes from the contexts of France and in relation to a wider global phenomenon – the decades following the Second World War are an 'era with "nothing to say"'.[27]

In the coding of this monolithic dichotomy as inseparable from the conditions of the modern epoch itself, the period of focus for this study is relegated to a slush pile of contended objects, with which 'critics relocate the borders of the two dominant movements'.[28] A process of progressive asset-stripping that has scarified the period's topoi *and* topography, and by which the era has become divorced from its cultural artefacts. In its treatment as the 'ambiguous intermediary period' where this sorting process takes place, the rapport between these years as numerical values, or points on the Gregorian calendar, and their material historicity also appears severed.[29] As a point in time, and a space of artistic generation and reception, the period 1945 to 1975 appears a spectral environment, indeed 'lost somewhere in the no-man's-land between modernism and postmodernism';[30] where these dominant cultural-critical structures have proved incapable of coherently mediating historical conditions and the literature they generated. This has acted to effectively dissolve the rapport between history, culture and artistic innovation, and acts to reduce the spatio-temporal environments of this study to near-unobservability. As such, the post-war period, the experimental novel within it, are characteristic of what Alain Badiou in 'The Three Negations' (2008) calls an 'intermediate multiplicity'.[31] They sit as a space caught between two opposing dominant elements in cultural history. And as Badiou writes, this intermediary is not 'excluded' by this opposition but is *cannibalized*. It is subsumed by these dichotomous polarities, that in this context present as two saturating historico-theoretical exegeses.

A wound in cultural history

After decades of retroactive critical re-historicizing of modernism and postmodernism back and forth across it, the post-war period appears to us now wrapped and warped in and by imposed obscurity. A palimpsest period, it and its cultural artefacts have been lost in, *de*-codified by, the vying of two historico-theoretical totalities bleeding out of points elsewhere in time. This, as Marshall Berman writes, does not just indicate a dysfunction in criticism, that can be adjusted and 'fixed' by critical reassessment, but is indicative of wider dysfunctional societal drives of which that critical practice is product, or perhaps, symptom:

> forms of modernist thought and vision may congeal into dogmatic orthodoxies and become archaic; other modes of modernism may be submerged for generations, without ever being superseded; and that the deepest social and psychic wounds of modernity may be repeatedly sealed, without ever being really healed.[32]

This reframes the application of the above binary as, not only obscurant in method, but obscuring of *something*. *Something* that would appear to be the generative centre of a performative dysfunction. As 'post-Jungian' Helena Bassil-Morozow puts it:

> The postmodern solution to the issue of evil has all been about casting history aside; forgetting its actuality and horror, trying to erase the memory of the trauma. Postmodern culture has been preoccupied with concealing the pain of realisation that the shadow is always inside, lurking [...] how does one come to terms with something of the scale of the Holocaust or the Great Purge in the nineteen thirties in Stalinist Russia? How does one face the fact that this did actually happen? [...] The loss of life and the subsequent ambient intimidation experienced by the surviving members of the social group are oxymoronically authentic in their nightmarishness because the first is a terrible fact and the second a projective mechanism aimed at the distortion of the victim's reality; it therefore maims reality, abuses it, blights it, manipulates it – in short, it hijacks the real.[33]

While I put no stake on the interaction of good and evil in the duality of the human as a misleading reduction of *biblical* proportions, and within which Bassil-Morozow bases her critique, what is highlighted is an internal-external amnesiac interaction of wilful dismissal of the full, horrifying potential extent of the environmental, experiential real. And it is the post-war revelation of the very real extent of that 'nightmarish horror' that here presents as both catalyst for dysfunction, and a moment of realization that itself appears occluded. While the sorting processes above now appear archaically congealed as Berman writes, the processes themselves appear to hold at their core the act of congealing itself from the outset. In these readings, the post-war moment would appear disappeared by faulty, inadequate reactions to the sheer magnitude of its dissolution of established frameworks of human norm; new magnitudes of traumatic violence that had in itself rendered the human ability to process reality faulty and inadequate. This posits a fundamental necessity in challenging the normalized dominance of this dead binary, and the fundamental necessity in attempting to access the literary artefacts, the historic societal conditions and human experience of these conditions that literature perhaps provides access to. Where the literature of this study re-emerges as evidence of these social and psychic wounds, wounds that themselves perhaps generated the critical practice described above, as a sort of obscuring de-historicizing-re-historicizing scar tissue. Wounds that this scarifying binary system seemingly continues to occlude, and has perhaps allowed to fester.

The experimental novel of the post-war positions itself as such an object of access to the socio-cultural conditions of its time. As, though perhaps perceived an oxymoron in English, what would be described in France as an 'avant-garde realism',[34] that tried 'to capture an image that resembles the life we live'.[35] However, as the word 'experimental' would suggest, this was not the product of a simplistic point-and-click reportage. As will be discussed at length below, the capture appears a complex aesthetic process, by which the novel is used as an instrument for attempting to carry out a 'phenomenological processing' of that 'imaging of life'.[36] The critical practice of relegation and omission of the literary artefact in this instance would then seemingly equally relegate and omit the image of life it attempted to phenomenologically capture and process. As such, I begin this study with the understanding that, by their constant bleeding into it, the application of modernist and postmodernist discourse is to some degree of use in unpacking elements native to the post-war period. However, in its reliance on dialectical *logos*, this critical standard has worked against a nuanced or complex understanding of movement within the cultural moment; of initial human living through the Second World War, and projected possibilities of human continuation within that war's after-*lives*. A status we have perhaps not yet exited.

Critical climate – current

With this study I aim to re-centre critique upon the post-war experimental novel as generative of revealing openings into the novel-object's potentials to socio-cultural functionality, and therefore too the conditions of its writing and initial reading. Relations of text and world, and understandings of those relations that appear here severed by historic critical treatment of the literary modern. I then do not commit to furthering critical structures that are not this literature's own, and that have participated in the perpetuation of the post-war experimental novel as cultural null. If the 1945 to 1975 period is a liminal ground, it is a space where the loose ends of critical threads that literary-historicize the twentieth century are found erratically untethered; a 'no-man's-land', or 'literary hinterland' as James Clements calls it.[37] And so, as demonstrated, in critically engaging literature of the post-war era the observer is presented with myriad modalities, formats, conceptualizations that neither align in agreement nor opposition. However, if the new prevalence of framings of the tone 'late-modernism', 'proto-postmodernism', 'soft-modernism' etc. represents a new opaqueness to these vast terms – comparable to the opaqueness of their conceptual tenets within the post-war period itself – this potential for critical re-framings and plurality has begun to slip into a series of re-totalizing constructs that again aim to concretize thought around literature of this era, and the modern epoch at-large, into blanket singularities.

I here think of the recent emergence in Britain of new terms and re-conceptualizations: 'intermodernism',[38] 'midmodernism',[39] a kind of 'permamodernism' etc.[40] The growing use of such terminology and frameworks is troubling: they are at turns de-textualized; de-aestheticized; de-historicized. The tone adopted in the studies that push these new labels is one of 'arbitrary selectivity':[41] intermodernism is established with a list of ninety-four names of 'intermodernist' writers (a critical tactic of eliciting copia I have taken to calling *listism*); midmodernism or 'mid-century late-modernism' is clarified as *the awkward bit in the middle*, a 'segue' in 'the years between the late 1930s (just after modernism) and the late 1960s (just before postmodernism)';[42] permamodernism makes claims for a perpetual Kafkaesque literary *angst* from Aristotle to the twenty-first century.[43] As Raymond Williams writes, such constructions in literary history give 'a highly selected version of the modern which then offers to appropriate the whole of modernity'.[44] Or in terms of permamodernism, far beyond that epochal delimitation. Following the apparent fracture of the modernism-postmodernism paradigm, presented with a newly opened field of critical potentialities, it would seem the old tendencies of trench-digging move to reclaim classifying dominance via universalization of reductive, definitional selection. A 'problematic tendency in critical commentary', it is demonstrative of an impulse 'to transform everything for use by adhered to narrative, a preference for accessing the grand narrative of art' to the detriment of the body of artwork itself.[45] And as such, they are projects that

> accept without hesitation a linear conception of history and, with it, the historical determinism that underpins the myth of 'the future,' and its resultant evolutionist implications.[46]

An assimilative, 'deterministic' tradition praxis that appears to produce what Jameson would call 'frail retrospective alignments'.[47] Projects that work on the culturally narcissistic assumption that history is a corpus of selection by which present conditions can be reified as a perpetual penultimate point in a constant building drive to some unknown total state of perfection, improvement, or utopian progression and development. A hysteresis loop in critique, where processes continue to carry out pre-coded interactions with environment, though those environmental conditions have long since altered. In terms of the post-war experimental novel, despite its recent burgeoning return to publication and scholarly discourse, it is not engaged by any of these new -ism labels; it does not easily fit these re-historicizing, de-historicizing lines drawn unbroken backwards. We therefore find it, and its period of emergence, once again lost within the modern palimpsest; a point at which these reductive line-drawings demonstrably fail.

While aporia and ambiguity appear inherent elements of the culture of the post-war, thus literature as part of it, the critical application of the strict totalities of established cultural narratives immediately preceding and following the period have served to misread, indeed intensify this confusion. Equally, the more recent labels that use prefixed formulations of -modernism or -postmodernism do not engage this newly observable space in literary history, but act to patch over holes not accounted for by discontinued dominant critical signifiers. They therefore perform a zombie-like continuation of cannibalization and mis-direct from the critical potentials of both our current space, and the space in question, that (for the time being) lack a native dominant critical doxa. Perceiving such an 'after the end of' postmodernism renegacy in literary criticism, in 2002 Christine Brooke-Rose entered a plea for attempts to develop the twenty-first century critical space's potential to plurality:

> a plea for an attempt to reunify all the many and now scattered ways of enthusing about a necessarily chameleon text and transmitting that enthusiasm without killing the chameleon through summary, ideology, a rigidly held theory, or imposition of abstract structures that have only a limited relevance to any text, using a sort of chameleon or even magpie criticism, that uses the best of past isms without fear of unfashion, and this or that theory if it can enhance understanding, but above all, genuine enjoyment, insight, imagination.[48]

In 2007, in *La Littérature en péril*, Tzvetan Todorov similarly perceived formulations of new critical reductions. Discussing new government directives in studying literature in France from 2000 on, Todorov writes that now:

> reading poems and novels does not lead you to reflect on the human condition, on the individual and society, love and hate, joy and desperation, but to critical notions, traditional or modern [...] are we studying, above all else, methods of analysis, which we then illustrate with the help of various works of art? Or are we studying works of art judged essential, utilising various critical methods of approach? Where is the goal in this, where is the middle ground?[49]

These growing orthodoxies of critical approach he calls 'literature reduced to the absurd.'[50] As both essays function as a kind of parting shot calls for preservation of critical openness and textual engagement,[51] critical reduction by historical/theoretical patching while perhaps a tendency, is not, or not yet, the only way to talk about books: as both Brooke-Rose and Todorov state, we have a choice. There are then new potentials for pluralized and integrally-nuanced critique within 'the literary modern', and the slippage by which the literatures of the post-war era have so far refused full recuperation into wider historical models again demands multivalent and nuanced approaches.

Attempting to access a point in the past as a synchronic, 'lived-in' space

Writing in 2018, Jacques Rancière meets this current critical climate of the modern epoch. As he argues: 'we could write a long list of the contradictions and paradoxes' that demonstrate the inadequacies of past and present attempts at classifying recent history by overarching linear progression models ('*the* avant-garde'),[52] or a singular developmental sequence of 'modernisms'. 'But it is enough to here state' that the liminality between, within, these critical classifications indicate that 'there is not one, but many "modern times"',[53] that exist in parallel, in conflict, in separation, and as such within a wide field of non-linear connectivity. After years of stunting debates of a sorting and re-sorting modernism-postmodernism, the critical image of coherent modernity, as viewed through the prism of canon-selection literature, as a kind of contiguous Bayeux Tapestry appears no longer a defensible position. As a structuring of history (an interweaved human/social/cultural imaging of past conditions), it has indeed acted to occlude comprehension of the many historical 'modern moments' that have interacted to generate the conditions of the lived-in past, and that have generated the conditions of our own current living moment, or moments. The drive behind this process is then that of refusal, of the many literary artefacts that both generated, and were generated by, these moments; artefacts we now find re-emerging. Recalling Berman and Bassil-Morozow and the hysteretic loop above, this process of refusal then appears symptomatic of an inherited impulse to world-reduction that, according to Jean Dubuffet writing from within the post-war in 1968, first properly took hold in that era. A societal drive, for Dubuffet, of 'eliminative reduction' that both 'asphyxiates culture' and in turn 'culturally asphyxiates' our cognition of social reality: 'this notion of great works of the past is completely illusory, that which has been preserved represents only a very shallow, specious selection'.[54] A further critical image of modern literary history seems to assert itself, of a vast pile of unsewn patchwork blocks; the few drawn into connection giving only a very small insight into the myriad left in the pile, and it cannot be agreed even how those few are meant to be sewn. If this inadequacy can now be perceived, recent literary history has come to present as a field of morphability, that, as access grows, and spotlights shift, takes on a sense of the fluid; it is a prismatic and fractured space both critically over- and under-determined. As Rancière writes:

> It is time to understand that, counter to what is accepted, the notions of modernity, modernism and avant-garde imply an overlapping of different temporalities, a complex play of relations between anticipation and delay, fragmentation and continuity, movement and immobility. Time is not simply a line stretched between a past and a future. It is also, and primarily, a milieu in which people live.[55]

Rancière here similarly links the dysfunctional reductions of cultural criticism to the occlusion of historic conditions of lived life; which would infer that this has not only warped our cognition of the past, but has had a knock-on effect on our ability to understand the conditions of our own current 'living' moment(s), and that these obscurant processes continue. This, amongst the vastness of discarded material to be met, infers that to participate in criticism as an essentially unfinishable discourse would perhaps be the optimal, 'chameleon', role taken. As opposed to re-imposing universalizing static totalities that function to re-scar over, rather than open up and attempt to investigate, newly observable spaces, or perhaps newly observable 'wounds', revealed by the generative fracture of dead totalities.

Then, critique that centres a continuation of totalizing -ism classification appears now upon unstable structural ground. As 'strategies of containment',[56] they have not become inadequate or archaic in the few short years since their re-emergence, but are conceptually so, as they build their newness upon inadequate and archaic foundations. The issue appears to develop from the observability of previously occluded subject matter as product of this new fluidity, that these *listism-segue-perma* theoretical stances struggle to engage with or contain. The old problematically limited figure-lodestones of Baudelaire, and Kafka, and Joyce, and Proust etc. no longer hold the universal ability to bring all other artefacts of literature into their totalizing orbit, and so the historico-theoretical positions built upon them, directly or indirectly, prove inadequate critical codifications of culture. This indicates similarities with issues raised by Wolfgang Iser, in apparent accord with Dubuffet above, of 'reductive abstraction' in his own era in 1972:

> [these critics] reduce texts to the proportions of their theories, instead of adapting their theories to fit in with the texts. Thus between texts and theories there has arisen a broad stretch of no-man's-land, and it should be the task of literary hermeneutics to map the topography of this region.[57]

Then, again, there is a sense that entering the critical space of 1945 to 1975 is to climb out of a trench, and stumble into the scarified, bombed-out topography of a no-man's-land. Now observable critically-discarded texts are not discovered as 'virgin territory' but surrounded by cannibalistic dominant structures that have warped their historical presence and in turn warped wider critical, cultural, narrations of recent history. A warping caused by both the totalities of asphyxiating established historical narrations, and the inadequacies generated by the drawing distance between observable texts and patching ('asphyxiated-asphyxiating') tradition projects in recent critique, from which the discarded material continues to be arbitrarily excluded or fringed, and yet continues to be cannibalistically spoken for.

Speaking of the post-war era in 1965, during that termed his 'experimental period', Philippe Sollers states:

> With the current silence of science, the novel is our era's primary value, which is to say its instinctive code of reference, the vehicle of its power, the key to its everyday, mechanical, closed unconscious.[58]

Then the occlusion of the post-war experimental novel has acted to remove a key by which we might gain access to this apparent transitory no-man's-land in literary history, and perhaps find it not quite as de-populated as we have been led to believe. Though these cultural-critical screens, or 'erasures', have perhaps acted to 'obliterate' the vast majority of the texts and writers of this study from our cognition of literature, in doing so these 'erasures' prove reflexive; they 'also reveal'.[59] The omission and cannibalization of this key literature itself presents as revealing framework of critical reception, whereby the abstractions that dominate our understandings of modern literature appear congealed, petrified, and through its cracks we might observe that which this abstraction drives to disappear. And so following this tack, I approach these erased texts as 'objective constellations in which "the social" situation [of their era of initial production and reception] represents itself'.[60] Where the experimental novel as socio-cultural artefact may be approached as a revealing, omitted code of reference of the post-war; a signifying entity within literary history.

1.2 On the literature of this study

Nationality, experience and social relation

Though limiting this study to French and British literature I do not affirm the tired doxa of strict national traditions in art; synchronizations of the experimental novel can easily extend across Western Europe and the Northern Americas in this period. As such, like 'what we call literary realism', the post-war experimental novel appears 'coextensive and, we can add without risk, concordant with the modern western world and its capitalist societies'.[61] As, I argue, a mutational form inherent to non-canon conceptions of literary realism, such wide-reaching cultural presence of the post-war experimental novel is, in itself, potentially revealing of the transnational historic conditions of the moment of which it is artefact. On a further scale indicative of the burgeoning globalization of the era, and perhaps of its catalysts, the *nationality* of the writers present in this study is often not quite so straightforward as French or British. In the wake of the Second World War and its accompanying fluid transgressions of border-limits, the Holocaust, mass continental displacement of people, and the beginnings of global Americanization – Jameson dubs the period 1945 to 1973 'the brief American century',[62] any sense of nation amongst these figures appears more or less arbitrary. A localized accent on the beginnings of a (still largely cross-sectional, divided) globalized cultural discourse.[63]

To then address this norm of nation classification. As stated, these writers' biographies often cannot so easily be reduced to French, or British, nor their writing to French and/or British concerns, however much Rayner Heppenstall might attempt to unify the two as exclusive, interlocking 'nation literatures' in *The Fourfold Tradition* (1961) (alongside – *of course* – the exceptions of the 'German provincials', Kafka and Kierkegaard; the 'two Ks').[64] To demonstrate this in some of those that haunt this study: Georges Perec and Roland Topor were both of Jewish Polish emigrant backgrounds, both narrowly survived the

Holocaust and never quite felt welcome in the country in which they were born. Sarraute was a Jewish Russian child emigrant following the First World War who also, under an assumed name, narrowly survived the Holocaust; Stefan Themerson, a Jewish Polish refugee; Eva Figes, a Jewish German refugee; Gustav Metzger, a Jewish Polish-German refugee; Pol Bury, Belgian; Brigid Brophy, Irish; Fernando Arrabal, a refugee from Franco's Spain. Wilson Harris was born in British Guiana (later, Guyana); Zulfikar Ghose in British India (later, Pakistan); Brooke-Rose, German-British-Swiss, wrote in English and French and lived in France. The great curator of the English literary canon himself T.S. Eliot was both American and, according to Hugh Sykes Davies, a Pétainist,[65] and so talk of nation tradition is discussed insofar as it itself is a constructed, and selective, cultural narrative.[66] This dislocation, or *dépaysement*, will come to prove central to several points that will be met (though in skirting the topic I have here committed something tantamount to *listism*, I intend it as an indication of approach and some of the figures that more or less pass in and out of this observation, not a demarcation or definition of any *thing*). Thus, it is not the writers who the national designation purports to classify, but the historic quotidian environments they are immersed in, the socio-cultural image communicated, and critical and readerly reaction to them; around them. This re-centres the positing of 'Post-War French and British Fiction' to socio-cultural cupolas in which texts were generated, presented and sold as novel-objects to be consumed.

This further posits a cross-generational space of production in the experimental novel of the era. As perhaps the first properly total war of the modern epoch for both Britain and France, the Second World War represents a shift in which war's violence broke from the boundaries of its venue and designated participants at the frontline and permeated the structures and routines of quotidian home life on a total scale. Unlike the officers who returned from the First World War trenches to publish their poetry (or left drafts to be published from), this post-Second World War reflexivity breaks from the heroic/anti-heroic thirtyish, male, upper-class mould, and also from therein inherent generational delimitations. The vast majority of participants in the Second World War were not so in the traditional, uniformed, sense. The post-Second World War experimental novel crosses both the adult participants, who in this study offer an immediate and continued sense of reflexion, and the hunted, blitzed, evacuated child participants who came to 'writing age' later in the period.⁶⁷ Both had by-and-large fallen into writing silence, or, more often, died, by the late-1970s (hence the period delimitation of this study: a window of production from, paper shortages notwithstanding, 1945 to a rough 1975 cut-off). From François Le Lionnais' *La Peinture à Dora* (1946) and Dan Billany's *The Cage* (1949), through Heppenstall's *The Connecting Door* (1962) and Figes' *Konek Landing* (1969), to Perec's *W ou le souvenir d'enfance* (1975) and the beginning of Johnson's unfinished trilogy, *See The Old Lady Decently* (1975), as some of the more overt examples, the narrative reflex of the brutalized-brutalizing experientiality of the Second World War pervades in the experimental novel of the years that followed.

To give further grounding to this reflexive cross-generational position, for example with Johnson, who dubs himself an 'evacuee forever':

> compared with that of those in Europe who suffered, say, machine gunning and dive-bombing by stukas on the roads of France, or the concentration camps [...] nothing, certainly, can have been worse than the concentration camps; but it is possible to compare a sudden and relatively short outburst of violence [...] and conclude that the psychological effects of evacuation would in fact be more severe.⁶⁸

This centralization of experience of the war upon him, and his specific experience, is characteristically narcissistic of Johnson, however, indicates a wider phenomenon. As Eva Tucker writes of Figes' childhood confrontation with that she had escaped, in *The Guardian* in 2012:

> 'One afternoon just before the war ended,' Eva wrote in *The Observer* in 1979, 'my mother gave me nine pence and sent me off to the local cinema ... I sat alone in the dark and watched the newsreel of Belsen...' It was a deeply shocking experience which haunted her in nightmares for years.⁶⁹

Similarly, Topor is quoted in title to a recent republication of his artwork: 'one fine evening, I was born across from the abattoir'.⁷⁰ Referring, it would seem, to the Hôpital Saint-Louis in Paris' 10th arrondissement, alongside which his father later queued for deportation, and a neighbourhood he himself as a child would have to flee in 1941. As Topor states of the intended aims of his writing: 'I want my existence to be a supreme affront to the vultures who have become so impatient since the Forties, by way of an uninhibited representation of blood, shit and sex.'[71] Hidden elements in human life Topor regarded as emblematic of a wider culture of occluding silence in post-war societies. Writing out of a very similar experiential background Perec, who lost his father at the Front in 1940 and his mother at Auschwitz in 1943, quotes Raymond Queneau in an epigraph to *W ou le souvenir d'enfance*: 'this insensate fog that churns the shadows, how might I ever clear it away?'[72] For Perec, an inability, or refusal, to remember is a central facet to human and societal continuation in the post-war, and is a recurring theme in his fictive and critical writing. As such, the experientiality of war would appear central to not only a reading of the experimental novel of the time but lived life within the post-war world itself. However, the nightmarish psychological effects here described draw this literature away from a simplistic reflection back upon that war as direct account or reportage of past events; it would be reductive to assign these novels 'war writing'. Though fictive reflex of this experience is one facet of its *œuvre*, as demonstrated above, and will be further seen, these writers draw the experience of that war and its fallout through the aesthetic prism of their own *post* moment of production. By which the experimental novel presents as product of wider, shared experiential conditions of a post-war world. As a literature that here appears to centralize nightmarish experience and its continuations within its novelistic project, it would indeed seem revealing that it has not, and currently cannot be, accounted for by the persistently re-historicizing-de-historicizing-ism narratives raised above. Nor are the human and societal conditions of which it is inherent product, presented here in the modes of silence, amnesia, psychological wounds, or a persisting nightmare found coded in such a way in dominant narrations of the era. Via the prism of the experimental novel we then find imaging of the period reformulated. As discussed below, we are presented with a confused, confusing world-environment suspended between projected points of total societal dissolution, of which that war here appears the point of origin.

The nationality figure-contexts, and figure-contexts of refugee, migrant or Holocaust survivor stated above then form a small part of a much broader spectrum of shared and specific experientiality the writers associated with the experimental novel bring to literature in the post-war. Within their biographical backgrounds we find struggles with mental and physical illness, addiction; the Blitz, evacuation, soldiering, occupation, resistance fighting, the POW camp;

amongst these writers are women, the working class, gay men and women, and former 'colonial subjects'.[73] These are all experiential bases of surviving the war, and continuing to survive in its post, that many of the lists classifying the period, and indeed the twentieth century at large, exclude. They are environmental-experiential contexts that not only often form topoi within the concrete narrative ground upon which the fictions of these novels are acted out but appear to permeate every level of their novelistic poetics (what I will come to describe as an 'experimental *romantics*'). These variegated differences in biographical-experiential background add prisms by which the texts these figures produced might be read. And yet, inclusive of this multiplicity, at the base-level of the texts themselves, they often appear to reverberate at similar frequencies of signification. This infers that the conditions in which these texts were generated goes beyond the sphere of personal, writerly-biographical critical interest. Though Brooke-Rose in 2002 cautions the twenty-first century critic against 'entering text' via biographical reading,[74] the prevailing tendency in current critique upon this literature primarily relies on the development of discourse around each individual writer as figure-study, and in almost total isolation.[75] However, as Michel Butor writes: 'a book must be a motor that gives movement to other books, a spark that reanimates their flame'.[76] With this understanding, there are revealing base synchronicities between these texts to be opened up, that might profitably draw these figures into a common critical space; that might in turn aid in opening up their novels' more diverging potentialities in mutual correspondence.

On the post-war experimental novel as an 'avant-garde realism'

At the time often dismissed, and in the decades after largely critically refused, re-reading the experimental novel will therefore offer a venue for the observation of further depths within the received image of the post-war period, that have been lost behind dominant critical literary-historicizing of the twentieth century, and the rather alienatingly dated – reductively 'cinematic'[77] – 'social realist' tendency in the novel that has come to vaguely represent the era (the experimental novel writer would perhaps add the prefix 'mis' to 'represent' here). The social realist novel's apparent successful cultural dominance very much contributing to the view that the post-war period is a dead-space in literary history, as diagnosed by Johnson above. There is a current turn in scholarship in both Britain and France to try to explore these further depths in what has been traditionally denigrated as non-literary: *Série noire*,[78] neo-fantastic,[79] the graphic novel,[80] and indeed the experimental novel (this last one often found inhabiting the genre tropes and bookshop sections of those preceding, points of contact briefly suggested in endnotes). The texts these studies tend to look to are, in a sense, unique. They appear to indicate that, departing from received understandings, for the first time, the innovative, or the avant-garde, primarily sought mass-market publication rather than presentation in art galleries, or dissemination to subscriber lists. They were sold in bookshops and tobacconists, at train stations and on magazine stands. They are now predominantly accessed via Oxfam or Amazon, rather than the glass presentation cases of the Pompidou, or by white-gloved appointment at the BnF. This alters the contractual terms on which the artefacts themselves must be met, and presents a pivot in the critical framework of approach required; where the experimental novel shifts from the eccentric art niche or fringe anachronism it is currently generally labelled under,[81] indeed to something altogether more revealing.

As an underlying thread of argument, this partition approaches the problematic question of what the post-war experimental novel potentially was or tried to be; what it came to be regarded as, and how that shades our access to it. However, due to critical and historical ambiguities raised, due to its status as cannibalized and/or discarded artefacts, it cannot be assumed that my mobilizing of the word would engender the same or similar signification in the reader. I therefore here give a baseline position of the parameters by which I apply the word, and observe the novel-objects ascribed the descriptor 'experimental'. In a post-war space of Dubuffet's cultural asphyxiation (that seemingly, at least critically, re-asserts itself today), as such a public entity, I posit that the post-war experimental novel is an art-object that, in its enaction by process of reading, attempts to generate complex channels of communication through increased formal engagement in content. This formal project draws its reader to its primary textual function: to prompt a process of analysis; in the first instance, of its own medium, and the role of reader and writer within it. By this process, the experimental novel therefore further functions as cultural staging-ground of wider, beyond-text, interactions of human and social and culture and world, of which the internal space of the novel presents as experiential synecdoche, or interactive symbiote. This interaction – described above in terms of phenomenological capture and processing – according to Sarraute writing in 1950, is 'the novelist's entire experimental effort'.[82]

With the post-war experimental novel then we observe the hypertrophy of an effect that, Iser notes in *The Implied Reader* (1972), is specific to the novel-genre: 'namely, to involve the reader in the world of the novel and so help him to understand it – and ultimately his own world – more clearly'.[83] That is, the novel writer formulates a textual space that is procedurally enacted by the reader, who draws to it their own external-to-text experience, and it is in that intra-extra-textual interaction these novels' experiments take place. To look to Robbe-Grillet in *Pour un nouveau roman* (1963), 'the function of art is never to illustrate a truth – or even a question – known in advance, but to bring into the world questions (and, perhaps also, in the end, answers) unknown to itself'.[84] Ghose goes further in *The Contradictions* (1966), and lays out three fundamental 'aesthetic questions of Cartesian doubt' he attempts to textually generate in a process of assertion and contradiction: '*How can we establish our knowledge of the physical world?*' '*How can we trust our senses?*' '*What is thought?*'[85] For Ghose, it is on the plane of 'daily experience' these questions must be prompted. This then does not speak of an eccentric unknowability of the schema of the artwork, but the field within which its internal mechanisms are intended to be applied to carry out the experiment; within its extra-textual affectivity and potentialities, where it is the unknown variable of the reader that acts as conduit. As Perec states in a lecture given at University of Warwick in 1967:

> I discovered what we might call the freedom at the interior of writing. How we can leave the reader free to comprehend, to choose, how we can influence them by distorting medium, how we might convince them if you like[86]

If this extra-textual process of engaging the reader in text by eliciting choices, questions, and perhaps answers, clings to this authenticity of indeterminate unknowing, novels 'can record', Williams writes, 'breaking through, in society and the novel': they may live out 'our future, the actual and probable direction of our society'.[87] A synchronic, rather than dialectical, indication of potential state of the past and present, and potential future consequences projected from those states, that would here appear refused; performatively misdirected.

Social engagement and the experimental novel

This paramount readerly concern brings the post-war experimental novel into synchronicity of project with Jean-Paul Sartre's call in 1947 for 'a literature of praxis', or 'engagement';[88] a call Perec claims to have continued to heavily influence literature until at least the late-1960s.[89] Sartre describes a confused space following total war, awaiting impending nuclear apocalypse, in which 'torn apart, without future, without guarantees, without justification, the bourgeoisie has objectively become a *sick man*, in a phase of subjective sorrowful [bad] conscience'.[90] It is here, with *Qu'est-ce que la littérature?* (1948)[91] that Sartre first formally re-injects the word 'experimental' into post-war discourse, and in doing so re-deploys the therapeutic and medicinal base tenets upon which Zola conceptualized the first iteration of the 'experimental novel' with *Le Roman expérimental* in 1880.[92] For Zola in the late-nineteenth century, the experimental novel functions as a 'white cell' within the 'social circulus'. It is an object of societal self-confrontation by which the social organism can 'cure' itself of its collective irrationalities, its dysfunctions and its delusions. 'Sicknesses' suffered and spread by the interconnected social human and propagated by 'rotten' dominant 'cultural organs'. Similarly, Sartre writes that in a post-war space suspended between points of total violence and societal dissolution the writer's 'only public' must again be 'helped',[93] by a literature that 'reclaims the right to write *histoire* [history/story] within a moment when we discover our historicity'.[94] Whereby these persistent nightmares and this silence they perhaps invoke, can be in some way mediated or confronted. Along with this word experimental, we then too find this sense of the experimental novel as a heuristic, or therapeutic entity harbouring the potentials of societal self-questioning and self-confrontation mutationally re-emerging in the post-war period.

This draws us to the point of contact by which the terms experimental and realism can be drawn back into connection and the phrase 'an avant-garde realism' can be reconciled. In France, as stated above, Sartre's tenets of a literature of praxis integrally align with that laid out by Zola; Sarraute's 1950 essay quoted above, and similarly first published in Sartre and Simone de Beauvoir's *Les Temps modernes*, is something of a response to that call; as too it would appear, are the essays that make up Robbe-Grillet's *Pour un nouveau roman*. Sarraute's essay in particular is heavily cited by the British writers of this study, to take for example Johnson in opening above. In further circumstance of connectivity, Butor wrote the introduction for the 1966 reprint of *Le Roman expérimental*, and elsewhere wrote at length upon it. In Britain, according to Jean-Michel Ganteau, writers like 'Brigid Brophy and B.S. Johnson' 'implicitly respond' to questions posed by Zola in that text.[95] Whether that is via a reading of Zola, Sartre, Sarraute, Robbe-Grillet and/or Butor, a shift in societal conditions that raised similar cultural reflex in literary product or a vague mixture of the two, synchronicity is to a considerable degree apparent.[96] However, it would not appear as a response to that earlier entity that these novels are written, but it is the questions themselves that are mutationally renewed; posited in different contexts and therefore, necessarily, in different modes. Then, such a correspondence within the application of the experimental itself draws this discourse out of *whateverism* or *the* linear developmental avant-garde and to a modern iteration of the novel; to correspondence with the literary debates of a pluri-realism rather than a modernistic (or perhaps rather anti-modernistic) opposition of 'social' and 'psychological' writing by which this literature has been, as will be seen, much maligned.

In English, this word experimental carries with it a myriad of connotations: it is the mad professor with their vials and lightning, it is a Jackson Pollock throwing around paint, it is a joint whichever politician toked – but did not inhale, of course – in the early-1980s; it is the sanitized lab technician carrying out empirical tests to ratify hypotheses. However, in French where it first emerged in relation to literature, and as we find it here applied, it means something else altogether. In French, it is the word *expérience* that specifically relates to scientific or sociological instance; an objective quantitative *expérience* that one can attempt to *scientifically* replicate. However, the word *expériment* in French is a word inappropriate for use in relation to modern scientific testing (or untoked joints, or Dr Emmett Brown); in relation to the novel it designates rather a mode of study, analysis, of probing – and is a word predominantly ascribed to formulations of literature since its first conceptualization by Zola, and, in French, continued in this Zolean sense in our era of study. It is a term that, in relation to the novel, primarily designates analytical critique. In English, there is no equivalent linguistic splitting of these processes, and in translations of French texts on the subject both terms are found unhelpfully rendered 'experiment'.[97] To look to the beginnings of the conceptualized literary word *expérimental*, to Zola, according to Colette Becker, the experimental does not claim direct scientific equivalence, nor a harnessing of supposed infinitudes of chance, but rather designates a renegotiation of what the novel could be when re-placed within the phenomenal real world (... like the then public function of science), as opposed to a Platonist transcendental idealism of Grecian water sprites and abject lyricism (which Zola perceived to be the dominant literature of his era, and from which he fled his earlier poetry into prose). As such, Becker clarifies the status of the book with which Zola brought the word experimental into relation with literature, *Le Roman expérimental*, with reference to the title of Robbe-Grillet's book of collected writings on the novel 1956–63 cited above, '*Pour un nouveau roman*'.[98]

In this text, Zola perceived a social sickness in the delusions of a communal false reality – built and fed of bad-faith belief, for Zola in the late-nineteenth century – in religion and spiritualism. That which dominant literatures participated in the construction and perpetuation of; that which the social human lived their life surrounded by, that encroached on, mollified, proper perception of the 'real world' itself. As such, he characterizes society as a body lain upon a surgeon's table, in which cultural entities function as organs: 'if an organ is rotten, many others are affected, and a very complex sickness takes hold'.[99] With this medical understanding, for Becker the 'scientific pretensions' of Zola 'regularly mocked' by critics overlooks his motive and application,[100] the term experimental demonstrates rather

> an opposition to an idealist tradition, [it is] a modern conception of the novel that took on the business of truth, not only of deveiling the social body and its antagonisms, but also the body of the individual and its dark margins [...] it is the exploration of what goes on within the flesh.[101]

No scientific direct equivalence then is here claimed, but the empirical, scientific shifts in perception of material reality around, within, the human could aid in renewing art's relation to the truths (therefore also untruths) of social reality, in a literary dissolution of the reductive, the anachronistic or the mythic comparable to the socio-cultural effect of contemporaneous public-engagement science upon the apparent delusions of spiritualism and religion. The novel as a public art space then would become hyper-aware of its status as 'a novel', and in this awareness work through itself to address elements within social reality; a socio-cultural space of interaction that had generated it, and which the novel intrinsically both inhabited, and is inhabited by. Then, the experimental novel is indeed a tool, or instrument, applied in relation to social reality and human experientiality upon developed content-form bases of confrontation and interactivity. There are three transitions presented in this formulation of the experimental novel: (1) where a 'motive' or 'catalyst' for its writing is environmental, (2) which would be critically presented in a 'content diagnosis', (3) which in turn would be drawn to a 'formal treatment' by complex interaction of reader with that form and content.

A novel written along the lines of such confrontation, would indeed then present as socially formative, heuristic, or therapeutic; it would function as a 'white cell' in the 'social circulus' as stated, that would 'reject romanticism and aspire to *more* realism'.[102] Such a cultural organism would then in turn fully accept a socio-cultural responsibility the novel, following a Zola-perceived observationally disengaged Honoré de Balzac, had been shirking. Similar to that stated by Williams above, in becoming experimental, the novel would develop as a questioning tool of 'the conception of the human and its future, and therefore that of the work of art and its role in society'.[103] This questioning reflexivity would then have a revelatory, or confrontational curative effect on society's cultural self-imaging of the truths and untruths of the world around it; the experimental novel could potentially re-deploy the novel genre's established socio-cultural role as fictive-space mediator – apparent Balzacian consensus-maker – of the extra-textual real to 'treat' the socially-networked, culturally-conditioned human for its 'sickly communal delusions'. Delusions Zola perceived to be a direct product of said socio-cultural novelistic processes of consensus making, that had spread from the rotten cultural organs throughout the social body.

Similar to the mass-market presence of the post-war experimental novel, Zola indeed wanted his experimental novels to 'access as many people as possible'.[104] And as such, as Butor writes, aesthetic affectivity is central to its project: 'to create an experimental novel is [...] to apply experimentation as effectively as possible upon the reality that it operates on through the intermediary of language'.[105] In terms of the affectivity of the experimental novel, it is not enough to simply state from a writerly position that dominant literary presences are rotten but that this must be an awareness disseminated amongst the public that they have made sick via readerly interaction with the novel-object; a judgement for themselves to make, to be convinced of as Perec states. Brophy similarly writes of the 'educadventures' of *In Transit* (1969): the project of that book 'my comrades, is no sentimentality. Indeed, it is cynicism. [...] our programme: – Undo the Normative conquest.'[106] Here it is the sociocultural 'bourgeois' 'normalizing' programmes of the post-war that are posited as the mechanisms of a sickly delusion; a forgetful silence. And the experimental novel programme that attempts to engage with it, or even perhaps roll that conquest back, depends on successfully drawing the 'dear Reader' to complex textual-engagement.

To expound upon the novel as such an entity, in 1955 Maurice Blanchot depicts such a socio-literary space of readerly textual praxis,

> This is why reading draws whoever reads the work into the remembrance of that profound genesis [its writing]. Not that the reader necessarily perceives anew the manner in which the work was produced – not that he is in attendance at the real experience of its creation. But he partakes of the work as the unfolding of something in the making, the intimacy of the void which comes to be. If this progression takes on the aspect of a temporal unfolding, it founds the essence of the *novelesque*.[107]

The genesis of the temporal void within the novel as something to be *experienced* (in the English sense (and an alternative meaning of the French word *expérience*)), a reality to be progressively generated, indicates the potential for actual and immediate relation to extra-page reality itself; it designates both a writerly, and most prescient for current discussion, readerly, *experiential* textual project. This writerly positing of a 'DIY space', as Brophy terms it, to be experientially generated by the reader appears a central project of the post-war experimental novel in which an authorial prerogative over text is deemed disingenuous.[108] As Harris writes in introduction to his *Guyana Quartet* (1960–3), the reading of the post-war iteration of the experimental novel would function as a kind of 'second death', which leads the reader to 'fiction's genesis or fiction's truths'.[109] It is the human here that is centred as cultural receiver and social disseminator, and in such the same routes of aesthetic contagion that had made the social sick, can potentially be put to use in a societal treatment.

Then the onus of the novel shifts from a perceived Balzacian authorial prerogative over defined reality, to a reader's ability to participate within experimental text-space. It is through the reader such a novel would intervene, by drawing them to a text-space that functions as staging-ground of extra-textual potentialities; seemingly the fictive would function in some sense as an interactive space of readerly analysis of the socio-cultural structures that they both inhabit, and inhabit them. An engaged reading of the experimental novel would then entail an active readerly self-analysis of themselves and the world they live in via increased formal engagement in fictive content. This firmly places the term experimental novel within the realms of non-canon conceptions of literary realism. As Williams writes of the meaning of the word 'realism' at its 1956 'centenary',[110] the meaning that led to first conceptualization of the experimental novel:

> when the 'realist' description arrived, a further development was taking place, both in content and in attitudes to it. A common adjective used with 'realism' was 'startling,' and, within the mainstream of 'ordinary, contemporary, everyday reality' a particular current of attention to the unpleasant, the exposed, the sordid could be distinguished. Realism thus appeared as in part a revolt against the ordinary bourgeois view of the world; the realists were making a further selection of ordinary material which the majority of bourgeois artists preferred to ignore. Thus 'realism,' as a watchword, passed over to the progressive and revolutionary movements.[111]

Later, as a word, re-appropriated to designate the pretence of 'simple presentation of things' and removing this confrontational 'revolution of everyday reality' quality. A quality of socially engaged experimental writing, described in France as an avant-garde realism, we here indeed find mutationally re-newed.

To plot this further in the post-war

The experimental novel of our period in question then presents as a historicized cultural staging ground of social interrogation in a post-war moment of social and cultural 'sorrowful, sickly' crisis, of which silencing asphyxiation is perhaps a symptom, in which the potential for a writer and a reader to break through, via entering into text, becomes a dynamic of immediate interaction central to wider socio-cultural discourse. And as such, it would indeed appear that 'the novel is the way this society speaks to itself'.[112] Through this sense of intra-textual engagement of external-to-text figures, the post-war experimental novel then functions as an out-folding frame, by which the reader might be 'helped' on the plane of the lived-in world. An interaction taking place on a scale of mass-market, everyday social contact with consumable cultural object. Therefore, as I will test below: the experimental novel here presents as instrument, which when applied generates a connective formative space in which the interacting, perhaps malfunctioning, dynamics of culture-human-social-world might be comprehended, or even, as Sartre argues, that this crisis, the apparent socio-cultural sickness that took hold following the Second World War though perhaps not cured, might be somehow treated.

This open potentiality of project then raises the prospect of a multiplicity of experimental approaches to the 'realist organism' of the novel,[113] and therefore an erratic spectrum of applications. This makes it possible to put distance between the reductive assumption that an experimental novel is simply that which 'plays games' with the novel artefact; what Vanessa Guignery refers to as a 'plasticity of writing'.[114] Guignery describes a formal *bouleversement* through the 'modernist inheritance' of typographical variation, or physical writerly imposition on the book-object itself, be that the inclusion of symbols, different type sizes, blank passages, irregular bindings or holes in pages. However, these aesthetic forms appear less a nostalgia for a Joycean modernism, nor to be preparing for the arrival of Barth's definitional corralling of postmodernism, and rather demonstrate a magnified warping of what André Breton describes in 1953 as the 'dismembering' and 'disintegratory' syntactic forms within Zola's nineteenth century experimental realist novel, as developed from 'pre-' or 'non-Balzacian' iterations of the novel genre, re-applied in the early-twentieth by 'Joyce for example' and forming a backdrop to surrealism's own 'innovations' (perhaps as indicated in *sur*realism's first Guillaume Apollinaire coined name '*super*naturalism').[115] Here, then, we do not find the revived 'optic tricks' of the 'spatial typography of an outmoded and futurist poem',[116] as Maurice Roche writes, but, as stated above, more a form of what Roche calls 'Sternean anamnesis';[117] a formal drive to extra-textual affectivity via reader-engagement. These approaches are then not eccentric to literature, but more a mutational re-newing, redeployment of historic applications of literary form and approach in new circumstances of generation and reception.

Pushing this tendency into the territory of the new, aesthetic treatment of text and book appear to re-emerge in widely varied dismembering and disintegratory modes in the post-war, that act to disengage the artefacts from an easy sense of ascribing stylistic continuity, or tradition heredity. Further, the book-object is only one of many limit-lines culturally defined and socially accepted as the definition of a novel as consumable item, that are 'the specific systems of expectation and hypothesis which spectators bring with them' to it;[118] that the novel writer, and novel reader, must colour within or crash against. Artefact and typography are two of the many genrefying structures of the novel that are here found not as rules broken but distorted constants: textual, linguistic, accepted inherent interior-exterior laws of physics, anachrony and/or the spatio-temporal, narratology, plotting, characterization, thematic indices, formal language, socially accepted moral norms, concretized social and gender roles, accepted factual historic reality as separated from alternative account, myth and hearsay, common shared knowledge, tone, error and inconsistency (be they in printing, editing or writing), and the very borders of genre separation and classification themselves that all these are traits thereof. This speaks of the above posited 'combined experimentation in form with experimentation in content',[119] and recentres the approach to the experimental novel not as the interpretation of effect of a writerly process, but observation of the acting out of text-space figure-presence processes. Described here are the constants of the novel observed during research to be doubted, questioned, indeed made changeable, that is variable, by experimental application. As Alexandre Devaux writes of Topor: his texts

> deploy the arguments of an authentic reflexion on the human condition. But, it's a reflexion where thought travels through deformed and deforming mirrors. Where reason undergoes mutations, absurd metamorphoses, it is exasperated to the point of insanity.[120]

That such an internally destabilized, externally destabilizing entity within literature would emerge in a space of socio-cultural crisis or social human sickness, implies here that 'vision of the world' is 'inseparable from literary technique used'.[121] The experimental novel at post-war therefore indeed appears a 'confrontational social form': 'a realist project, a critical project'.[122] By this the experimental novel presents as skeuomorph, an art-object of manifest social confrontation and analysis, dressed in the familiar skin of a popular cultural medium of social entertainment and interaction. As seen above, the writers of these books often deployed forms and contents developed in what has been regarded their more extreme texts in the skins of popular genre-fiction modes (which indeed goes so far as the social realist kitchen sink drama itself, for example, in Billany's *The Trap* (1950), or Queneau's *Zazie dans le métro* (1959), or Johnson's *Albert Angelo* (1964)). For Perec, 'as a kind of formal jazz', the 'new experimental' literature's interactions with 'other aesthetic forms' had the potential to provide ways by which 'traditional forms might be saved',[123] in a moment when literature-at-large appeared also to succumb to sickly crisis (echoing Zola's apparent rotten cultural organs prognosis). Then counter to much current critical perception of the post-war experimental novel as reduced to singular over-troped sub-sub-genre, or troped out of literature altogether; the application of the word experimental here is descriptive of hypertrophied modes of both writerly production and readerly reception of the novel as consumable object.

To look to Heppenstall writing in 1948: 'one of the commonest fallacies inherent in all expressions of taste [...] is that, in literature, the arts and public entertainment, there are certain fixed *genres* or kinds, with standards of their own which may not be transgressed.'[124] Then in their experimental adherence to the fallacy, or rather, fallacies, of the novel, these objects, extreme and applied, are both an inherent product of the phantasmatic novel genre itself and the historic socio-cultural climates of their era, of which, as Sollers states, they functioned as part of its primary value; as the object through which post-war societies speak. It would seem that we are presented with a relation of the social space to the novel object in which 'a kind of collective unconscious speaks to itself by the voice of a novel, that is the transcription of a mental reality'.[125] In a space where the anachronistic dominant, that is social realist, novel progressively minors its genre-at-large from critical societal participation, the re-newing experimental novel object is a cultural artefact where the constitutive genrefying elements of the novel are actively included, altered, magnified, generated or disintegrated. Through this active critical shift these variables form a kind of destabilized, destabilizing *romantics*. That is, an experimental poetics of the novel, employed as a historicized formulation of a content-form confrontation with perceived inadequacies and issues in the interconnected spheres of literature, culture, social, human and their relation to the world-environments in which these entities must function, in a moment where we appear to find them mutually malfunctioning.

1.3 Conflicts in cultural production

Contemporaneous cultural climate

This then leads to a second screen between us and the experimental novel at post-war. That of the societal climates that fed, and fed out of, the dominant cultural structures of the era by which the 'vast majority' of literature was perceived to have 'dropped the baton'; where the image of this avant-garde entity of social engagement was diverted to a kind of masturbatory writerly eccentricity. A screen erected contemporaneous to the post-war, that has been concretized in subsequent critique as yet another highly selective, oppositional construct. From the end of the Second World War the development of cultural discourse within the then arbitrary territorial borders of France and Britain at a cursory glance seems polarized. In established perspective, appearing out of the smoke and mirrors of the instant post-war years in France is found the development of a post-Breton literary landscape, the persisting formation of movements; groups, manifestoes. Further, the first tentative debates of that termed 'structuralism' and 'post-structuralism' and elements that would form the brunt of what would later be heavily appropriated into Anglo-American constructions of postmodernism, as employed to also retroactively classify difference to an earlier modernism. In Britain, the climate appears starkly flaccid in contrast: a strong house of social realist and oppressively provincial writers dominating a diaspora of loosely linked solitary experimental novel writers of intermittent novel production, that at every turn were denied, by censors, critics, editors, publishers, prize boards, typesetters, printers, booksellers, bookshops.[126] As such, there is a current in established understandings that characterizes post-war Britain, an apparently isolated cultural entity 'left out of' transnational discourse,[127] as a kind of hell of artistic innovation, and France a sort of heaven. And indeed, in Britain this dominant cultural refusal of innovation appears particularly prominent. It forms a staple of critique on the British post-war experimental novel, however it is largely used as a stylistic polarization of an arbitrarily evoked 'experimentalism' vs. an arbitrarily evoked 'social realism'.[128] An oppositional conflict the latter is perceived to have *won*, and as such, instances perhaps revealing of potential reasons for this apparent opposition are rarely tracked beyond Johnson referring to social realist writers as 'dead',[129] lumped in with the, equally 'dead', 'cunts' of what he perceives as a retrograde academia.[130] It is this conflict or confrontation within the novel as primary value of the post-war era I then here look to dilate to clearer observability.

From the very early years of the post-war period in Britain, the hostile application of the critical antinomy of experimental and realism that claimed to have definitively removed innovative modes of writing from British literature – to have 'balanced the literary budget' by 1938 – continued to 'victoriously' dominate cultural discourse.[131] As Heppenstall raises in a roundup of the effects of the Second World War on the arts in *Imaginary Conversations* (1948): 'the novel remains very largely what it was. The experiments of Virginia Woolf and James Joyce are admired and by-passed.'[132] Literature carries on as if the wars, the economic crises, the fundamental societal ruptures, and the earlier innovations of figures like Woolf and Joyce, had occurred as a sort of sideshow, and as such project false-continuity from a Victorian, or Edwardian cultural status quo. It is this climate we find the post-war experimental novel emerging into in Britain; a climate in which it is allotted no cultural part to play. As Themerson writes in 1950 to Swedish writer Lars Gustav Hellström, who was keen to translate Themerson's novel *Bayamus* (1949):

> you asked me to send you some of the reviews, because you want to quote the English critics' point of view as a typically 'reactionary one.' Well, it will be rather difficult to quote silences, will it not? The fact is that the book has been passed over in perfect silence.[133]

The 'reactionary' point-of-view the Swedish translator thought typifying of England couldn't be edified, as the reactionary response to an experimental novel was not particularly grounded in reading and measured critique of a text's perceived shortcomings, but general distaste; the simple idea of irresponsibly experimenting with an established genre during a period of societal instability and paper shortages was enough.

Bayamus itself a macabre invocation of the refugee experience of wartime London, it is the kind of text that might be deemed culturally integral, for, in some sense, aesthetically accessing reflexions back upon that experientiality within the initial post-war moment of realization. As Bertrand Russell describes it in 1953: '*Bayamus* is nearly as mad as the world.'[134] And yet, refused in Britain, it apparently went unread and dismissed from cultural discourse. While in France, Heppenstall's own *The Blaze of Noon* (1939) was regarded by 1967 as 'inaugurating the *nouveau roman* [in the wider, beyond Robbe-Grillet sense, externally, reductively, blanket-applied in newspaper culture sections]',[135] Themerson's 'Semantic Poetry Translation' ('SPT') method introduced in *Bayamus* was foundational to Queneau's later conception of 'Definitional Literature'.[136] And yet, despite the apparent centrality of these innovations to post-war literature in both France and Britain, upon publication the texts themselves were greeted with silence.

However, later in the period, the refusal in Britain of innovation in the novel as not-literature had become more pronounced. At the 1962 Edinburgh International Festival, Scottish poet Hugh MacDiarmid publicly denounced Scottish novelist Alexander Trocchi as 'cosmopolitan scum, a writer of no literary consequence whatsoever' (seemingly missing the 'International' bit in the festival's title).[137] MacDiarmid described both Trocchi and William S. Burroughs as 'vermin who should never have been invited to the conference'.[138] The episode is indeed typifying of reactions by a grouping of dominant-at-the-time British writers and critics against what they perceived as *otherly*, or *foreign*, that what can only appear to us now as newer, or different, forms of writing; of writer. To follow the echoes of rejection, in his journal Heppenstall (who was also in attendance at Edinburgh) reports that critics of his books think him either redundantly eccentric, or a mad man. Of newspaper reviews of his novel *Two Moons* (1977) he writes: 'Harwood says nothing whatever about the content, but simply makes clever remarks about the form. To him, I am, though a distinguished man of letters, in this novel merely eccentric. To Sage, I am mad.'[139] In a 1963 letter to the printers who had refused to put to press his novel *Albert Angelo*, Johnson writes,

> I understand that you have refused to print my novel *Albert Angelo* because of the use, perhaps a dozen times, of certain four-letter words. I write to make known to you my opinion that your refusal is an act of moral cowardice:

the *Lady Chatterley's Lover* case [R. (crown) v. Penguin Books ltd., 1960 – which Penguin won] gave serious writers a freedom to express the truth as they found it in life which you, sirs, seem determined to limit by imposing a form of censorship of your own.[140]

To reanimate Trocchi a moment, his *Cain's Book* (1960) was 'banned, burned, prosecuted, refused by book-distributors everywhere, condemned for its loving descriptions of heroin use and coarse sexual content'.[141] And this hostility in Britain was not reserved just for British writers and a resident Burroughs. In a 1997 obituary of Topor, his publisher in Britain John Calder remembers:

> his play *Vinci avait raison* (*Leonardo was Right*) was a farcical comedy where a policeman and his wife invite a colleague and family to spend a weekend in their new house, where the lavatories are blocked. Piles of excrement emerge all over the house and only the constipated visiting policeman escapes suspicion: the end of this unusual detective play confounds everyone, but at its Brussels premiere and at a public reading at the Arts Theatre Club in London in English, not many of the audience waited for the end.[142]

Challenged with a metaphor depicting a very normal process of the human body, the British (and Belgian) audience walked away, surely to commit such horror to taste in the sanctity of a locked bathroom. The idea of such a total rejection seems almost comical, unbelievable (they had, after all, seen the poster, bought the book, bought the ticket), the kind of thing we would associate with reactions to early twentieth century Dada and a Sunday-best-to-theatre public perhaps more conservatively naive to artistic attempts at 'transgression'.[143] Such performative outrage and refusal then seems to indicate something further than anachronistic defence of 'good taste'.

Away from the sanctity of the toilet, this refusal of 'pungent' French literature appears on a wider scale.[144] As Heppenstall writes in his journal of British reactions to Robbe-Grillet:

> our middlebrow, consolidating interest is marvellously dug-in. Earlier in the year, its artillery had shot up M. Robbe-Grillet's position before we, the mere infantry, got a chance to see the whites of his eyes.[145]

Experimental modes of literature in post-war Britain were dismissed for a *foreignness*, as without roots within British national tradition. Laurence Sterne

(1713–68), cited heavily among their formal inspirations by both the British and French writers of this study, would assumedly disagree (unless he would here be perceived too Irish for qualification). However, Sterne's *Tristram Shandy* (1759), was contemporaneously met with comparable scorn. As *Dr.* Johnson incorrectly claimed in 1776 'nothing odd will do long. *Tristram Shandy* did not last'.[146] Similarly dismissed as odd in this very loaded sense, the post-war writers were therefore deemed, seemingly paradoxically, both socially irresponsible, and culturally inconsequential. Whether that was in an externalizing internal cultural othering of the experimental novel in Britain, or an externalized cultural othering of the 'pungent' experimental novel perceived to be taking over France. The novelist William Cooper – whose 'optimistic' social realism in books such as *Scenes from Provincial Life* (1950), *Scenes from Married Life* (1961) and *Love on the Coast* (1973) was much-lauded at the time – writes in 1959:

> Aren't the French wonderful! Who else in these days could present a literary avant-garde so irredeemably *derrière*? Avant-garde—and they're still trying to get something out of Experimental Writing, which was fading away here at the end of the thirties and finally got the push at the beginning of the fifties. What a garde! [...] The point not to miss is this: not only are these anxious, suspicious, despairing French writers nullifying the novel, but they are weakening the intellectual world as a whole, by bringing one part of it into disrepute.[147]

As is perhaps becoming clear here, it would appear these refusals, as too the placing of innovation in literature as product of a (by-)*passed* moment, are not primarily being carried out by a popular public (as reduced to homogeneous mass) uprising of moral outrage, but being orchestrated and performed by dominant presences that held a monopoly in cultural strata, and in defence of specific social and cultural agenda.

Dominant literature as societal 'normalizer'

Morton Levitt writes in *The Rhetoric of Modernist Fiction* (2006): 'invariably, "experimental" as used by English novelists and critics from 1945 to about 1980 was a pejorative'.[148] And as such, with the experimental novel refused, a British literature of the era is found delimited to the listism presented by James

Jack Gindin in *Post War British Fiction* (1962): 'Kingsley Amis, John Wain, Keith Waterhouse, David Storey, John Bowen,[149] and others have made the novel a fresh, energetic, and responsible statement of the fifties and the early sixties.'[150] According to Marina Mackay and Lyndsey Stonebridge in *British Fiction after Modernism* (2007), the writing of these social realist figures represents 'a new ethnography turned inwards to observe an ever more precarious-looking Britain'.[151] Their responsibility is then within their role as a literature of cultural consolidation within an era of precarity; it is a prescriptive/ proscriptive literature that feeds into and out of wider dominant cultural processes of social reality norming following the Second World War (Brophy's 'Normative conquest' above). As Peter Brooker writes,

> [they] participated in the broader making and unmaking of post-war national identities, where England returned to an insular realism.[152]

A process defined by Pierre Bourdieu as a performative process of exerting 'symbolic violence', which describes the reorientation of cultural forms as 'symbolic structures' in order to re-exert a new 'symbolic power'. Symbolic structures being cultural entities such as art, language, religion, Bourdieu writes that they are 'instruments of knowledge and communication': the structuring tools with which symbolic power 'constructs reality, works to establish the *gnoseological* order; the immediate meaning of the world (and in particular, the social world)'.[153] These symbols are the tools '*par excellence* of social integration',[154] the modes of communication by which the 'logical' and 'moral' social order is unnaturally reasserted, and the veneer of a communally shared, persistent, constructed illusion of objective reality are established. The novel and *writing* here is a central cultural symbol of this post-war consolidation, and in this return to an anachronistic insular realism, the ties to which communal identities were searched for and asserted by the dominant novel were not established within the new, immediate environments of the post-war, but looked to consolidate a canon image by alignment with a highly selective, warped, tradition heredity. This was an understanding held by the experimental novel writers of the era: for Johnson, Gindin's writers listed as responsibly edifying a post-war literary Britain are 'neo-Dickensian', they 'simply imitate the act of being a writer, a deliberately anachronistic act, like writing a five-act verse drama in Shakespearean English'.[155] For Billany writing in *The Trap*, these dominant modes of literature form 'a vulgar tower of insincerities, an unreal world [...] an ivory tower which I shall help to pull down, I hope'.[156] This perhaps begins to indicate something of what this societal and human sickness or crisis was that had to be confronted, within interactions within literature itself.

In this sense of cultural regeneration of social identities, the social realist novel here feeds into and out of a post-war drive for societal re-stabilization; normalization. Presented with a world beset by war and instability, these dominant novels conjure an optimistic image of nostalgic idyll – 'love on the coast' – and position that image as the true, empirical reflection of lived-life; a precarious imaging of the world that demands a performative refusal of elements that might contradict it. The acted-out public othering of the experimental novel as *foreign, impure, immoral* by dominant presences in culture appears then demonstrative of what Sigmund Freud would call 'cultural narcissism' (which, in another context and another mode, I have applied above): a propagation of the public's 'right to despise outsiders [as] compensation for the restrictions placed on them in their own circle'.[157] In this compulsion, a communal narcissism is employed to offset the instability and hardships of a post-war world, in defence of the 'cultural ideal' and to 'combat hostility to culture within [and without] the cultural unit'.[158] Within these groupings this process is propagated as a cultural form of peace-keeping, and yet the interior societal cogency that is produced by this creation of an 'us' and a 'them' is forged on the basis that 'every culture gives itself the right to look down on the others. This is how cultural ideals occasion rupture and hostility between different culture groups – most obviously amongst nations'.[159] For Freud, this is a narcissistic opposition based on cultural ideology and a fundamental sense of social insecurity that is inherently 'self-destructive', and can only ever end yet again in dissolution and war.[160] As Dubuffet similarly writes: 'culture is enamoured with counting and measuring; the uncountable disorients it, makes it uncomfortable. Its efforts are to restrict the numbers in all areas, to be able to count them on one hand. Culture is essentially eliminative and because of this impoverishing.'[161] As such an eliminative entity, according to Dubuffet, dominant cultural processes 'have become a tool for dealing with the stable and only things that are stable' in a post-war world that would appear to be characterized by continuing societal instability and insecurity.[162] In an era of wider global shifts and internationalization of previously national societal hierarchies and processes, it further appears precarious in a space in which internalized nation as self-separated from the world by island, *outre-mer* or metropole status is something of a foregone conclusion.

The notion of dominant literature in Britain taking up dysfunctional, consolidatory cultural positions was a common criticism at the time. To refer to Henry Green, 'Amis and Wain [...] are both really bad writers. *Lucky Jim* [(1954)] is disastrous because it pretends to make something pretentious out of nothing without a thought that the whole thing was nothing from the start.'[163] Perec's 'hatchet job' review,[164] *L'Univers de la science-fiction* (1963) is devoted to how very reductive, 'reactionary', and simply wrong he finds Amis' perceptions of literature and its potentials (or lack of) to societal critique. From the viewpoint of the French writers of this study, dominant British literature suffered from a particularly bad case of a post-war societal malady of eliminative reduction, and indeed acted to cleanse cultural representation of the confrontational, challenging, or unsanitary. As Hélène Cixous writes bluntly in *Le Monde* in 1967:

> The English novel suffers from a realism close to reportage, where non-critical factual account replaces ethical perspective. Such idealistic diagnosis is partial: it signals not only a lack of morals, but a vertigo when faced with the dimensions of the contemporary real.[165]

From this standpoint, the dominant British novel looks to have reduced itself to a vanity mirror for British society to admire itself nostalgically airbrushed and eschewed the diagnostic 'social ethics' of fiction writing. To refer to Figes, speaking of Johnson's neo-Dickensian judgement:

> a belief that Ann [Quin], Alan [Burns] and I all shared with him: the belief that the seamless 'realist' novel is not only not realistic, but a downright lie. Of course all fiction is a form of lying, but the realist novel is a dangerous lie because people have come to believe it.[166]

Asserted is the complicity of the novel-at-large in a post-war persistent collective self-delusion; the novel-at-large is assigned a function in the post-war process of world rebuilding. This presents an apparent paradox within the projects of dominant British literature in the era: as a driving force of post-war social identification, the symbolic violence of this social realism primarily functioned within a role of social mythicization. Its mimetic relation to the real was not grounded in reflection, but selection, rejection and construction. The dominant post-war literature in Britain then appears as that described by Roland Barthes: a 'realism of regression', it generates an 'effect of the real', and positions this effect as direct 'referentiality'.[167] With a mask of 'simple presentation of things', it hid a toxic ideological drive.

'Reactionary' Vrance

Though Heppenstall bemoans British 'middlebrow' rejections of Robbe-Grillet as opposed to a kind of mythical 'highbrow' general French reader, the refusal of new forms of literature, and new forms of participant and participation in the cultural sphere occurred too in France. Robbe-Grillet himself writes:

> my novels were not welcomed at the time of their publication with the greatest warmth, to say the least. From the disapproving half-silence that met the first (*Les Gommes* [(1953)]) to the out-and-out violent refusal by the broadsheets of the second (*Le Voyeur* [(1955)])), very little progress was made.[168]

France, Sartre writes in 1947, was a place of 'literary inflation', in which French writers who attempt to 'engage' with the difficult 'truths' of the era (as opposed to 'disengage' from them into entirely idealized realities; romantic fabulations) were 'more read about than read'.[169] Sartre describes a Paris-centric salon atmosphere where the romantic myth of the eccentric writer was of more interest in gossip sections and radio vox-pops than the books they wrote. In terms of literary presence, it was rather the idealized romance of the social realist novel that again claimed cultural dominance. Further, Sartre seems envious of the English writer's apparent isolation from the salon culture of being expected to entertain 'politicians and bankers' with witticisms: 'the English writers make a virtue of necessity and, in adding to the singularity of their traditions, try to claim their isolation from high society as their own free choice'.[170] This raises that cultural strata, what Robbe-Grillet describes as the 'literary caste system', in France was also dominated by a consolidatory, traditionalist presence. A traditionalist presence that corresponds closely with a similar element in Britain which, that, as demonstrated below, also possessed an *othering* anti-cosmopolitan eye to post-Second World War nation idealization.

While in Britain, Green states, as a kind of re-imagining of Cinderella, dominant social realist writers 'Amis and Wain in their novels often put their young men to rise [erectile/social class] on the backs of [upper-class] women in the red-brick universities',[171] this apparently responsible dominant literature appears little different in France. According to Perec, dominant, again social realist, post-war literature in France was typified by stories 'chiefly interested in the liaisons of rich young men with poor young girls'.[172] This returns us to the debates of a pluri-realism above; of dominant literature as an idealism dislocated from the real world, that adopts the toxic visage of total objectifying mimesis. The dominant literature was indeed regarded in France as, and claimed to be, 'neo-Balzacian' on, Butor states, a reduced interpretation of Balzac generated by his received cultural figure-image as formally conservative, rather than a reading of his novels.[173] And it was upon this corrupted image of heredity realism they were sold as authentically real, taking up positions of direct opposition to an internally *othered* 'non-Balzacian' experimental novel. Thus, aiming to, again, ideologically balance the literary budget by which the innovative would become a cultural zero-value. An oppositional conflict described above of Britain that would indeed appear to equally dog the experimental novel in France throughout the period. In 1950, Sarraute describes the emergence of a new experimental 'literature of analysis', that would internally oppose a dominant obsolete novel that was acting to minor the critical social role of the novel genre at-large:

> the novel, which only a stubborn adherence to obsolete techniques places in the position of a minor art, pursues with means that are uniquely its own, a path which can only be its own [...] that is the uncovering of the new.[174]

A drive to obsolescence Queneau regarded as harbouring the intention of removing literature's aesthetic potential to analysis and confrontation of societal inadequacy and malfunction. As he writes in 1955, the reductions of the dominant novel would soon lead to the disappearance of literature from culture altogether: 'in a few years, there will no longer be any "books," they'll be used as nothing more than a "mechanical" medium for the simple transmission of information via language'.[175] A statement he fashions in paragraphs surrounded by thick black chain links. Later, by 1967, we seem to observe this neo-Balzacian dominant entity achieving its apparent ideological aims. In that year, Le Lionnais and Noël Arnaud led a ten-day Cerisy conference entitled '*Paralittérature*', at which they attempted to weaponize claims that innovative writing in France, such as their own, was not literature; *para*-literature. Debate largely centred around the idea that experimental novels like Roche's *Compact* (1966) (who was also in attendance) were a kind of 'literature of non-literature'. A 'literary-para-literary' centre to the many artefacts of written language disavowed in culture's pursuit of 'bourgeois' literary – thus representational – purism, or 'canon' writing; ergo 'canon' selective imaging of the 'real world'.[176] Which indicates a dominant tendency in French post-war literature, in the same vein to that in Britain, towards a kind of proto-Instagramization of the real. A dominant literature that would appear societal product and producer of a fundamental 'nihilism, a neurotic idealism that presents the allure of a metaphysical pseudo-materialism' according to Sollers;[177] its social function is that of a disingenuous, self-totalizing *pseudo-realism*. This posits a retrograde, regressive dominant literature in both Britain and France with more in common with medieval prescriptive romance and proscriptive morality tale rather than a cultural artefact engaged with the new realities of a post-Second World War world.

Then the assumed positioning of eyebrows on a face does not present as reliable modelling of dichotomy between the literatures, or wider cultural climates, of Britain and France in this era. In terms of material access, just as in France, in Britain within the years 1945 to 1975 experimental novels found regular publication (which would infer an engaged, consuming and considerable public (whatever cross-section that might be), that by these statements of refusal appear disappeared from history), and following this period in both countries the vast majority of these texts were kept out of print. As Nick Bentley writes of Muriel Spark and Robbe-Grillet: 'both writers were affected by a similar social, cultural and intellectual climate and were responding with similar experimental narrative techniques'.[178] Therefore, it would appear to see France as a 'heaven' of innovation and Britain its 'hell' is indeed to take conclusions on a cursory glance. Nation oppositions Henri Peyre describes as 'frail generalisations';[179] it would be to adopt yet another reductive paradigm. In both countries the experimental novel appears reduced to a marginalized, minor role in literature, by a romantically idealized realism of the social realist novel. Then, established Anglo-American perceptions of post-war France, predicated on the fetish of Robbe-Grillet, as I have termed it, indeed appear a further, reductive, romantically *othered*, selection. This acts to misread, further occlude, the socio-cultural presence of these texts in both Britain and in France.[180]

Case in point

Beyond a cross-channel glance, rather than received with finely-arched plaudits, the French writers of this study often came up against similar claims of irresponsibility, immorality, and calls for their exclusion from cultural participation. While Sartre was complaining about the tedium of the salon, also in 1947, Boris Vian was taken to court for moral indecency (involving incitement to murder) over the book *J'Irai cracher sur vos tombes* (1946).[181] In first his denouncement by a private lobby group called the *Cartel d'action sociale et morale*, trial by the press, then that by the judiciary, Vian first had to prove that he was simply the translator (he was not), and the pseudonym he had adopted, Vernon Sullivan, was a real writer; a real – American – person (he was not). Vian then had to prove that the nature of the book was 'art', and not 'writing': it became a trial of what is 'literature', as opposed to a non-artistic 'para-literature ["*extra-littéraire*"]'.[182] This he successfully won and resulted in the novel swiftly becoming a bestseller. Before, in an amnesty in 1948, Vian admitted his part (the fortnight jail term for admission commuted, and the rights to the book forfeited to the French state), and the book was re-banned in 1949. And yet while the outcome of this trial legally positions these texts as of artistic interest – similar to Johnson's perception of the 1960 *Lady Chatterley's Lover* judgement – Vian's bartering of what literature potentially was came with a very real threat of failure; potential result of the trial itself being a bankrupting fine (300,000 francs) and, perhaps more bizarre for the twenty-first century observer, years of jail-time (two years, to be precise). In his later study of 'the affair', Arnaud writes that this was a product of the 'taste of the time' in post-war France, as a carry-over of the Vichy principles of 'Work, Family, Nation'.[183] Or, as he phrases it on the back cover of his 1974 *Dossier de l'affaire 'J'irai cracher sur vos tombes'*:

> Between the two wars Freidrich Sieburg posed a question (which became a famous headline): God, is he French? A reading of the *Dossier de l'affaire*... raises an analogous problematic and by no means less profound: ARSEHOLERY, IS IT FRENCH?[184]

'Arseholery' here compounding both 'idiocy' and 'vindictiveness' ['*connerie*']; the primary issue taken with Vian's book appears not his pastiche deployment of the exploitation tropes of the *roman noir*. Rather, that the protagonist, Lee Anderson, is defined legally in the US as black, but has pale skin and blond hair, and, in segregated America, 'infiltrates white society'. And this apparent obscene narrative horror was being visited on the French public by a *foreigner*; the made-up American spectre of Vernon Sullivan (the *Cartel d'action sociale et morale* had also gone for, the potentially more real, Henry Miller on similar charges). Here, Vian appears to be trying to draw the reader to question segregation in America, thus vast fractures inherent to the supposed post-war Free World at its very supposed centre. Reaction against the book further reflexively indicates these fractures; of an underlying social continuity in France of the principles of Vichy, as Arnaud argues. Principles that were supposed to have dissolved abruptly in 1944, with the 'Liberation' of France.

In his *dossier*, Arnaud – who was editor of the semi-clandestine surrealist resistance review *La Main à plume* under occupation – presents an image of what Louis-Ferdinand Céline in his post-war writing calls 'Vrance'.[185] As a former very much invested Nazi-collaborator, Céline uses the term to refer to what he views as the hypocritical disavowing French society collectively employed in order to avoid reconciling their participation in the Holocaust and upholding fascism throughout the Second World War. Whereas for Arnaud it is a general continuity arseholery that potentially defines the French, for Céline, post-war Vrance was an inherently fascist populace, wearing a Marshall Plan-friendly 'liberal' mask.[186] With a similar understanding of post-war France from a very different perspective, Topor writes that with his writing he wants to confront society with its disavowed, with 'the blood, shit and sex' they try to ignore;[187] for his entire existence to be an affront to those who had tried to have him and his family killed for being *foreign* and Jewish during the war, and continued to people the post-war world around him. In this depiction of the post-war cultural climates of these countries in this era, this conflict within, around the cultural entity of literature appears integrally tied up with societal conditions. And, it is the societal influence of traditionalist or reactionary presences that monopolized cultural strata that are here framed as elements to be confronted; that functioned to delimit and reform social reality itself, which here appears a fundamentally exclusory process. This realigns the frameworks of interaction between the experimental novel and the social realist novel and their writers. In a space of experience of total war, its fallout, and post-war societal normalization and rebuilding in process of dominant cultural mediation, minored presences in literature that questioned that process, or brought societal narratives of re-continuity and re-stabilization into contention, are here found refused.

The predicament of cultural refusal

And yet, the reactionary rejection of these modes of literature; defined by Arnaud as 'arseholery' or by Johnson as 'cuntishness', does not appear to reside only in Britain and France in the period. Themerson's Swedish translator didn't manage to secure publication of any of Themerson's translated novels. And, as Calder above alludes, the Belgian audience walked out on Topor's play too. When *Vinci avait raison* (1976) was staged in Belgium at the Théâtre de Poche in Brussels in 1977, it caused a national scandal. In the newspaper *Peuple*, Philippe Genaert wrote:

> We must put the idiot in prison... for creating such filth [...] it's a matter of the public moral good.[188]

Five years earlier in 1972, with the first theatrical performance of *Joko fête son anniversaire* (1969), Genaert had called for Topor's execution: 'in some countries, the author would be shot'.[189] And despite continuing obscenity trials and concerted outrage in both Britain and in France around these books, in a period beginning with a late-1940s and 1950s dominated by McCarthyism and the loyalty checking agencies, many of the writers taken now to describe an American post-war literature were published in London (much to the delight of the publisher Calder) and Paris; or bodily fled America for these cities (a displacement seen with the bizarre historical moment of 'vermin' stand-off between Burroughs and MacDiarmid). And so, on a scale of societal post-war consolidatory reactions against the perceived internal/external otherly, non-traditional and/or obscene in literature, neither Britain nor France appear particularly eccentric in their dominant cultural strata's refusal of the experimental novel. This socio-cultural climate of rejection of critical presences in societies' art of primary value appears an effect of a wider dysfunction inherent to post-war capitalist societies in an era when much hay was made of apparent dogmas of 'artistic freedom of expression',[190] and indeed individual human freedom of action.

And as such, claims of immorality function as a mask by which the underlying motive for refusal is obscured. We seem to be presented with dominant cultural mediation of the post-war world as an idealizing, homogenizing entity of reduction of access to the field of real itself. The removal of the aesthetic dimension of societal critique in the experimental texts by relegation to an assigned unfathomable eccentricity (for example, in France, in cutesy filmic re-imaginings),[191] or to cover band-style anachronism, or out of literature altogether, further demonstrates this dominant cultural process of elimination. As Brooke-Rose recounts of the era, 'the resistance was great, in France but especially in England, where traditionalist critics and realistic novelists organized strong campaigns, which they no doubt feel they have won'.[192] Writing in 1981, Brooke-Rose had a clear view of the experimental novel's apparent defeat. As the here applied post-war delimitation infers, as stated, I peg a rough discontinuation to this formulation of the novel in 1975, as by the mid- to late-1970s the vast majority of writers of the experimental novel had died, succumbed to long-term illness, exited mainstream publication, or stopped writing altogether. And this discontinuation in production and authorial lobby was accompanied by their texts' apparent disappearance from literary history. It is the point at which many of the books fell definitively out of print, out of access and out of discourse.

Then, it is this native-to-period refusal of the experimental novel by 'traditionalist critics and realistic novelists' that appears to have first successfully pushed its artefacts out of readability, and its writers' names out of ken, before this dropped baton image of the post-war was later opted into by the cultural-critical discourse of a cannibalistic ouroboros modernism-postmodernism. Where the assimilation of the term experimental from an engaged literary realism to a generic term for artistic forms as wide-ranging as 'edible art' and spoken-word poetry, and experiment in the post-war novel was reduced to de-historicized leftover or prototype, would demonstrate complicity in that warping reduction. If the post-war experimental novel here appears confrontational, as questioning of dominant cultural mediation of the lived-in world – Johnson's 'truth as is found in life' – this refusal constitutes a denial of what that minor cultural interrogation might signify. A de-selecting cultural refusal that would appear intrinsic facet of a period of socio-cultural normalization; the result of a societal process of nostalgic, optimistic, occlusive self-mythicization. Social realism and its seemingly successful impulse to silence the experimental novel therefore appears to centralize as novel project the unquestionable propagation of a 'hypostatic illusion', a drive to 'make fiction a reality'.[193] Sollers states that this is an 'irresponsible impulse to be without contradiction which each society must check and try to keep under control'.[194] With the reduction of the experimental novel to 'ivory tower' eccentric anachronism; socially irresponsible and culturally inconsequential,[195] we then appear to witness the dismantling of these socio-cultural checks and balances. This opposition within and around the novel then takes place as a conflict within the cultural formation of post-war social reality itself. Between an unnatural symbolic violence, and entities that attempted to cut away at the mythicized façade in process of violent assertion. Within these conflicting positions within reality mediation, of a consolidation and a confrontation, an idealized evasion and a critical interrogation, social realism then presents as literary conduit of the socio-cultural *horror vacui* of the era. The writers who people social realism here performatively refuse a further cultural reflex of those societal conditions, an experimental novel that questions that cultural void-stuffing as a damaging process of propagating a deluded, deluding imaging of the world. And as such, we are confronted with the image of a dominant, claimed post-war sovereign, 'literary realism as a kind of Disneyfication'.[196] It is a literature that adopts the mask of socially engaged realism to perform an illusory reconstruction of socio-cultural world-norms, where the reader participates in a collective '"cognitive estrangement" [that] here takes the form of an unworlding';[197] whereby claims social realism is responsible in its idealism, and the experimental novel is irresponsible in its critique appear here reversed.

Thus, this idea of a defence of cultural ideal presents within the sense of a defence of culture-built social delusion, a pathological illusory removed from the post-war experiential real. As Butor writes in 1955, the social realist writers 'are imposters that critique must denounce, because such works, despite their charms and merits, both maintain and obscure the blackness, lock consciousness in its contradictions, in their blindness they risk bringing about the most fatal of disorders'.[198] This implies the defence of such idealized imaging as *the* reflection of the real is not only regressive and integrally irrational, but indeed self-destructive. If social realism here appears the literary mouthpiece of post-war cultural pacification of the social through mythic communal identification, then at the very base level of the human, by rejecting the new of the world around them, and a new literature that tried to engage with that, the dominant writers and the collective social communities that appear to have taken up their texts as truth indeed seem 'revealed to be caught in a terrible compulsion to repeat' the wars, the economic crises, the societal dissolutions and divisions they appear to intend to mediate by evasion.[199] An evasive illusion unreconciled with the conditions in which the social human must live, and therefore propagating of instabilities and ruptures unmet that indeed, echoing Zola above, appear contagious. As Charles Sugnet writes of the societal effect of the dominant novel in the post-war: 'the whole public has been conned (or has conned itself) into accepting as fixed, "natural," and "real," an order of things which is a human artefact'.[200] The collective opting in to this 'love on the coast' imaging of reality, the upholding of this dominant culture as dominant, then takes on the sense of a retreat from the real itself; a palliative interaction of culture and social that does not cure the societal wounds above raised, but cedes to a collective impulse to occultation. By which the wounds of the past, and present are not confronted, and perhaps allowed to heal or even acknowledged as such, but grow, renew and mutate in ever greater societal disorders that must again be cyclically, performatively hidden by ever-increasing magnitudes of delusional remove.

1.4 Historical contexts

Writing out of the 1945 event

This leads us to a further screen to clear comprehension of these texts, the figures who generated them, indeed the readers who received them. This is the dissonance between received narrations of this period as a moment in history, and the image presented of it by the experimental novel and its writers. By drawing these figures and their writing back into cultural signification, we then also draw established historical understandings of the decades following the Second World War into contention. Within the reflexive projects and projections raised in the above, the 'vast ruptures' of the Second World War do not appear to have ended with formal surrenders in 1945 and the signing of peace treaties in the mid-late 1940s.[201] As the reflexive prefix *post-* itself infers, the decades following that war indeed appear locked in relation to the experience of that war, a moment that appears to be the catalyst of inherent societal dysfunction that dominant cultural structure appears to here double down on, and seemingly continued – perhaps hysteretically continues – to do so.

The experimental novel of the era is unique in its historical position and content-form interactions, but not so as texts: they are amongst 'literally thousands of narratives written since the end of the Second World War [that] turn irrevocably on some written "event"'.[202] Christopher Nash here pinpoints an international epistemic break in 1945, a cultural event that is inherent in writing of the period that followed. A point of no return where literature became 'grossly incompatible with the writing premises of a *Madame Bovary* [(1856)], a *Père Goriot* [(1835)], a *Middlemarch* [(1871)], an *Anna Karenina* [(1877)]'.[203] I argue here that it is more or less possible to follow on that list with a *Mrs. Dalloway* (1925), a *Metamorphosis* (1915), a *Nadja* (1928), a *Ulysses* (1922).[204] As Green says of post-war innovation: 'I think Joyce and Kafka have said the last word on each of the two forms they developed. There's no one to follow them. They're like cats which have licked the plate clean. You've got to dream up another dish if you're to be a writer [...] it isn't that everything has been done in fiction – truly nothing has been done yet.'[205] The dish has been emptied, there are no nostalgic scraps left to be licked, thus necessitating replacement with the new. Here, the new state of things cannot be said to seamlessly reconcile with what had gone before. The relation of the end of one dish with another, this 'event' and 'the new', writes Badiou, is exclusive:

> In a given world, we have something new only if the rational or conventional laws of this world are interrupted, or put out of their normal effects, by something which happens, and that I name an Event.[206]

In terms of this study, then, it is perhaps not that earlier writers had licked the plate clean (both Kafka (d. 1924, at forty) and Joyce (d. 1941, at forty-eight) died prematurely, before they could assumedly exhaust said plate), but that the material Event of the Second World War and its ending smashed the plate altogether. According to Harvey, both what he calls 'literary modernism' and an 'optimistic' sense of 'moral progression' within the 'modern project' was 'shattered' by this culminating Event, by 'death camps and death squads, militaries and two world wars, its threat of nuclear annihilation and its experience of Hiroshima and Nagasaki'.[207] This is the position held by Sartre, who writes that the Second World War had 'killed' the 'poetic-political' projects of surrealism, and the reality-mediating projects of the novelists that 'came to prominence around 1927'.[208] The surrealist group was formally disbanded in Britain in 1947,[209] with a statement presented at the same 'meagre' *Exposition Internationale du Surréalisme* Sartre takes as signalling its formal end too in France;[210] few of the '1927' novelists survived the war.[211] Then the end of the Second World War, in terms of presences in literature, does harbour the sense of a plate cleanly broken, though that breaking from the before appears the product of an Event that wasn't all that clean. This new post-Event period does not present as a fresh start, passing of the baton or clean beginning, but more in the sense of an abrupt beginning of the end. As Marc Alyn writes in 1956 of the human, and the novel they produced and consumed, in the period: 'a wind of existential pessimism blew through the spirits, marking literary works with an indelible seal of the event. It wasn't necessarily that all was lost, but that everything had in common a certain taste of ash, of tears and blood. Whether their authors wanted it or not.'[212] Similarly, for Victor Gollancz in Britain, the world found itself in an end times, with 'ashes in the mouth and ice in the heart',[213] and this experientiality permeated the novel as art-object.

This Event that new forms of literature fell out from under initially appears very much similar to that of the First World War; the post-Second World War indeed appears within a renewed sense of *entre-deux-guerres* (a moment not just pushed on by the past, but pulled on by the impending transpired), of uneasy triumphalism. However, unlike that earlier demarcation, it seems fed by the understanding that these World Wars were not repetitive but cyclical, and their accumulating violence was growing in total reach. As such, Sartre writes, '1918 was a celebration [...] today, such a spirit [of return to continuity socio-cultural norm] has extinguished itself, or refuses to take; the time for celebrating isn't soon to return.'[214] As late as 1972, Pierre de Boisdeffre relates, 'everything changed in 1940 [with the fall of France]. Our humanist and Christian civilisation suddenly slipped into the abyss.'[215] Then, after the Second World War this is not a seemingly historically blind champagne Weimar of Bright Young Things unaware of impending return to foreign slaughter, but this violent dissolution and its projected re-arrival is unavoidably present. As James Knowlson writes of France, 'after the initial euphoria of the Liberation, the dominant mood became one of intense disappointment, disillusionment and depression.'[216] In both France and Britain, the mid-1940s to early-1950s are discussed as the unstable 'unravelling black years'.[217] They are characterized by an overwhelming sense of irreconcilable 'anxiety'.[218] Within each and every family's living room, it is a post-Blitz, post-Occupation, post-Holocaust, post-Hiroshima/Nagasaki period of paranoia. A permeating sense seems apparent in the initial post-war period, of yet another *interbellum interregnum*. On a localized scale in Britain it is a moment product of the common 'experiences of bombing, of universal military and civil defence service'.[219] In France, it was a continuing period of national division following partition, in which 'revolution [or perhaps rather, civil war] seemed imminent'.[220] And as such, as Gollancz writes in 1946: 'Hitler is dead, and Germany is in ruins. But has the horror passed? I do not think so.'[221]

This then speaks of an inherent continuation of realized fear born in the traumatic violent moment, that as seen above would appear to have become culturally buried in the social psyche. That though the violence of that war had been made primordial by its formalized, normalized, ending – it was *The Good War*, it was *The Liberation of Europe* – its realized horrors actively continued in the POW camps, the rehabilitation of concentration camp survivors, the liquidation of German cities in Central and Eastern Europe, French legal and illegal social purification executions (*L'Épuration*) and humiliations (in particular of women, *Les Tondues*). As too the trials and hangings of perceived traitors in Britain, and the Nuremberg Trials. Across Europe, 'the continent was disorganised and impoverished; millions of refugees, or "displaced persons," as they were known in the language of the Allied bureaucrats, had to be given some sort of shelter and nourishment. There were millions of prisoners of war in Allied hands: many of those in the Soviet Union did not return home for years.'²²² The fear that military dictatorship would inevitably take hold in France led, in the early years of strict rationing, failed harvests and famine, to the money provided to keep the country vaguely liquid bearing no mention of a *'République française'*. As too, the exclusion of French representatives from Yalta,²²³ and plans for setting up 'France' as an Allied protectorate. As well as contingency plans for a communist reaction to that eventuality resulting in a 'Soviet Paris-Berlin-Moscow axis' that would bring the USSR to Britain's Calais doorstep,²²⁴ at a time of that country's own internal social, cultural and economic instability and fracture. To refer again to Gollancz, he gives the image of the British and French newspaper reader passively reading of the new atrocities of the week in the Sunday edition, over breakfast and before church. As he quotes what they passively read over toast, or perhaps a croissant:

> In Danzig evictions take place street by street [...] between 12,000,000 and 14,000,000 refugees [...] typhoid [...] cattle trains [...] in the woods around Berlin corpses are hanging from the trees. Other men, women and children throw themselves into the rivers. Hundreds of corpses are continually drifting down the rivers Elbe and Oder [...]²²⁵

For Gollancz, these years embody a brutalized, brutalizing, Europe in disarray, that had learned to become passive to, stupefied by, an ever-present brutality within quotidian life, and as such was already in or on the cusp of a decay into 'barbarism'. Where the 'high values' of 'European civilisation' had been, over the course of the war, and would continue to be 'reversed: good becomes evil, and evil good'.²²⁶ Then, with the fallout of that war still so active, so very 'black' in these years following, the sanitized narrations of civilizational victory (Good War etc.) appear difficult to reconcile with material conditions. If these narratives, to which the dominant novel subscribed and propagated, were intended to permit societies to re-coalesce around nation identity, they appear to have had further effects beyond that intended. The narration of these years in France as the beginning of *Les Trentes Glorieuses* (1945–75), and claims of moral victory and universal post-war consensus for the greater good in Britain – that this was not only a getting back to normal, but the beginnings of a new utopian drive, a getting back to better than ever – appear entirely removed from the plane of experientiality. To quote Max Horkheimer writing in March 1946:

At the moment of this writing, the peoples of the democratic nations are confronted with the problems of consummating their victory of arms. They must work out and put into practice the principles of humanity in the name of which the sacrifices of war were made. The present potentialities of social achievement surpass the expectations of all philosophers and statesmen who have ever outlined in utopian programs the idea of a truly human society. Yet there is a universal feeling of fear and disillusionment. The hopes of mankind seem to be farther from fulfilment today than they were even in the groping epochs when they were first formulated by humanists. It seems that even as technical knowledge expands the horizon of man's thought and activity, his autonomy as an individual, his ability to resist the growing apparatus of mass manipulation, his power of imagination, his independent judgement appear to be reduced. Advance in technical facilities for enlightenment is accompanied by a process of dehumanisation.[227]

This throws into question the justness of retroactively justified action, the objective, universal justness of an Allied violent victory,[228] the morality in morals not inherited, but arbitrarily asserted as a codified aesthetic of belief that works to bury killing committed and suffered; Sartre's sorrowful – bad – societal conscience. Whether the payoff of being allowed to go on as if socii are not both killer and victim within that war, within that occupation, has achieved anything but a dynamic of a social subject perpetually relying on reduced narrative to fill the gaps of their confusion, in a constant cycle in which the phantasm of belief is evermore sclerotic. All of which returns us to this wilful amnesia, to refer to Themerson's *Bayamus* in 1949:

> There are some dozens, or dozens of hundreds, or hundreds of thousands of people living, working, eating, drinking, discussing problems and going to the cinema, who have also something in them definitely and irreparably broken. Nobody knows that, and nobody ever will know that, because they hide the very fact that there is a small nothing broken in them; because they pretend to be the same as they were before the war; and because they want to take that secret with them into the grave.[229]

It would appear here that the societal and human trauma of that war and its ending 'can therefore be thought of as a kind of transcendental shock'.[230] As catalyst of a series of material and phantasmagoric dissolutions, reversals and disintegrations in what was perceived to have been a previously stable world-norm, and that had the effect of progressively concretizing a dehumanizing remove of the individual and the communal collective from the conditions in which they must continue to function.

Despite the 'blackness' of these years, for Gollancz there is worse to come. As he writes in *Our Threatened Values* (1946) in the rhetoric of Western civilization on the precipice of ultimate peril: 'most of us are uneasy, and a few of us are downright frightened, about the atom bomb: we feel that another war, far more painful and degrading than the last; may sooner or later be upon us'.[231] Sooner or later, the world will return to war, and the impending slaughter is at home, at *your* place of work, it is for *you*, *your* family and *your* children. To refer again to Sartre, the human in the immediate post-war is horrifically aware of this 'historicity' 'in a kind of stupor':[232]

> There was a collective project that was forged for the future and that will be our project [...] something we await in the shadow of the future, something that might perhaps be revealed to us in the illumination of the final moment before we are annihilated; the secret of our actions and of our most intimate moments lies before us in the catastrophe in which our names will be inscribed. Historicity drowns us; it is in all that we touch, in the air that we breathe, in the page that we read, in the page that we write, in the love we might feel, in all of this we find the taste of history, a bitter and strange taste mixed of the absolute and the transitory.[233]

If this stupefied anxiety, this de-humanizing performative remove from experientiality, characterizes the black years of the early post-war, by the later years of the period, as viewed through the prism of the experimental novel, perception appears to have little shifted of 'this stage of civilisation's peril'.[234] It is in those later years that Gollancz and Sartre foresee the final atomizing, ecocidal, end of everything, and this sense remains there ubiquitous. Anna Kavan writes in 1967, 'this uncertainty, and the resulting tension, provoked escalating crises, each of which brought nearer the final catastrophe. An insane impatience for death was driving mankind to a second suicide, even before the full effect of the first had been felt.'[235] As Brophy similarly begins *Black Ship to Hell* (1962): 'the theme of the book is man as a destructive and, more particularly, a self-destructive animal: a theme whose urgency is obvious at a time when he is threatening to commit suicide as a species'.[236] For Sollers writing in 1966 the period was very much still within 'the end times', for which the experimental novel functioned as an 'atomised Babel'; a communicating 'mnemopolis' within this 'necropole' space of continued deathly societal 'stupefaction'.[237]

The new 'new'

However, counter to that posited by the writers of this study, the black years of precarity are now widely held to begin in 1945, and, as cited above, abruptly end in and around the early-1950s. When this blackness was apparently cleared away and a period of 'unprecedented', 'miracle'[238] economic growth and societal 'modernisation' and 'progression' that was 'to flower so powerfully'[239] by the 1960s apparently 'burst onto society [...] with all of the force, excitement, disruption, and horror of the genuinely new'.[240] An apparent new 'new' that seemingly delivered societies to their late-twentieth century states of norm, where 'it *appears* as though we live a kind of universal peace'.[241] This has led, according to Mackay and Stonebridge, to critics classifying the 'post-war period' as a delayed beginning; in and around the early 1950s,[242] with the ambiguous, confusing, stupefying black years discounted from history. And yet concrete examples of violence and instability over-spilling that war continued beyond the vaguely pegged black years which end in 1950 in the violence invoked across the globe by Britain's sporadic attempts at maintaining empire, or walking away from it, and the violence inflicted by France in doomed interventions intended to preserve their own. As, too, both countries' development and deployment of nuclear weapons. Further, on the home front for France, the 1950s and 1960s were harried by an almost annual series of bloody and bloodless continued attempts at *coup d'état* and regime change, some of which were successful: the Fourth Republic established in 1946 was dissolved amidst violence and crisis in 1958. France found itself in circumstances so desperate, French governments of the era repeatedly sought national unification with *la perfide albion*, which Britain, in its own moment of instability deemed untenable.[243] In Britain, the 1950s and 1960s were a period of weak governance, labour disputes; societal division and 'Rivers of Blood'. As a product of this instability, the later years of the period brought the introduction of the three-day week, and Britain's new-found status as 'the sick man of Europe'. None of which find much of a place in current received normalized nation images of either country's recent history. It would perhaps indicate that the classification of an ended violent, unstable black years between 1945 and the early-1950s as oppositional construct to whatever it was that followed, seemingly characterized as a stabilized new enlightened period of reaffirmation of civilizational progression, moral good and universal peace, is a further misleading cultural othering of elements within human experientiality and societal conditions. As a new without Badiouean 'material break', without 'Event', it would appear that it is no 'genuine new' at all.

1968 as performative re-adhesion

Looking for an Aristotelian reconciling narrative *teleute* to the instability and violence of the early years of the era, Mackay and Stonebridge pin the student protests of 'Paris May '68' as culminating proof of this new 'new'.[244] For them, May '68 functioned as a sort of correcting manoeuvre to the sense of overwhelming anxiety or civilizational decay that dominates the years that precede it; a moment where Western societies finally re-arrived at clarity of civilizational project. They write, it is 'only when the post-war sensibility violently sheds its historical and ideological skins in 1968 that we can really say (again) that on or about a certain date something in human character changed'.[245] A clarity which, for Mackay and Stonebridge, is found in the deliverance of history from the ambiguous post-war to the clarity claimed by postmodernism; a construct we have already found itself ambiguous and unstable above. In a similar impulse for sea-change, Joseph Darlington goes further, claiming this moment as the 'total zenith' of the experimental novel.[246] Darlington appears to frame the experimental novel as conduit of French students' permutations of the Maoist Cultural Revolution, despite none of the writers of the post-war experimental novel participating in May '68, close to no artefacts of the experimental novel finding publication in that year, and those in Paris at the time directly refusing affiliation. In apparent agreeance with the writers of this study, much current discourse regards the zenith of social and cultural freedom critical imaging of May '68 as a misleading fallacy in narratives of recent socio-cultural history. As Benjamin Noys writes in *The Persistence of the Negative* (2012):

> The historical irony, pointed out by Jacques Rancière, is that it has been left-wing thinkers (or ex-left-wing thinkers) who have done most to popularise

the critique that May 68 was simply an effect of the cunning of capitalist reason. This position puts a perverse twist on the concept of recuperation: capitalism does not recuperate radical struggles, it has already moulded them in advance – hence capitalism is the only game in town. Christopher Leigh Connery describes this as the position of 'always-already co-optation.' In fact the US based Telos group came close to this position in the late 1970s. They argued that many, if not all, of the protest movements of the 1960s embodied an 'artificial negativity' that was actually incited by capitalism to create a certain amount of friction that would improve its functioning.[247]

As suggested above, this understanding was not only a position to be critically assigned *a posteriori* by (ex-)Marxist critics. When Perec was commended for auguring the student riots with his book *Les Choses* (1965), he vehemently denied any connection: 'there is no causal relation there';[248] 'the characters aren't mounting a revolution, but a process of critical thinking'.[249]

The position presented by the writers of this study is that there is no easy out from the violence and inadequacies of the post-war world; that this moment of realizational stupefaction suspended between points of total human and societal dissolution in the recent past and impending future appears inescapable. And as such, the human locked within stupefying experientiality, within a palliative relation of culture to social has no access to supposed Cultural Revolution. In their stupefied now suspended between two apocalyptic Events, Perec's characters in *Les Choses* attempt to critically apprehend rather than avoid or overthrow that confusion and ambiguity. For these writers, the socio-cultural climate of the era is indeed defined by an inherent asphyxiated-asphyxiating always-already co-optation, that itself was a reality the social human must try to meet. As it was not some abstract hyper-hydra mythical capitalist machine that dictated this process, but the human collective itself. In a societal climate where the passivity of the newspaper reader performatively self-removed from the violence outside their window had mutated by the later years of the period into the dominant orthodoxy of socio-cultural norm as perhaps demonstrated above in relation to social realism; a performative, collective act of mutual self-unworlding, Horkheimer's societal process of de-humanization.

To look to, arguably, the only experimental novel to appear that year in Britain or France, Queneau's *le Vol d'Icare* (1968), the narrative follows figures inescapably imprisoned within layers of fictive reality built and maintained by their cultural codification, social ties and communal interactions with those around them. The point at which they believe they have changed their circumstances enwrapped in a further layer of codified virtuality. As Johnson similarly depicts the human in 1964, revised and filmed in 1967, and screened in 1968, with *You're Human Like the Rest of Them* (1967):

> The locusts couldn't get away, of course/
> They had no defence against getting killed/
> The only thing a locust could do was/
> To make itself an awkward thing to eat/[250]

This would perhaps indeed put a perverse twist on the term People Power. Writing in 1967, and reprinting in 1968, Sollers refers to 'counter culture' as 'pseudo-transgression': 'a fantasy of experience, the forbidden has disappeared from the field of cognition, and what would appear "liberation" is but a mask of repression redoubled'.[251] Brophy criticises a May 68-esque sit-in at-length in the final section of *In Transit*, as for her such internal societal conflict is 'the pretext for a grand collusion' of implicit 'self-interest'.[252] It is not a process of revolution, but functions as a petrifying re-adhesion of the social to dominant cultural ideologies; the stupefied, self-destructive delusions of civilization, here revealed an abstracted re-narration; *ruins* façading as synecdochic whole. As such, the position given by the writers of the experimental novel of the period can be succinctly presented in the words of Dubuffet, for whom May '68 was a 'struggle against culture by minds that are themselves entirely spun of its thread'.[253]

Similar to the critique given by Noys, raised here is that there can be no authentic counter to culture; like for Queneau's Icare, there is no authentic outside whereby the societal body might be clearly, coldly objectified and consciously altered. The inability to meet with the barbarism of the war and its fallout, and the impulse to keep on keeping on amongst it all had seeped across and into the fundamental structures of relation of culture to human, to social, to world. As Paul Virilio states in 1972: 'from the moment the world status quo was guaranteed by an atomic umbrella, it's clear that public action is no longer possible [...] the nuclear umbrella forbids all action, except the parasitic'.[254] As such, the critical perception of a 1950s/1960s sense of new centred on freedom of expression, youth revolt and counter cultural consumption indeed appears as a disingenuous moment of new or fundamental change. It was, after all, Charles de Gaulle dragged out of retirement, whose public oration 'ended the crisis of May 68'. Rather, these years of new clarity would appear as a moment of redoubled collective repression, in a period of societal reconsolidation. A re-adhesion to the self-destructive, dysfunctional, bombed-out socio-cultural structures that remained following the Second World War, and that only a few years before are now regarded to have been utterly, unknowably broken. And as such, 'by 1972', Mark Fisher writes in 2016,

> the counterculture's dreams of overthrowing and replacing dominant structures have devolved into a series of empty gestures, a congealed rhetoric [...] its libertarian rhetoric not only serving as a legitimation of familiar male privilege but offering new rationales for exploitation and subjugation.[255]

A 1950s pseudo-new culminating in a 1968 zenith of new human freedoms then appears an illusory reconciliation with, and moving beyond, that which precedes it. The accelerating consumerism and cultural pill popping, free love and kitchen sinks that apparently brought delayed social renewing and stability,[256] following the total dissolution of the established norm that the war here represents and the resultant barbaric and confused black years, harbours a false sense of forging new terms in the human-social contract. This re-posits Topor's 'vultures from the Forties', and critical position on the socio-cultural silence of the post-war above. Or, as Kavan writes in *Ice* (1967):

> The endless celebrations here seemed both boring and sinister, reminiscent of the orgies of the Plague years. Now, as then, people were deluding themselves; they induced a false sense of security by means of self-indulgence and wishful-thinking. I did not believe for one moment they had really escaped.[257]

In this sense, if the later years of the post-war brought a new 'new', it would appear new in the sense of a cultural veneer applied; where the wilful dismissal of the experiential real was formalized into societal structures. With which the wounds below that veneer might be further repressed, and these inadequacies, breaks and traumas became concreted into dysfunctional quotidian human norms. As Horkheimer writes, the re-initiation of societies into these narratives would appear to reveal a paradox at their very centre: this renewed sense of 'progress threatens to nullify the very goal it is supposed to realise – the idea of man'.[258]

As such, this emblematic May '68 moment falsely compartmentalizes the material and phantasmagoric, societal and human, continuing violent effects of the Second World War and its fallout into the safely (by-)*passed* past. Further, by drawing the adhesion of this veneer into direct connection with the emergence of postmodernism and our dead binary above, Mackay and Stonebridge demonstrate that posited; that this critical practice and this cultural construct itself was generated by the wishful-thinking of the post-war processes of self-delusion. That the de-historicizing dominant cultural artefact, as discussed above as social realism, following that raised by Berman and Bassil-Morozow, fed into the de-historicizing scarifying processes of a dominant postmodernism. This in turn largely jumped the period altogether, and chose reflex to what would generally appear a Roaring Twenties, champagne Weimar, 'ex-pats' at the Paris salons modernism, and as such, in its cultural dominance, indeed appears complicit in this process. As Themerson begins, and ends, his later novel *Special Branch* (1972), four years into Mackay and Stonebridge's new clarity: 'the world will have another washing day; the decadents decay; the pedants pall; [. . .] I think I will not hang myself today'.[259] Taken from G.K. Chesterton's *A Ballade of Suicide*, this sense of living a banal moment on the precipice of global suicide would demonstrate a continuity of that raised above of the late-1940s and early-1950s, as too the 1960s, entering into the latter years of this study. And as such societies of the period appear trapped in an inescapable interaction of reductive evasion, thus cyclical repetition. A cycle that recalls, in the words of Freud, 'the regular alternation of melancholic and manic phases that has found expression in the formulation of cyclical insanity'.[260] Then, viewing the period through the prism given by the writers of the experimental novel, counter to the current vague understandings of both this literature and this era, we are presented with a sense of the blackness of the early years seeping out of its allotted temporal cage like an amorphous sludge, and into what is held as the enlightened beginnings of our own contemporary. As Noys writes in *The Culture of Death* (2005): 'despite the fact that there has not yet been a world war since 1945 we all live under the abstract threat of nuclear destruction, which threatens the survival of humanity [. . .] we [still] live in the wake of the concentration camps and under the threat of nuclear war that seems to expose us to the threat of mass death'.[261] And this sense of ecocidal instability, and violent societal division is once again, by the violent, traumatic events of our own beginnings of the twenty-first century, brought closer to the surface of collective cognition.

The old new veneer

In this apparent sudden post-war repolarization of black horror to flower power we find the sense of a weird *Edward Scissorhands* real-unreal in the post-war, where the cultural processes of normalization above indeed appear to have 'locked the human into its contradictions'. And culture, in its relation to social takes on a sense of coercion; 'the manipulatory'.[262] As Alyn describes the era, it was a space where reality entered the realms of the 'Fantastic'; where 'the pieces of the puzzle' were put back together.[263] With the social human in a state of 'sleep', similar to Sartre's stupefaction, in which the 'chaos' of these wounds and their re-coding went largely unobserved.[264] However, without this cultural process of re-mythicizing social reality, re-formulation, normalization, performative purification, it would appear there would be no possibility of societal continuation. As Fisher writes, 'the mythic is part of the virtual infrastructure which makes human life as such possible';[265] the re-adhesion to societal progression structures was necessitated for society to go on at all. It is understandable that after such a brutalizing, lingering, Event a new norm would be desired, would be necessitated: Jameson writes, 'a process of compensatory exchange must be involved here, in which the henceforth manipulated viewer is offered specific gratifications in return for his or her consent to passivity'.[266] However, as found in relation to the dominant presence in the era's novel as primary value, this dominant cultural normalization, this exertion of Bourdieu's symbolic violence appears to have foregone its apparent intended aims of soothing societal wounds and returning the social to a state of communal cogency in assigned peacetime, and became an inescapable socio-cultural doxa; a culture>human>social>culture etc. feedback loop of contagious phantasmatic eliminative nullification of the lived-in world. This echoes what Tacitus writes of Agricola's coercive, manipulatory conquering of Britain:

> The following winter was spent on schemes of social betterment. Agricola had to deal with people living in isolation and ignorance, and therefore prone to fight; and his object was to accustom them to a life of peace and quiet by the provision of amenities. [...] And so the population was gradually led into the demoralising temptation of arcades, baths, and sumptuous banquets. The unsuspecting Britons spoke of such novelties as 'civilisation,' when in fact they were only a feature of their enslavement.[267]

If these comparable, manipulatory cultural processes in the post-war here act to shunt the horrifying past and horrifying future into some unknowable adjacent, the post-war space begins to appear a weird holographic parallel present environment, a rationalized irrationality displaced from its own historicity. These normalizing processes then do not appear to act to reconcile, or fleetingly hide experience, or realized historicity, but attempt to entirely displace it, overwrite it, purify it; *re*-write it. To refer once again to Kavan: 'the past had vanished and become nothing; the future was the inconceivable nothingness of annihilation. All that was left was the ceaselessly shrinking fragment of time called "now"'.[268] It would seem in the period, as Brooke Rose writes, there is a sense of a

> new consciousness we have of the real having become unreal, because brutally endowed with significance and then as brutally deprived of it. With the death of the planet in the conveniently displaced background, the feeling that not only can no one be trusted but that we ourselves cannot, and contribute constantly, makes us unavoidably aware of the real's meaninglessness.[269]

In a frenetic, transitory space suspended between points of apocalyptic violence and societal dissolution, of shifting unbelievable realities, it is collectively willed unreal phantasmagoria that becomes the believable; the normalized real. Thus, in the chaos of living in the post-war, 'the sense that empirical reality is not as secure as it used to be is now pervasive at all levels of society'.[270] Giving a schema of comprehension to these concerns, as a kind of Hollywoodized re-imagining of Plato's cave, Brophy describes the period as locked within socio-cultural interactions that had produced the effect of 'living in that unrealistic world' of 'the perpetual cinema show'.[271] Where the open blackness of the early post-war years has not been cleared away, but had been marginalized by the imposition of a dominant projected image. Brophy employs the language of Freud, and writes: 'primitive and neurotic thought are created when the Ego clings to the psychic reality of the unconscious world and fails to test whether the unconscious narrative is true in the external world as well'.[272] Which builds a sense of collective cognitive dissonance, in which the interconnected individual within the communal social, works to continually opt out of the lived-in material real, and opt into the collective delusions of a culturally built idealized environment-image; a dystopian post-war world overlaid by utopian impulse, which does indeed bring the dominant processes of world-building into the realms of a coercive Fantastic. It would appear that, to refer to Ghose's *The Contradictions*, 'engrossed in the story, we have mistaken the fiction for reality'.[273] Which raises that the processes of reductive rationalization of the imaged world had indeed become a delusional ideology; that centred unreconciled violence and trauma at the very core of societal subsistence.

This process of re-norming then functions as a kind of feedback loop, in which the collective impulse to idealized projection image magnifies a sense of unease with the blackness that surrounds it, which would enforce disengagement from the blackness and passive reception of the projection. It is a perception cycle of unease and reduction in quotidian living by which 'the repressed returns, and returns doubly so'.[274] The reduced interior-exterior projection must be continually reified as *the* reality, as its inadequate constructedness constantly threatens to fall apart; in a perpetual act of co-opted-co-optation, reality appears no stable totality, but locked within a cycle of spiralling reduction. The perpetual cinema show was not saving people from a return to war, but was delivering the social human to two eventualities for these figures: a kind of anxious-utopia-by-zombification as transitory period, an inadequately non-perceiving socio-cultural epic-homogeneity, before the final end of apocalyptic nuclear annihilation. And as such, as Perec states in 1972, it is as though 'we've begun to live within something that resembles science fiction'.[275]

Era as here presented

Then the post-war period presents as an ambiguous space of frenetic contradictions. The Second World War was *The* Good War, the Allied invasion of France dubbed Operation Overlord was not a violent process of regime change, but Liberation from an othered uncivilized, inhuman animalistic 'Nazi' entity. The late-1940s and early-1950s that followed are the impenetrable black years of social fragmentation and open fissures, of rationing, starvation, imminent civil, continental and/or global war. As such, these years of fall out, the years of war that precede them and the earlier years of fundamental instability that generated that war, are retroactively assigned a civilizational, historical non sequitur. And yet, in dominant cultural narration of these post-war years in France, they are the beginning of *Les Trentes Glorieuses*, of abundant wealth and consumer happiness; in a period when France frequently came to the brink, and indeed over that precipice, of violent societal dissolution. In Britain, these early years are omitted from discourse of the period following the Second World War, they are classed unknowable. Before a pitch-shift in the collective social conscious, 'that was to flower so powerfully in the 1960s',[276] took hold and brought progressive social and cultural clarity, these glory years themselves taking hold in a climate of continued threat of impending apocalyptic dissolution. This series of abrupt irreconcilable, overlapping, socio-cultural reversals following the Second World War are presented not as a sign of inherent brokenness, but developmental progression and unpreventable non sequitur to, blips in, that continued development. And as such, we appear presented with the model of a de-humanizing collective social insanity raised by Virilio, Perec and Jean Duvignaud in discussion at the close of our era of study, in 1972.[277] As Duvignaud states: 'I wonder if these forces of [cultural] coercion are not themselves locked in a process of destruction, or self-destruction. A nihilism. I believe we all accept that societies are preservational [...] [but] the industrialised societies appear to be exerting a process of slow but sure degradation of the living human.'[278] Which, similar to Horkheimer, they link back to a beginning in the Second World War. As Perec responds: 'the delirium continues: concentration camp fascist society'.[279] And Virilio clarifies, but 'a linear concentration camp, which reveals its object: a road, a bit like the stairway at Mauthausen. That we build to go nowhere ["*nulle part*": here a place of "nothingness"], but go there all the same.'[280]

The period as a whole appears within a confused slippage of material and narrated 'realities'; a confused, confusing loss of causality, a splitting of *histoire* (in its French double meaning of 'history' and 'story') from (experiential) historicity. As Queneau writes in *Une Histoire modèle* (1966): history 'is not a science. It rests at the same qualitative level of alchemy, or astrology. It is a basic story, accompanied by qualitative judgements and claims blind to causality'.[281] Here it would seem dominant cultural processes function to actively reformulate that *histoire*, in a moment when its stable civilizational narrative appears to have dissolved and has been unnaturally, irrationally re-asserted. We then do not find the received norm here inherited via a sense of 'thrownness' into established, accumulative historical continuity or progression, but in a moment of active selection and re-construction; alchemical re-narration. However, *experientiality* appears to have rendered that narration inadequate, indeed faulty. This draws us to Michel Foucault's diagnosis of the era in 1962: 'it is the point where history is immobilised by the tragedy that both generates it and dissolves it'.[282] A status of the era which in turn encourages the positions raised in opening to this partition; that retroactive cultural, critical coding of that termed the modern epoch as a singular developmental entity, that we find emanating from the latter half of the twentieth century, both suffers from and propagates this dissolution; that continues to deprive the human of 'the tools necessary', as will be discussed below, to process the dissonance between experientiality and social reality. A cultural-critical asphyxiated-asphyxiating process inherited in discourse, thus societal conditions, today, that continues to propagate this remove.

In the critical perspectives here raised, it is then the experimental novel that positions itself as reflexive cultural, confrontational, product of this self-destructive, dysfunctional, conflicting predicament in stupefied, asphyxiated post-war social reality. A disintegratory, dismembered literature, it is mimetic of the conditions in which it was initially generated and received. 'Frozen', in societal reversals, contradictions and removes the human is complicit in, and under which: 'experimentation [...] has a historical role to fill: to fuck with prejudgements, thaw normalities, and unbutton the uniform of fear'.[283] It inhabits a frenetic, virtual marginality within a formational period in active flux, within which the process of asserting a homogenized image of social reality was still underway. As Topor describes the potentialities of an art of critique in the era: 'it is an art of rage without abdication, a fencer that covers his adversary with a thousand cuts [...] [these writers] share a common disgust for voluntary servitude'.[284] We are presented with a literature locked within socio-cultural relation; not one which primarily works 'to dissolve or explode',[285] nor towards a 'capitalistic' 'dismantlement of the great social machines that precede it'.[286] But more, it exists as artefact of a space of ambiguous crisis. As an analytical entity, it presents an image of a people, a community, a culture, a reality warped and broken; product of a brutalizing experiential Event, and ensuing self-mutilating social milieu that would appear here both myopic and amnesiac. And as such, returning to this notion of an avant-garde realism, it is a minored literature that signals to the minored in collective experientiality through mass produced object, thus individual engagement and subsequent networked transmission. As immersed within these dysfunctional processes and interactions, these writers then appear to write out of the *vague* to the *vague*; from and to a human margin that fails to be (ir)rationalized by dominant cultural coding. Both the experimental novel as an object, and the dominant refusal of it from cultural participation would then appear product of these sickly post-war conditions. This refusal would appear to function as a sort of auto-immune disorder, by which the societal body rejects its cultural 'white cells' as foreign bodies, and societal delusion, dehumanizing socio-cultural mass manipulation, is thus permitted to continue unchecked. If this process propagated by dominant cultural monopoly functions as a palliative, as a cultural pain-killer, it would appear the experimental novel attempts to function as a kind of antibiotic in this sense. The post-war experimental novel would then, by reflex, indeed appear a socially engaged re-newed avant-garde realism that attempts to meet these societal inconsistencies, this apparent sickness. And, as has begun to be demonstrated here, through which it would seem 'something rotten is revealed' in the occlusive, violent 'law' at the core of the formational beginnings of 'normalized' contemporary societies.[287]

PARTITION TWO

Diagnoses: The Confused Narrative of the Post-War Human

2.1 The sense something is missing

Moving into the second phase of this study, the window of observation passes from approaching the historical topoi of the period, from both native and post-mortem obscurity and obscuring of the era – which here appears in Zola's terms inherent to a social sickness, or that at the close of partition one was equated to a Benjaminian social rottenness – to a, perhaps, clearer contemporaneous view of the realities of societal shift, rift, reinvention and continuation post-war. A (relative) clarity of diagnosis perhaps afforded the experimental novel, in both its effaced role as socio-cultural interrogator, generated from a doubt emanating from an experiential sense of unease, and perhaps given potency in its positioning of experimentation in the novel at the intersection of cultural structure and quotidian social life. In this sense, the points that made themselves apparent in the preceding partition here set the constellations by which this study might navigate another.[1] If in the preceding we have established the conditions that generated the post-war experimental novel, and to which it attempted to respond, in this second partition the study shifts to content diagnoses of these societal conditions within the text-worlds of the experimental novel itself. The sections that follow draw that posited of an inherent socio-cultural delusion, amnesia, collective normative estrangement from the real further into encounters with positions taken within the participatory internal space of the novel-object. Below, I track through these concerns within the experimental novel as cultural artefact of the post-war moment; as artefact of a period of fundamental epistemic societal rupture that went unreconciled. It is a spatio-temporal moment that finds framing in a fractured novel as a cultural artefact of an integrally fractured socially held perspective. Therefore, the experimental novel here functions as instrument by which the reader might carry out a process of phenomenological self-diagnosis of the state of their own internal human space, which would in turn potentially throw critical light upon the connectivity by which they as participant in society are culturally codified and socially networked. I therefore begin by looking to interactions of violent trauma and the stupefied social human as myopic-amnesiac as represented in this literature, before pursuing that critical position into a broader societal critique of the human-in-society post-war.

A mimesis of violent stupefaction

From war to its reflexive post, as seen historically in the previous partition, appears as a sudden brutal moment on-going. As a brutalized environment of shift within the normed tenets of reality, in which these texts demand to be viewed in a critical schema of effaced yet persistent trauma and the mutational, travelled effects of both this experiential trauma and its performative effacement on-going. While in the previous partition, the perceived delusional sickness begun with the 1945 Event presents itself as an obscurer of violent trauma in the mode of retroactively assigned Good War, *Les Trentes Glorieuses*, 'love on the coast' and we never had it so good, placing both itself and its precursor beyond clear ken, its source is perhaps indicated by its conspicuous absence from these optimistic narratives, as too the dominant social realist novel that participated in the building of this seemingly veneer-thin imaging. As seen, these processes are here framed as a re-writing; an active project of communal self-delusion, which imposes the tenets of a socio-cultural utopian impulse, predicated on narrated nostalgia and optimistic return, carrying the implication of falsity, in place of experience, and experiential memory. According to Figes' favourite, William Sansom, this failure in art is both casualty and causality of these post-war crises in reality.[2] Speaking of the experientiality of war that first generated this sense of a remove, an impossibility in experience itself:

> The experience is too violent for the arts to transcribe; there will never be an adequate reportage to convey to posterity a living idea of the truth of such experience. Posterity may indeed speculate on the battle's trailed miseries,

on the histories of courage and endurance, on the vigil before the battle and the tired aftermath, even on the appearance of the battle itself with its reported volumes of shell and blood and tactic – but of the real sensations of the thick of the battle it will know nothing. It cannot. The pace has become too violent, machines move too fast for the nerves' perception, the din outsounds the ear, movements and winds and lights strike with such great impact that this can scarcely be perceived and even then never, neither in the symbols of language nor in the tones of paint, be recorded.[3]

The battle Sansom refers to is not some mythic, distantly othered Somme or Stalingrad of ultimate and transitory breakdown of normed imagining of the world, but Blitz London through the eyes of a fireman. This speaks of a dilemma of loss present in the violent moment, present upon a spectrum of immersive and myriad scales. Which as Perec writes in relation to the concentration camps, caused literature to succumb 'to the temptations of a naturalism characteristic of the historico-social novel':[4] a 'neo-Balzacian' faux-reportage with processes twisted to perpetuating an 'inefficacy, daze and stupor' in social reality.[5] An entity that, as argued by these writers, propagated the seemingly irreversible societal dysfunctions that generated it. According to Butor: 'the traditional techniques of story are incapable of integrating all the new experience that has occurred. Which has resulted in a perpetual malaise, it is impossible for us to put our consciousness in order, all the information that assails us, because we lack the necessary tools to do so.'[6] In this position there can be found correspondence with Theodor Adorno's own oft paraphrased statement in 1949:

> Cultural criticism finds itself faced with the final stage of the dialectic of culture and barbarism. To write poetry after Auschwitz is barbaric. And this corrodes even the knowledge of why it has become impossible to write poetry today.[7]

For Adorno, the post-war moment is the culmination of *the* civilizational dialectic; the jumped precipice of an end where 'barbarism' and 'civilization' as supposed opposing concepts had become, as we have seen in the preceding exposition, indiscernibly interlocking. Where below the semblance of plentiful food and blood-flushed organs are Gollancz's ashes in the mouth and ice in the heart; the flowing corpse rivers of the Elbe and the Oder running their way through Europe, feeding its failed harvests.[8] A climate in which art, and art's potential to analytical reflex can no longer coherently function as such.

The implication being, where events are commonly divested of human influence and become not orchestrated but occurred, where a subjective violence is arbitrarily othered and retroactively assigned objective justification,[9] violent events do not divest the perpetrators' guilt, the survivors' guilt, but conversely shifts this sense of responsibility, from *their* catastrophes, to a lingering *ours*. A product of a process of 'closed rationalization', 'dead rationalism' that these writers perceived to be bringing about 'the death of the word';[10] an impossibility in perception, communication, thus communicative representation. There is no external position from which these events might be objectified and understood, as the events themselves are immersive, and are drawn by a persistent proves of refusal into the core of societal continuation itself. It is perhaps this, alongside, apparently, the post-war paper shortages, that had first shaken the dominant novel to stupor, and that, steeped in violence, makes this moment seemingly so very unknowable. It is a silence, an unsaid, that becomes the grounded cultural keystone of post-war societies, which forms the inherent nature of the co-opted–co-opting social subject. Who, in this delusional societal coding of the individual becomes collectively both the guilty perpetrator *and* fearful victim. The zombified subject in a weird faux-civilizational drive to ever greater magnitudes of crisis, and an accompanying ever greater magnitude of estrangement from that instability, by which these crises are reframed as continued proof, as proving ground, of developmental progression, or are wholly dismissed from narratives of civilizational continuity. This implies the real is concretely present, concretely indeterminate and different, concretely ill-defined and incoherent. It is the new received perception of it where the limits are imposed, where its sci-fi smoothness is irrealized and human, societal action is arbitrarily re-narrated, thus inadequately, damagingly vindicated. Perhaps both externally co-opting upon the human in social and cultural interrelation, and wilfully co-opted internally by the human themselves. To refer again to Perec on the effect of this levelling in literature and social process:

> in all the other works of concentration camp literature [other than Robert Antelme's *L'Espèce humain* (1947)], there is a privileged passage to experience of it: but this sudden discovery and unveiling of suffering and terror does

not reveal the camp as it purports to, as if to *effectively* open up that space to new arrivals: it only elicits in the reader a falsifying pity that conceals a refusal, pure and simple. This pitying refusal has wide reaching effects beyond itself. The universe in which the concentration camps exist is translocated to somewhere else.[11]

This is perhaps further demonstrated in relation to Sansom above, where he speaks of the Blitz as a battle performed, while it later became coded as an unmoored violence grittily outlived. This dilemma in reality is noted by Queneau, as he wrote on 16 June 1945: 'six weeks after the freeing of millions of slaves to the Nazi yoke, a cheerful racist wrote in the corridors of the metro: *the Jews are coming back bigger and fatter than ever* (another person had added: *from Buchenwald*, there you go, the black humour is still there)'.[12] The post-war would appear an unbelievable space of black farce where reality had become a double (triple, quadruple etc.) entendre, where the same people who had committed to a newly othered norm under/counter the cultural construct of 'Nazism' and the epic-homogeneity of total war now haphazardly adhered to another. Where the blackness of that war persisted, within the continuity human itself. And as such 'human nervous systems and memory' would appear here as vessels that carry within them 'relics of traumatic events that humans must either [attempt to] decode or repeat'.[13] The post-war individual returning from war, prison camp or evacuation, it seems, could not approach the horrors around and within them, and as such threw themselves into the latter of these two options: the post-war human committed to a new social subjectification, the prescribed post-war cultural narrative of normalization, of progression and affluence at the expense of both individual and communal comprehension and catharsis. And as such, as Sartre writes: 'no doubt they are victims, and innocent, yet still tyrants and guilty'.[14] The in-life vivid experience of wartime and post-war quotidian continued horror would appear to act as a 'lure which prevents us from thinking' in this respect,[15] and the socio-cultural interactions that muster societal cogency functioned to encourage that distancing refusal.

This is a product of the both actual, and symbolic, violent moment, for Adorno, of ultimate reification of culture. All innovation is ended, experimentation can be no more; there can be no complex criticism beyond opiate voyeuring of the new smooth surface under which the human's shared, individual guilt and fear may be hidden. The social subject is adrift, unknowing beyond a persistent sense of unease, in a communally shared deathly violence, bereft of the space of cognition or freedom of thought. As Themerson writes, 'the surface of the earth is now becoming smoother and smoother. We level it, we remove its roughness and projections, we smooth the roads and paths', and for a number of 'psychological and social reasons':[16] 'the environment – is also: you'.[17] However, it is Adorno's later revision of his statement in 1966 that might offer the possibility of comprehension of reality as inadequately constructed, smoothed, and the veneer's subterranean horrors; that may allow some space of cognition, despite lacking the tools to do so. Where he writes:

> There is no getting out of this, no more than out of the electrified barbed wire around the camps. Perennial suffering has as much right to expression as a tortured man has to scream; hence it may have been wrong to say that after Auschwitz you could no longer write poems.[18] But it is not wrong to raise the less cultural question whether after Auschwitz you can go on living—especially whether one who escaped by accident, one who by rights should have been killed, may go on living.[19]

The inertial scream, or rather screams, that open here in spite of imposed silence and do not close offer expression of quotidian fearful unease and that conceptualized as 'misery', the uncanny feeling something is horribly wrong; that it is indeed living, that had become impossible. This must essentially bring to quotidian living post-war a perpetually malignant sense of disbelief, that must be constantly, fantastically, suspended. As Slavoj Žižek approaches Adorno's statement before its later realignment of poetry to living, Žižek claims it is not poetry that became impossible, but prose: 'when Adorno declares poetry impossible (or, rather, barbaric) after Auschwitz, this impossibility is an enabling impossibility: poetry is always "about" something that cannot be addressed directly, only alluded to'.[20] It is for this, Žižek claims, the poetic gives his *awry* look at the violence of the 1940s, however 'realistic' prose fails in the face of this trauma, which Sansom at the time similarly raises above. A failure that Robert Pinget's *Passacaille* (1969) finds,[21] where only the cyclical structure of musical poetry can novelize the forgetful experience of a, potential, murder-suicide. In the unknowability of the Event, the act itself, Pinget's novel becomes a space where prose leaves 'music' to come in 'where words fail'.[22] Which draws us to a post-war socio-functionality of the experimental novel, to its content-form avant-garde realism. To look to how Edmond Jabès' fragmentary *Le Livre des questions* (1963) begins:

> What is happening behind this door?
> A book is in the process of being read.
> What is the story of this book?
> The discovery of a scream.[23]

This further speaks of a communicative centre of the novel genre that can only authentically exist self-consciously broken, confused, dis-genred, 'schizoid', thus encompassing of both fractured experience and necessarily fractured observation. If the scream is essentially poetic-musical in nature, it is the fracturing of culture, thus genre within it, which allows the freer potentials of these non-prose modes of communication to slip within the structures of the novel, to distort them in immediacy. The novel itself here contracts this ambiguous immediacy; it becomes an essential tenet of the literary form. To this end, Jabès writes that the novel may be disintegrated in order to indicate the shortcomings, cracks and limits hidden in society, and indicate, potentially, a view of the screaming horrors below; indeed, the very impossibility of living itself. In a place where cultural criticism is inauthentic even in opposition, and the social, reality itself, charades as made of a singular quality, there is for Jabès only 'the innocence of the scream'.[24] In a scream can be perceived the frustration of an inability to act, or a victim attacked, and in this form the experimental novel offers an immediate, urgent – if essentially ambiguous – form of authentic communication that alludes to an essential dysfunction inherent in on-going life. But this is not a parallel of the screams of a born baby, of a group, Octavio Paz writes, emerging 'purified and strengthened from this plunge into chaos'.[25] This scream does not augur a new peaceful world forged by the chaos and violence of a deathly womb of fighting, genocide, purges and the atom bomb. It is a fragmentary, inarticulate articulation of terror turned horror; of a perpetual deathly taint that will not wash off. And within which, as Jabès writes: 'We do not communicate. We signal.'[26] In a place of breakdown, of arbitrary, unnatural ordering of reality, it is, as raised in partition one, a novel that is hyper-aware of its status as such that would appear faithfully, perhaps 'hysterically' mimetic of those conditions;[27] to authentically mediate these slipping realities via the indeterminate incompleteness of participatory experimental praxis, and by which disingenuous, coercive modes of communication can be redeployed.

As demonstrated, the experimental novel writers claim no separation from these processes of confused amnesia, myopic distancing and reduction of lived experience, they do not objectify the societal body from without, but are engaged. They are *involved, analytical observers* and as such inescapably participate in its functions, as too malfunctions. To draw this closer to text, David Madden writes of Alan Burns' *Europe after the Rain* (1965):[28] 'an air of illogic pervades all actions and much of the dialogue. Ardent patriots are double agents, macho commanders are actually feeble old men,[29] and police control revolutionaries – in short, the usual expectations do not pertain, and the reader is constantly forced to redefine characters and the fictional universe until all frames of reference have been dissolved.'[30] Burns evokes a deathly, visceral *demi-monde* of wreaths and discarded rubbish, as he writes:

> I did not realise it was my last chance of seeing lights, I saw nothing but small white wreaths for the dead, the trees had been cut down, there were no trees in the place, no gardens, the land not built upon was covered with rubbish. The last man missed his footing and fell. He was already fifty yards away, he threw his arms into the air, the fatal instinct, the body was not recovered.[31]

To take on Madden's critique, *Europe after the Rain*, following the Max Ernst artwork of the same title (1942), works to evoke within the reader this very experiential field of hazy, deathly double entendre following the horrors petrified, reduced, by post-war socii, as observed in the previous partition. The norm is revealed as socii's fantastic eternalizing narratives, that warp the realities of broken and tragic quotidian experience. In a culture of reduction, the fantastic ideal and the horrifying real are forced to resonate on the same frequency. Where the most violent, rampant nightmares unavoidably, persistently come into focus too stark to contemplate. Just as Burns himself looked to the concentration camps in Poland for reference for *Europe after the Rain*, and yet 'I did not read (don't think I could have found it possible to read) books on Polish concentration camps [...] I did not want, was not capable of, journalistic accuracy, I was interested in something a lot hazier, yet composed of razor sharp details, splinters of fact.'[32] He states in *Imagination on Trial*

(1981): 'I came across a book by an English reporter who'd been to Poland and written a strong, straightforward journalist's description of post-war life there in about 1946 [...] what I did was, I put the book to the side of my typewriter. Then I "looked" at the page. I looked yet I didn't look. I did that thing painters often do, which is to screw up their eyes so only bits and pieces percolate through.'[33] Burns, still in the mid-1960s, could not look the *matter* directly in the eye. Thus, mimetically, he portrays splinters of fact, Madden writes, to hand in the experience of the book's contemporaneous reader, and yet, as for Burns himself, they are but splinters haemorrhaging meaning. This is a space where perceivable fact appears *impossible, unapproachable* – the splinters are too sharp – and everything appears believably unbelievable. Where the limits of possibility have retreated beyond view irrespective of boundary or border, and yet the arbitrary wall of societal normalcy appears to stand unbroken as a betrayed sense of quotidian stability.

In his book *Violence* (2008), Žižek describes a schema with which we might better comprehend this dysfunctional functionality, and which might offer clarity in relation to a novelization of unknowability. Žižek writes that violent traumatic events cannot be approached directly, but must indeed be observed *awry*; with a sidelong glance. For, he argues, 'the truth' and 'truthfulness' are two very different concepts. He gives the unsettlingly detached example of a rape victim:

> The very factual deficiencies of the traumatised victim's report on her experience bear witness to the truthfulness of her report, since they signal that the reported content 'contaminated' the manner of reporting it.[34]

According to Žižek, the veracity of the subject's statement is in its fragmentation, inaccuracy, confusion, jumbling and falsehoods. A report which is entirely accurate and unfragmented presents a cold report of the truth, and as such is not truthful; it does not present a 'faithful' portrayal of experience, nor event. Coherent narrative itself is disintegrated by experience of violent trauma. This offers schematic clarity to that discussed above of the damaging reductions of dominant tenets of social realism as faux-reportage, and the seemingly broken tropes of the experimental novel. Burns' narrative haze, for example, would function as a sort of traumatized, traumatic (re-)telling by this schema; an articulation of the inarticulate scream. This would infer that these writers follow an understanding of their writerly position similar to that described by R.D. Laing and D.G. Cooper in 1964:

> The only valid theory of knowledge today is one which is founded on that principle of microphysics which asserts that the experimenter is part of the experimental system. Only a theory so founded can eliminate all idealistic illusion and show us a real man in the midst of a real world.[35]

The employment of the word experimental as stated then reformulates the intra-textual interactions of extra-textual figures, and displaces the writer from prescriptive/proscriptive role to just another participant in social world, in symbiotic text-space. To continue a quote from Themerson's *Bayamus* already seen, on the human that lives within this post-war space: 'they pretend to be the same as they were before the war; and because they want to take that secret with them into the grave. I'm one of them, and I'm fed-up with them as well.'[36] The novels that here pass through the remit of this study appear to share a fragility of aim in this central drive of critique, a problem raised by Peter Krapp: 'can one seek what one does not know?'[37] A drive to seek the disappeared in experientiality through its minored persisting presence, that would appear to be revealed by a stumbling against the unnameable or unknowable in the disintegratory and the dismembered, invoking a sense of dissolution of all frames of reference by which fiction might be normally received, and as such perhaps reflexively reveals its violent source as too the dysfunctions that cloud it.

Impossible confrontations

To ground this further, again, what is described here is not so much a shady mass manipulation of the innocent by some abstracted inhuman machine, but as discussed above, the complex give and take of guilt-free-guilt-ridden social subjects' demand for soothing cultural narrative, congealed into a systemic drive. Where the impossibility of accessing past experience fundamentally destabilizes present experientiality. As Burns states,

> It seems 'a quarter million Germans' were killed in Normandy. How many more of them throughout the war, and Brits, Americans, impossible to list how many more, and 20,000,000 Russians [...] I know the grief attached to

the death of one young man, my brother Jerry. Can human consciousness begin to grapple with what that all means? Life is tough enough. We all die. But deliberately to smash another human being's skull in [...] why am I going about this, no point.[38]

Burns here echoes the characters of Johnson's *House Mother Normal* (1971), who for all their woes drift in the mindset of 'never mind', too mirrored in Jean Tardieu's *Dix variations sur une ligne* (1951), which ends 'all talk is useless'.[39] Which speaks of an effort made to grasp at something that cracks to shards as the fingers fold around it. We are presented with a faulty human cognitive process that chimes with that written by Johnson in *Trawl* (1966): 'the mind tries hard, does its best, to forget what hurts it, has hurt it, has threatened it to any point, let alone to destruction'.[40] As Carol Watts writes of Johnson's attempts to 'exorcise' his memories of his friend dying in *The Unfortunates* (1969), or his childhood memories of the war in *Trawl*,

> 'I fail to remember, the mind has fuses,' he writes [in *The Unfortunates*], in a simple line, its own paragraph. This is a registering not simply of the inability to remember, but of a short-circuiting, as if the mind, faced with something traumatic, will blow, like a fuse box [...] a source of pain that Johnson's mind can't bring near.[41]

And again, as a reading of the medical definitions of narrating characters in Johnson's *House Mother Normal*, Guignery writes, 'the aim is to attempt, temporarily, and rather in vain, to put at a distance the effects of a personal emotional engagement, which would be too painful'.[42] The trauma itself cannot be brought near, it is so very stark in its horror it is unapproachable. Whereas for Johnson, this is, according to Guignery 'in vain', it is a void that demands he 'return to it again and again'.[43] The realities of this trauma are themselves terrifying and unknowable, hidden away, overrun by disingenuous representation, and leave perhaps nothing to say, but a malleable, suggestible void. And yet it is a void that is ever-present, as Figes writes of her own amnesiac writerly figure, and indeed perhaps herself, in *B* (1972): '(I am drawn to this house not only by a wish to recapture the past, a sense of loss which is, I suppose, a recurring theme in my writing, but by a wish to confirm isolation in physical surroundings. My wounds are the only way I now have of knowing I continue to exist.)'[44] This bracketed, perhaps, intervention appearing at the end of twelve numbered sections, each largely made up of one single running sentence, before a following dissolution into chunks of text scattered across the pages.

What is posited here is not only an inability to remember, but a compulsive return to the wound where that realization should be, that is here inadequately hidden by socio-cultural palliative. Where this absence 'erupts' into 'empirical reality', and with it 'the gap that is opened up and the perturbations it produces',[45] bring closer to the surface of human cognition the traumatized mechanics of this persistent quotidian malaise. To look to Perec, as he writes in conclusion to *Je me souviens* (1978 (composed 1973–7)):

> These memories stretch for the most part from when I was 10 to when I was 25, between 1946 and 1961. When I evoke memories from before the end of the war, for me they refer to a time tantamount to the domain of myth: this explains why a memory may be 'objectively' false.[46]

While he recalls plotting the movements of the Allied armies across France from *Radio Londres*, distinctly missing from Perec's book are his mother and father killed during that war. Lost somewhere between the horror of the war and the rhetoric of liberation is his family, and his childhood. His was a childhood, similar to Topor's, spent in Vichy France, renamed and christened a catholic; hiding in plain sight. And as such, a childhood, along with the building blocks of formational individual identity, cast adrift out in the forgetful sea of memory. As seen in another of his novels *W ou le souvenir d'enfance*, Perec writes:

> The memories assert themselves, fleeting or enduring, futile or unbearable, but nothing puts them back in order. They are like non-joined up handwriting, made up of isolated letters incapable of coalescing together to form a word, like my own handwriting until the age of seventeen or eighteen. Or like the dissociative sketches, dislocated, of which the scattered elements almost never manage to connect with each other, and with which, at the time of W, between, say, the ages of eleven and fifteen, I covered whole notebooks. Figures for whom nothing connects them with the ground that was supposed to support them, ships whose sails did not fit to the masts, nor the masts to the deck, machines of war, machines of death, aeroplanes and vehicles with illogical mechanisms, with their floating gun barrels, their untied ropes, their wheels turning in the void; the wings of the planes were detached from

the fuselage, the legs of the athletes were separated from their bodies, the arms separated from the torsos, the hands had no grip. What characterises this time is above all its lack of landmarks: memories are pieces of life torn from the void. They have no mooring. Nothing anchors them, nothing fixes them in place. Almost nothing endorses that they are correct. There is no chronology except what I have, over time, arbitrarily reconstituted from time passed.[47]

Despite his attempts, like Johnson, to return to this trauma, there is only a void of disjointed scraps with no foundation, no mooring, no route of approach to anything other than their fragmentation and absence. Indeed, this memory-work carried out by these writers appears typified by stumbling failure to both build and retain an image. Perec must necessarily approach experience indirectly, as he states in an interview with Franck Venaille: 'I put together the autobiographical elements of my childhood from descriptions on the back of photographs, the photographs served as a conduit, a medium of approach to a reality of which I have no memory.'[48] A point succinctly put by the formal mechanics of Topor's *Souvenir* (1971), in which all text inside and out has been written, printed, violently scrubbed out in black ink, and printed again. We are presented with the image of the present as a space of unmoored drift, within which, as Perec writes: 'there was no beginning and no end. There was no past, and for a very long time, no future; one simply endured. We were just there.'[49] Here, the disjointed fragmentation of memory, and the unease of the unknowable, inherent in post-war life, a life made possible by the ambiguities evoked by reductive, coercive dominant culture, becomes the very engine of the experimental novel. There is, to quote Pinget's *Cette voix* (1975) and to echo Roche, an 'impossible anamnesis' present.[50] This provides a key by which we might better understand this textual project of a faltering memory-work, as too content presentation of that faltering memorialisation. Where 'life would not be there without memory',[51] these stark absences and fractures indicate that somewhere there is a missing link; a remove within life itself.

The short circuiting of Johnson's project appears to attempt to put this failure down in ink, to bind the pain that emanates from this impossible anamnesis, and to place it safely at a distance, away; over there on the bookshelf. As Johnson said in conversation with Burns:

> I call it exorcism. I wrote those three books to get them out of my head. I wanted to unburden my mind.[52]

While Perec appears to write to a very different purpose: to solidify these broken images, senses, and as such make solid their fallibility. As Teresa Bridgeman writes: in his linking of fantasy, quotidian and memory 'Perec not only weakens memory through the number of links in his citational chains, but also undermines belief in *text* as authorised *evidence*'.[53] This preoccupation with an impossibility to remember is indeed then a diagnostic reflex of the dominant cultural symbol that purports to define a *whole* reality, and does so retroactively. Where the scrubbing of memory is developed into a concretized socio-cultural doxa of re-narration of human life, where that narration does not adequately fill the gaps in the memory it attempts to scrub. In this destabilization Perec does not, like Topor and Johnson, attack his experiences, or loss of, but performatively documents their essentially broken nature, and this very interaction; to try to document the on-going accumulating and disappearing nature of human experience on a foundation already shaken to scraps and void against the promises of social realism and normalization above. A textual process of impossible anamnesis which raises that this societal distancing of experience; the translocation of violence into a somewhere else is ineffective. And the experience itself is drawn solidly within the space of impossible living. This chimes with the theme of immovability in Marcel Béalu's *récits*,[54] or the novel of thematic fragments, *Journal d'un mort* (1947) in which he writes:

> You believe that the most distant star remains to be discovered, that there is a *something else*, that there is a *somewhere else*, that the final word has not yet been said. But at the core of the immobile eye rests a buried darkness. A sunken universe that has been too quickly replaced by another. The something else is the same as this. The somewhere else is here.[55]

Within this image of a liquid unreal-real lies that of a dissolving ouroboros, a shrugging sense of end and beginning, whereby the states of the figures present in the virtuality of text-space, appear to display synchronicity with the states of figures present in the virtuality of the socio-cultural field. This frames the transitory genesis of post-war realities, the internal space of the post-war human; as will become clear later, social communities. The projected utopian state is not a future to be attained, but a state of fantastic anticipation within the now, as too the alternative projection; a global nuclear apocalypse. These anticipatory projections reside upon the same plane as the glory years, as too the black years; 'dig for Britain!' and a continental genocide. These states of cognition of world slipping amongst one another, in a confusion of incomplete, fragmented coda of symbolic ordering, to which Davies gives the image of a spider at its web in Andrew Melmoth's manuscript on the vindication of rats in *The Papers of Andrew Melmoth* (1960):

> If you break one of the bridges between the radii of a spider's web while it is in the process of being made, the spider continues its work, but never manages to re-make the broken bridge. On it goes round and round, groping with its forelegs for something to guide it, and always fixing threads in wrong places. More and more confusion follows in its architecture; nevertheless it sticks to its lifelong duty, the making of its viscid spiral. At last it ceases; its business is done. It has spread its spiral, or at least the erratic maze that should have been a spiral. Satisfied with its work, it seats itself at the centre, surrounded by the hopeless tangle of its crazy threads...[56]

Spinning a crazy maze that is taken as a natural, perfect spiral from within the maze itself, and yet to traverse that maze, to live that overlaid imaging of environment, is to constantly trip while walking along radii of the web that should be there, but are not. Post-war reality then appears a chaos of unreliable systemic coding that can only be reconciled by an individual interaction of pathological forgetting, and myopic refusal of continued proofs of that disappeared from the topoi of the lived-in world.

The act of forgetting

Such chaotic unknowability, a sense of drifting lack of reconciliation, as demonstrated, seeps from the experimental novel of the period. An inability to approach the war and its continuities of breakdown that speaks of a demand, a need, for a reappraisal of that reality, that these writers and these texts appear to attempt to carry out, and that appears a central ground of confrontation in experimental text-space. To look to Green's *Back* (1946), to what Mr Grant tells protagonist Charley Summers:

> 'Mustn't complain, mustn't complain at all,' Mr. Grant replied. 'When you come to consider, there's compensations in not remembering, as I dare say you've found, eh Charley.'[57]

Here Mr Grant assumes Charley has met his second daughter, Nance, the half-sister and spit of Charley's fiancée Rose who was killed during Charley's time as a prisoner of war, and yet he has not. When he does, he is so shocked he blacks out and cannot accept that Nance is not Rose – he cannot accept the evaporation of his pre-war reality; the peaceful married life post-war he had promised himself. The story itself rolls out as a broken hallucinatory re-normalization in which Nance is progressively recuperated into the Grant family as Rose, to Charley as his bride to be, and Charley never really does accept that she is not Rose after all. Indeed, he thinks that Rose has 'forgotten herself',[58] as an accidental oversight while forgetting everything else. The amnesia required to return to a normal that is not normal at all; that is a smoothness that belies its fragmentation, selection. It is an amnesiac version of nostalgic pre-war life evidenced here, a hallucinatory cognitive estrangement which returns Mrs Grant's sanity, a process which Summers' missing leg offers the most inescapable reminder of that missing six-year space. As such, we are presented with a state of human cognition similar to that in Heppenstall's *The Lesser Infortune* (1953), where Frobisher would appear quite right to ponder: 'I feel about this war as some people feel about God. I keep wondering if it really exists.'[59]

Green's novel follows a soldier coming back, and forgetting, seeing the back of, a war that is, in the text, still in its final stages; building a reality that, like Nance, looks a lot like another when not looked in the face. It is a return to some semblance of normalcy that does not fit, like jigsaw pieces punched into holes that can no longer house them. And yet it eventually goes unquestioned. The trauma of return slips into a vague unease as the social constructs around Nance slowly mould her into a not-quite Rose, where Nance's self is edited, remoulded; forgotten. Whose internal space is terraformed by communal, external societal coercive desire to fill a deathly absence. The collective cognitive dissonance apparent is dual, it is a façade of bloodless post-war peace; a rejection of wartime trauma, and the acceptance of nostalgic narratives of great nation states, in a period where the rhetoric no longer (if ever) aligns with that witnessed in the full quotidian copia of the real-world. But it is good enough for Charley, who then can move from a chaotic confusion to continue his public life and hide his trauma at home, crying with not-quite the girl he had thought of everyday in the prison camp. Family and work life begins anew, but continued obscured is the endless public alcoholism and private weeping; the trauma continues, the brutal, violent source wilfully, haphazardly, forgotten.

Thus, the idea of an accepted common reality, a concrete, objective truth to which the standard is pinned is a disingenuous artifice of vindication of past, present, and future action. Just as Charley meets again his dead lover and is encouraged by those around him to accept her as such, though the community around him exonerates him, it takes an unreal, fantastic, arbitrary process to return to that supposed as reality, to efface violence witnessed, violence committed; violence suffered. Similarly, in Jacques Yonnet's *Enchantements sur Paris* (1954) (republished as *Rue des Maléfices* (1995)), the protagonist is tasked with murdering an assumed Gestapo informant within his resistance group in the closing years of the war. Yonnet himself is drawing from his own experience as a resistance hitman when he describes the following process:

> I did once take courses in anatomy, even dissection, and I was terribly lucid in my project. Even so, I went about it like a very clumsy child. Instead of properly disjointing my stiff at the pelvis and shoulders, I began to cut at the waist as one saws a tree trunk. I thought it would be so easy. The butchering, packing and cleaning lasted all night. His detached, pensive head, his half-closed eyes, watched me take care of the rest. I'd put it on a copper platter bought at Bicêtre.
>
> The upper part of the body, which made the bag bulge a little, was deposited at the bag check at Montparnasse train station. The lower at Austerlitz. We'll see how it goes.[60]

The protagonist cannot, like Charley, at first move on from the butchery he has experienced: 'my obsession, my shame, my sorrow is above, below the judgment of man. I do not have to think, to calculate, to weigh my rights and my duties to find myself guilty of an affront to human nature itself'.[61] It is uncanny in the way the guilt, the violence of the performative moment and its ensuing trauma sticks to the static variable of Parisian geography, the head-platter from Bicêtre, the body hidden in the commuter hubs of Montparnasse and Austerlitz. Where 'physical spaces condition perception', here these quotidian 'terrains are stained by traumatic events'.[62] The end of the war does not represent a clean break from the past in this respect. The fields of combat – Liberated France, Blitzed Britain – are spaces within which people continued to live; where they did not return from war as such, but normalized peaceful living upon the battlefield itself. This had rendered new points of reference of internal-external human life; where there appear fundamental 'ruptures in the very fabric of experience itself'.[63] A fabric of experience by which these ruptures would appear a quotidian, continued, confrontation that must be perpetually evaded. And as such, Yonnet's protagonist has his own moment of fantastic slippage parallel to Charley's nightly breakdowns with his head on Nance-Rose's lap. The protagonist goes to a homeless mystic who lives below the Pont au Double, 'he said to me, touching his forehead: – in there, it doesn't seem to be running so well. You must be very overworked. If only he knew… he laid the Sleeper's hands on the pain in my side, and on my head. On Sunday I'm going to my third appointment. I'm amazed at the real benefits of this mysterious therapy. It was high time I get back to normal: we have much work to do.'[64] Referring to the protagonist's sudden newfound post-war role as a normalizing newspaper propagandist and police officer; the hollowness of which with this text Yonnet attempts to indicate.

The implications are twofold, for both Yonnet's textual projection and Charley there is again this weird, hallucinatory moment of moving on, of going back to work: an oblique ritual of peace that passes from the violence of war to the violence of peace in which these figures appear emblematic of the human locked in a kind of *zugzwang*. As Jacques Derrida writes of a social space post-total violence: these figures appear 'suspended in a void or above an abyss, suspended by a pure performative act, that is accountable to no one'.[65] Vindicated by the necessities of post-war societal norming, there is no point at which the missing leg, missing people, or indeed this apparent PTSD is met, processed, or even acknowledged. However, the realities of the experiential moment are a hatchet, after all, shallow buried, the wrong rose too quickly won. Secondly, that the violent reductions of reality, of the cultural curtailing of perception reliant on a pretence of total mimetic reflection cannot hold to the horrifying Tartarus of war and its reflexive post. As discussed throughout this section, this crisis of reality positions the individual on the phantasmagoric tightrope of belief, where a fantastic, hallucinatory, dreamlike ambiguity shrouds experience. It is a space where dominant mimetic structures appear delimiting, and a process of real observation that must not mime the disingenuous image, but mime the way that image is built; to embrace the fantastic, the unknowable, the fragmentation is asserted. To refer to China Miéville:

> 'Real' life under capitalism [a 'capitalism' for us found in post-war societal norming] is a fantasy: 'realism', narrowly defined, is therefore a 'realistic' depiction of 'an absurdity which is true,' but no less absurd for that. Narrow 'realism' is as partial and ideological as 'reality' itself [. . ..] In fact, the fantastic might be a mode peculiarly suited to and resonant with the forms of modernity. The usual charge that fantasy is escapist, incoherent or nostalgic (if not downright reactionary), though perhaps true for great swathes of the literature, is contingent on content. Fantasy is a mode that, in constructing an internally coherent but actually impossible totality – constructed on the basis that the impossible is, for this work, true – mimics the 'absurdity' of capitalist modernity.[66]

This experimental novelization of experientiality as avant-garde realism thus portrays not a reconciliation, or realization, but what post-war reality is; a decentred, fantastic oblique adjacent. The portrayal of these fantastic normalizing processes in action through these figures parallels, as seen above, that experienced by the writers themselves, and is a process they attempt to script. In text, Yonnet states that if he were able to narrate his experiences entirely uncensored he would 'be hacked to pieces' by the same 'mob' he himself participated in forming.[67] Just like his protagonist, as a propagandist following the war, he worked to obscure the barbarity he and wider French society had committed and suffered, both in his newspaper work and also in his scant novel *Le Cabaret des inconnus* (1945).[68] Where the violence of war was ascribed to primordial, 'Nazi' entities presented within a 2D aspect as rapists, torturers and murderers, and *the resistance* and the French populace in general took on a similarly 2D aspect as pulpish divine beings.

In Yonnet's normalizing culture-work, all violent action is shifted to a discontinued entity whose humanity is rescinded and become sort of demoniacal creatures, that a purified France had forced back into the void. A reality in which systemic, everyday collaboration and complicit inaction, the *Vel d'Hiv*, did not, cannot have occurred. This is the critical perception of a number of writers present here, especially those with Jewish backgrounds, of a communal inaction or complicity that gives the impression, as Topor biographer Frantz Vaillant quotes his subject, that 'many French are just Germans that speak the French language'.[69] As further demonstrated in a favourite joke Topor liked to tell, mimicking the sudden revelation that the entire French populace during the war had actually been exceedingly humble members of the resistance: 'I too, saved a Jew'.[70] Topor had managed to survive attempts to have him and his family killed for being Jewish throughout the war, which were not carried out by 'Nazis', but by the French police, their Parisian neighbours, people in the street; their landlady.[71] This crisis of reality raised is then, in a dual sense, the *verdunization* of human experience.[72] And it is this ambiguous space of falsity that, on a societal scale, Yonnet and his protagonist acted to re-narrate, to warp that experientiality, to bury that actual violence in violent symbol. And it is with this later novel Yonnet attempted to roll back that enforced, socially complicit, cultural amnesia; what Brophy describes as a 'Normative conquest', to which he had been complicit. A normative amnesia Green similarly draws the reader to confused-confusing confrontation with, an impossibility in the present environment and experiential recall that the wider spectrum of experimental novel writers of the period, as seen above, centre in their textual project.

Sorge and the continuity human

The texts here raised entail a reflexivity upon the genesis of the post-war social crisis of reality, and its fractious continuation; acceleration. This draws us away from the descriptions of societal 'anxiety' or '*angst*' in the period as a sort of general, shared fearful 'imagination of catastrophe'[73] and closer to what Heppenstall calls 'Sorge':

> 'Angst' is the mood of affective tonality which reflects the void of non-existence. The mood or affective tonality which reflects the daily commonplace (*Alltäglichkeit*) is 'Sorge.' This is translated by the French as '*souci*' [...] 'preoccupation' and 'care' are English words which have been used, [...] there is an English word etymologically related to 'Sorge' and to some extent still contained in it and that is the word 'sorrow.'[74]

It is not within an *angst* regarding the arching over apocalyptic Event and its return that we find the human primarily living under the effects of, but the contagious, mutational presence of that *deathliness* within the commonplace, the quotidian of human life and human interactions with the world and with others. This would appear to further clarify the post-war collective 'sorrowful sickness' described by Sartre. To look to Pinget, who depicts a street scene in *Entre Fantoine et Agapa* (1951), from the eyes of one pedestrian amongst the crowd, he writes:

> When you walk down the street you are surrounded by decorticated beings. They present a spectacle of monstrous psychological division. I met almost none for whom the present had any importance. They project everything into the future. A future constituted of present and past preoccupations. Encumbered by this impossibility, they trudge from distress to downfall. They are dangerously haunted by eternity.[75]

For these decorticated beings there is no stable now, only a confused distress relying on societal narratives emplaced they struggle to fully, continually, reify, and a present that can only ever be experienced post-mortem: where there is a 'nothing where there should be something'.[76] And so we are again presented with an interaction in which a fantastic delusory remove intercedes between human and world. Where this individual sense of break in experience became concreted into social life and societal world-norm itself; where the war, the camps, the atom bomb are indeed translocated to somewhere else, and damagingly so.

As Béalu echoes Pinget, on the human self-reductions of quotidian perception, 'they move through a world of miracles with glasses with blacked-out lenses covering their eyes from quotidian reality. A reality that they themselves create to fill their artificial needs: a car, tobacco, alcohol and television.'[77] With the yielding of reality, the trauma ostensibly subsides, and yet the sacrifice of that experience takes other aspects of humanity with it like Pinget's beings, like Horkheimer's man, 'decorticated';[78] with the bath water goes the baby. The imposition of this amnesia requires a perpetual myopia, by which the recuperated individual, the social subject, does not see that saving money for a car, that being turned away from the *tabac* due to cigarette shortages, if the building itself has not been shelled, that poor wine with added anti-freeze, that the seemingly empty airwaves of post-war broadcasting in France, but for the BBC world service,[79] belies these as opiatic mechanisms – indeed both Perec and Heppenstall recall the dubious yellow bread available in post-war France after the failed harvests noted in partition one.[80] They become emblematic partialities of an intention; simulations of living. It is a dissonant illusion acted out by Charley Summers, who will go on forgetting, perilously gliding across the new veneer of normalcy, needing the realities invented to fill the dislocated gaps, to moor some sense of the stable.

It is through this 'that the whole panorama of post-war England [and France] is seen from a strange hallucinatory angle',[81] as Philip Toynbee wrote in a review of *Back* in 1947. While as Nance becomes Rose, Charley (who, according to Toynbee, in his hesitation is apparently the very 'device for throwing doubts on the normality that surrounds him', though he is allowed to keep his name, it would appear he too is inadequately re-formed in this process) and the Grant family and everyone else falls head first into the new states of things, what Toynbee calls 'a new revelation of the real world'.[82] In relation to *Back*, Toynbee sketches a communally willed 'new hallucinatory real' in which the normal is a delimited reduction within a sea of abnormality; a groundless façade of sense in a space of unmoored, foundationless, fractured meaning. This is borne out by memory-fractal-ghost-risen Atha in Heppenstall's *The Connecting Door* who drifts in a 'protective amnesia' that masks 'that the purpose of his coming here [to Strasbourg] was suicide' with the narrative disguise of it as 'a happy place' in recollection.[83] This chimes with that indicated above: what came after the unmitigated violence of the Second World War, on a transnational scale, was the social desire for getting back to normal. A performative getting back to work, which in its rapid and arbitrary shift has a shruggingly transient quality in a place normally described in the grand, eternalized narratives of re-establishing civilization. A civilization that here appears in ruins frozen in grotesque forms mid-crumble. In a social space in which amnesia demands a perpetual myopia for the veneer it protects to be maintained, for these writers normalcy itself is a bizarre collective performance; life itself is a theatre of the absurd, or cruelty, which drags with it both the illusory palliative, and the Sorge to which it is integrally connected. As François Jost writes channelling Dubuffet, 'disquiet comes to us at the very moment when the presentation of things and their representation become confused',[84] when the believable and unbelievable reverberate at the same frequency, where the fiction usurps the reality. To apply a practical analogy, to look to John Ruskin on the ambiguities of perception:

> Draw on a piece of white paper a square and a circle, each about a twelfth or eighth of an inch in diameter, and blacken them so that their forms may be very distinct, place your paper against the wall at the end of the room, and retire from it a greater or less distance accordingly as you have drawn the figures larger or smaller. You will come to a point where, though you can see both the spots with perfect plainness, you cannot tell which is the square and which the circle.[85]

The culturally generated distancing, rewriting of experienced reality altered its communal perception, to the extent, as noted above, the fact and the fantasy, the truth and the lie, slip within one another, and within this fantastic vibration the latter usurps the former in referential primacy. The believable unreal frenetically overlays the unbelievable real. And as such, as Ghose writes giving his own practical analogy: 'clearly we cannot trust our senses. The rod, when immersed in water, *is* bent: to explain the distorted image in terms of behaviour of light is only to have constructed the phrase, *distorted image*, and to have given rise to another question about the fallibility of human sight which is so subject to being misled.'[86] A dynamic that raises the ambiguity and unreliability of perception and recall, that demonstrates the very impossibility of objectively recording the real itself. Echoing Béalu and Pinget above, Yonnet wrote in a piece for *Bizarre* in 1955:

> We have eyes not to see, ears not to hear. How much time have we lost, how many wonders of the world are forever sullied by the facts of herd-like sufficiency, of the falsely blasé calm that people communicate by discrete smiles that betray a hidden meaning, an invite to vertiginous complicity, to those addressed by these smiles, and at one time or another, and much more often than one thinks, by an obsession with things.[87]

To such an end it is the 'hysterically' mimetic ruinous nature of the experimental novel's tenets itself that offers a degree of relative clarity. An approach, inherent in experimental romantics, as I previously termed it, of a reality born to the reader, the social individual, already bombed out. Indeed, to draw into question the internal-external illusory remove that is 'sometimes so complete [...] that we perceive the external world within a 2D aspect, as if in a dream: we have become strangers to ourselves'.[88] A shrugging unreality that emanates from the required cognitive dissonance, distancing of the traumatic violence collectively committed, witnessed and suffered, a total violence that had shaken away the very foundations, walls of normalcy, and the acceptance of the fantastic cultural image of what had, and what was, occurring around and within societal communities. This positions normalization within the spectrum of at its most benign grasping at straws, at its most extreme a 'systemic "casualness, indifference, mass carelessness"' in which cultural narratives as 'generalisations are taken at their literal word', in a climate where 'violence produces violence'.[89] An interaction which indeed appears here to act to estrange the human from themselves; where 'an absence erupts into empirical reality'.[90]

And this appears to offer itself to be taken in a number of ways, it is a wound to be obsessively returned to. Or it is a sort of stumbling Libet gap, by which sense is forever given in the past tense to hide the horrors of the impulse of externally given desire, within which, like Yonnet's protagonist, the human might attempt to bypass their trauma. *He* did not commit murder, there was no individuation in the action: it was simply 'Paris that avenged itself'.[91] And yet with this evasion, Yonnet presents both the culturally defined place and the communally self-defining people as the impetus for this active obscuring, warping, of the war and its aftermath, that goes on with an artifice of supposedly liberal, humanist principles, apparently unaware these 'values' had 'slipped into the abyss' opened in that absence. This is a dualism demonstrated in the processes of amnesia and myopic distancing cited above, from Béalu's prescription of a delimited, inescapable sameness, to Charley Summers in *Back* being gradually reconciled to that lie in a void of reliable memory. A rupture that for the social subject runs off beyond knowability, leaving perhaps only the hidden break from which it launched, a reduction, a de-synched confusion; the 'insane contradictions' of these overlapping projects. The wound, however bypassed, whether willed and/or coerced, returns. This turmoil is perhaps the impetus for wishing deterministic, airbrushed civilizational narrative grounding, a past to hold to, a future to reach to – a perpetual penultimate moment within an arbitrarily asserted utopian drive – when there appears here neither and none. This is accompanied by a vague, often overt fear of the violent communal demand for reductive stability; the *deus ex machina* of *Back* hinges on the communal rewriting of Nance's consciousness in order to fill a shared deathly void. Yonnet's mob demand a space of remove from a previous reality at disjuncture to that they lived in post-war, in which they might semi-convincingly state 'I too, saved a Jew.' Then, in the confusion of the post-war in which violence had made a phantasm of reality, where Yonnet must write falsehoods to sate the mob, it is the disjuncture of the war and its peaceful post which are locked in unnatural reflex. Further, it is this reflexion itself, socii's communally, culturally generated self-representation, that cements this sense of Sorge, that these pale realities are artificial; that according to Dubuffet 'restricts the field of perception, [and in so doing] brings with it a darkness'.[92] A Sorge that would appear to encumber the most rudimentary goings-on with an unreal, sorrowful quality that constantly threatens to break the social subject's suspension of disbelief, a persistent *veisalgia*. Framed here is the 'insane cycle' of fear that perhaps drives an ever more aggressive forgetfulness and acceptance of dominant cultural re-narration. That described in partition one as a 'social Mauthausen', that generated the effect of cultural relation to social of Brophy's inescapable 'perpetual cinema show'.

Cycling violence

If in the above is demonstrated an imposition of myopia, of amnesia that was necessary for the social human to continue post-war, then we are led to confrontation with the human void that these processes acted to mask. If in the above is introduced how these interactions had affected the writerly process, and entered text-space as a foundational, broken, structure, that became itself a novelistic scaffolding, we are left to clarify *how* that structure might function in relation to the reader. In doing so, finding some schema of comprehension of the internal-external interactions of confusion and evasion above presented within human interaction itself. To look closer at Johnson's *House Mother Normal*, where each account of an evening's events in a nursing home is begun with a generative definition of the extent to which the following section's narrator will be able to receive, process and relay via internal monologue the same unfolding events in front of them at the same paginated timing. There are eight character narrators and a writerly intervention. All nine are graded by their level of physical and mental deterioration, which structures their narration and plot participation. In this the internal to external readerly unfolding of the text's inherent realities hinges, as Nicolas Tredell writes of the novel in *Fighting Fictions* (2010), on 'old age' which, 'like death, is a historical variable'.⁹³ In this way the inescapable amnesiac elements of the narrative reflect, and are tied to, the experience of life lived and the shortcomings of the grand continuity narratives of civilizational history.

Sarah Lamson	
Age	74
marital status	widow
sight	60%
hearing	75%
touch	70%
smell	50%
movement	85%
CQ count	10
pathology	contractures; incipient hallux valgus; osteoarthritis; suspected late paraprenia; among others.⁹⁴

By this method not only does Johnson impose personal experience on a seemingly faux-objective sense of communally shared historico-cultural event, but in doing so both imposes the fragmentary nature of perception on these grand, seemingly full images, and also generates the narrators' differing levels of reliability; the extent to which they enter the story from the stupefied phenomenal set-space where unravels the novel's plot, lurking as too the individual does to history, as vague partialities in the shadows of the narrative inferred and never fully shown.

This fracturing marginality is similarly present in Heppenstall's *The Connecting Door* which Gareth J. Buckell writes, implying a critical subscription to the Britain-France oppositional paradigm met above, is an 'attempt to narrow the gap between post-war English and French literature'.⁹⁵ Aside from this sorting, *The Connecting Door* is a novel in which event and characterization slip along the common axis of the frenetic border of France and Germany between temporal plateaus, the three of which most edified describing before, during, and after 'Nazism', with characters and reader unaware, and the narrator largely forgetting, that like the Sartre film *Les Jeux sont faits* (1948):

> The lovers danced on an empty *café* terrace to the faint sound of an invisible orchestra. They were dead, but did not know it, as they whirled in slow motion round and round.⁹⁶

The three main plateaus are designated chiefly by tense, the first two – 1931, and 1936 – slipping largely into past tense, rather than the largely present beginning in 1948 – which too slumps to past when progressing to 1949. The setting is malleable in this sense: at the top of the page the narrator enters the café Gallia, asking for the menu in the café Germania, before leaving, by the end of the page, the newly renamed café Gallia. The churches at once ringing bells to wake the narrator, yet when looking out of the window he sees the church bombed 'for strategical reasons' by the Americans,[97] the ringing bells that awoke him orphaned. And like this these dead past characters slip amongst the three, to the point at which it is entirely ambiguous which of them are still alive in that time frame, and which are 'ghosts rising'.[98]

This offers clarity for the elements of interaction within the internal-external spaces of the human and immersive society at post-war discussed above: first by which the arbitrary degeneration of event by aging memory is, like historically stabilized, narrated reality, reduced in Heppenstall to a solipsistic confusion, and in Johnson to a variable defined by socially deigned percentages and pathological disease. While Kate Connolly finds 'a tool for the operation of disciplinary power' in Johnson's language of pathology,[99] it appears paramount rather that the alienating array of complex terms act as an oblique simulacrum for the precarious state of lived experience itself, to stand in meek place for the suicidal confusion of Heppenstall. While perhaps what Connolly calls a 'Foucauldian disciplining' is occurring in this arcane lexicon, it may perhaps stand as the dismembered terms on which the individual has palatable access to experience at all, a thing defined, indeed, by oblique limits it cannot access. To refer to Foucault himself, 'an illness only has its reality and value as an illness at the interior of a culture that recognises it as such'.[100] Thus there is perhaps a social *discipline* present here that asserts itself before the concerns of cultural structure *disciplining*.

With Sarah Lamson, the reader is afforded a relatively padded out back story, and albeit fragmentary, running commentary of what is occurring. As can be seen from her stats she is a relatively involved and clear narrative machine with high plausibility of information given, high possibility of cognitive presence for in-text narrative events with the mobile ability to be an involved mechanism in the series of plotted actioned culminations. Sarah Lamson here is one of the more generative sources of narrative story and progression, setting, theme and mode; as she relates her participation in the events of the evening she recalls snippets of past experiences as a banal quotidian flowing into and out of these wider global tumults to which she is present but seemingly inessential, which would appear the extra-textual key. She recalls her dead husbands, the war, constant loss, meals and family holidays all of which, entangled, stand on the precipice of being forgotten:

> It seemed as though it would go on for ever, the summer, the sun, and for the first time since the War I really felt that things were getting back to normal, though all the ones who could remember better than I could were saying that things would never be the same, never could be, after the War, which I could understand in the case of someone like myself, who'd lost their husband because of the war.[101]

The War here is again this shattering event, before the reader is told that the holiday retold was 'in that seaside town in France, France where Jim had got Gassed,[102] and it is the unsaid communication, somewhere suspended between the capitalized Gas and Lamson's age that her first husband (one of three apparent dead husbands) was killed in the First World War. The working holiday-cum-pilgrimage to the place of 'Jim's death' several years after the fact,[103] though she describes it as the most perfect moment of her life, acts as a second traumatic experience that forces the reconciliation of a past trauma and ensuing confused amnesia. On this pilgrimage Lamson was sexually exploited by her boss, took the blame and was sacked – it was then, for the first time she could accept the violent verity of her first husband's death coughing up 'bits that were him' after returning home from the front. Yet it does not signal the calming end of past violence and ability to build back up, reclaim lived life and move on, but appears as another indent in a cyclical series of violent traumas done to Lamson, not the end of some terrible epoch of her life but a moment of simply 'going on' from it to the next.[104] Her husband's return from the First World War, the repetition of this trauma in her sexual and economic exploitation, the Second World War where 'we were there all right, slapping the sandbags on the incendiaries, ducking down the shelters when the HE started. All that sort of thing,' burying her third husband long after that war and the disconcerting absence of her second dead husband (dead in the Second?) retreat into a forgetful and repetitive haze of 'the good old days'.[105] If violent traumas here in societal life can be said to be cyclical they are not repetitive; it is the problem of death, in its birth, throwing a boomerang and expecting it not to return, ad nauseum. As Watts asks: 'is there a constant quantity of violence in the world, continually circulating?'[106] Here, within the reminiscences of pre-Second World War horrors, lies a disjuncture between the very concrete way in which the First World War we as societies discuss at a distance as a comparative chart of numbers killed and wounded, and the Second that still appears without comfortable number.[107] This difficulty of reduced comprehension of traumatic event forces a process in which, as for Atha in Heppenstall's *The Connecting Door*, the 'mind had undergone a partial black-out'.[108] Memory, like the Rhine, became 'icier and less easy simply to drop into but irrevocable and slower to yield up its corpses'.[109] Just as contemplations of suicide are for the fractal character Atha made inaccessible, the Second World War here it appears is unfathomable, qualitative; all too human.

The minds that render these attempted reminiscences here have, as Tredell writes, historically deteriorated beyond an ability to fully grasp the received whole image of the past. Thus, does this speak of the cognitive fragility of Sarah Lamson, of Heppenstall's memory-tourist narrator, or the unreal nature of the image of the Second World War not present in first-hand experience, but re-assigned as the infallible good war afterwards? A socio-cultural artifice these inmates locked away from society no longer have any need, or perhaps on the precipice of death a reduced ability to strive to maintain. An artifice in Heppenstall slipping confronted with the difficulty in properly grasping the event. As Ron Lamson laments in his narrative in *House Mother Normal*, and appears to characterize the internal human space in the post-war, what remains is a self-perpetuating trauma and little cognisance of its source: 'it's constant, the pain, what else is there to think about, it goes round and round in circles in my mind'.[110] What is present here is a cultural element, and societal presence, perhaps singular to the experimental novel of the period. What was at the time obscured, unapproachable, performatively omitted, that may perhaps now be approached at distance, may be contemporaneously indicated as a confused void within these texts, pouring out from this event-break. What is indicated by these texts is the active nature of the reflex classified by the prefix post-, and the unease and pain, this Sorge, emanating from somewhere within the inadequate, shrinking lived present. Where the experimental novel here attempts to bring these borders into focus, the mechanisms of a rebuilding and maintenance of the veneer of singular reality, where the limit or border 'of language is to stand at the edge of what we know on the threshold of the undefined and unknowable',[111] and be, momentarily, perhaps aware of this limit. A status that is defined by the interactive dynamic of two modes of human processing of external reality here presented: culturally eliminated, socially marginalized human experience and the confusion of the individual; where one perpetually begets the other.

If this slippage of experiential confusion and arbitrary ordering is presented in the contents of the book as such, this content is amplified in form. The textual mechanics, in particular here the narrative mode, would appear to function as construct by which these qualities might project beyond text-space. As Connolly writes of Johnson quoting Jonathan Coe, the text must be read '"vertically" as well as "horizontally"';[112] 'in order to piece together an exchange between two individuals, it is necessary to move forwards and backwards through the text'.[113] It might be assumed Coe draws this description from that raised by Themerson as an aspect of 'SPT', which he calls 'Typographical Topography':[114]

> you may read horizontally [...] you may also take each of its words vertically [...] you may give each of them the flesh of exact definition; instead of allowing them to evoke the clichés stored in your mind, you may try to find the true reality to which every word points, and that is what I call Semantic Poetry.[115]

To grasp some idea of the sequencing of events, this readerly interaction of Typographical Topography is also necessary in *The Connecting Door*. And therefore both texts break with what Genette calls 'the paradoxal logic of fiction',[116] which forces the reader 'to define each element, each unit of story by its functional character' and 'by its correlation with another unit'; where chapters commit to an Aristotelian march towards a final culmination of the text's monolithic meaning.[117] Coe's process implies a displacement of this march, but it remains a, albeit confused-confusing, linearity; a readerly act of parallel reading akin to Derrida's use of marginalia in essay,[118] or Heppenstall's parallel novel *Two Moons* where one page might simultaneously unlock another.[119] However, as accounted for in the opening up of this process in

Themerson, and as present in the texts here cited, the narrative mode appears more akin to the asymmetry of the marginalia present in Johnson in *Albert Angelo*,[120] Roche's *Codex*,[121] Burns' *Babel* (1969),[122] or Quin's dual writing in *Passages* (1969),[123] which requires a roving eye between the pages. And which returns us to the formal concerns of the 'second death' writerly-readerly textual genesis raised in partition one. Thus, it goes much beyond 'parallel reading' here. The readerly act of moving back and forth implies a jumping back and forth seeking confirmation of multiple parallel fragmented accounts rather than a cogent act of parallel reading itself: it implies rather something like a tumbling through wisps of information, of attempting to build a shadow of a whole from fragmented, shifting connections in a constant scan reading of each section of the text that impairs the rationalization of a readerly desire to impose contextualizing world-image synecdoche.[124] This in itself presents as *effectively, affectively* mimetic of the degenerative states in which we find the narrating entities, and their attempts to function in-world.

To some extent this again chimes with the rudiments of Iser's 'reception aesthetic' described in *The Implied Reader* and *The Act of Reading* (1976),[125] a recentring of text towards a space of readerly praxis, presence and participation, as Terry Eagleton puts it:

> We read backwards and forwards simultaneously, predicting and recollecting, perhaps aware of other possible realisations of the text which our reading has negated. Moreover, all of this complicated activity is carried out on many levels at once, for the text has 'backgrounds' and 'foregrounds,' different narrative viewpoints, alternative layers of meaning between which we are constantly moving.[126]

Iser gives the example of Northrop Frye who 'once wrote: "it has been said of Boehme that his books are like a picnic to which the author brings the words and the reader the meaning." The remark may have been intended as a sneer at Boehme, but it is an exact description of all works of literary art without exception.'[127] And yet in the texts here present there is a destabilization in this realizing of the readerly, in which the reader's ability to make 'implicit connections, fill in gaps, draw inferences and test out hunches' is not a passively standard textual element but a responsibility.[128] It is brought to the fore as the conscious mechanic of the experimental novel in the vein of a Zolean formal treatment. Though not hesitating in stating the importance of text-space 'cooperation',[129] more interested in the theoretical formulation of 'real', 'contemporary' or 'ideal' reader figure,[130] Iser perhaps would not appreciate this writerly deviation. But this is at heart a divergence from the totality of his positioning of an idealized 'implied reader', that traps itself in its own paradox of interpretative privilege that Iser argues so much against in writer figure and critic. There would appear to be an inescapable presence within the textual space of the novel of each of these entities, amongst a further gamut of potential textual presences on a wide spectrum of participation, engagement and, as already seen, out and out refusal.[131] Rather, in relation to this Typographical Topography, it would appear as Roche quotes his own *Compact* in *Codex* (1974): '(writing/secret) evaporates itself a little for a reading to condense it in itself (unknowingly) later on as its own anagram'.[132] As Sollers states of a more or less engaged reading of the experimental novel, in the introduction to the text Roche quotes, *Compact*: 'the reader would comprehend that the book is not an object at all, but a realist representative organism, that relies on a typographical costume, for which reference must be searched for outside itself'.[133] And as such, as Eagleton writes of Iser:

> The whole point of reading [...] is that it brings us into deeper self-consciousness, catalyses a more critical view of our own identities. It is as though what we have been 'reading,' in working our way through a text is ourselves.[134]

As Iser writes, 'thus we have the apparently paradoxical situation in which the reader is forced to reveal aspects of himself in order to experience a reality which is different from his own'.[135] And this potentiality is variable, as it 'will depend largely on the extent to which he himself actively provides the unwritten part of the text'.[136] Then the confusion and re-ordering presented, the horrors indicated in these texts are not projected by these texts upon the reader: rather, they ratify a shared uneasy marginality, a doubting interiority; they do not cause a destabilization, but induce it. It is in this sense, rather, that Heppenstall's deathly confusion; the isolation of the individuals present in Johnson, the alienation of their degenerating memories and their current predicament, is too invoked within the reader – the point at which this premise finds its extra-textual opening up, in which the terms of quantification are found wanting, and no one present in the text stands upon stable, concrete, grounding. A sense the reader of an experimental novel is perhaps momentarily drawn to experience, indeed as a margin within themselves and their own world, like Pinget's reader according to Anthony Cheal Pugh, 'pulled violently in opposite directions';[137] torn at from all axes. This in itself was perhaps the catalyst for 'traditionalist' revulsion and refusal. An experiential mimesis that includes both the writer and reader, who are dragged into the text by this participatory formal dynamic as too, in Johnson, the concluding writerly intervention, and in both, second person direct address of the reader. What is reinforced in this section is that the experimental text is not created in opposition, but within the tenets of reality's own inadequacies, it is not an *I*, or a *you*, but a *we* 'without eyes to see'. And the increased interaction with text the experimental novel posits brings the reliability of the touchpoints of objective reality into doubt, an effect of interacting slippage between confusion and order the reader is obliged to participate in. This perhaps acts to reveal that, as Fisher writes:

> The material world in which we live is more profoundly alien and strange than we had previously imagined [...] an enquiry into the nature of what the world is like is also inevitably an unravelling of what human beings had taken themselves to be.[138]

If this constitutes experimental romantics in action within the text, then this formal application (a textual treatment) represents the treating of these concerns in content (a content diagnosis); of a perceived human, societal delusional sickness. It would appear the failures of the novel, of the claimed reportage of social realism, are themselves by-passed in centring that object's own broken inadequacy; the functionality of the experimental novel is indeed found in its dysfunctional *incompleteness*. And it is through which, perhaps, Adorno's inarticulate scream might be given articulation. Formal participation, or textual treatment, I will return to at length in the final partition, however here I continue with the diagnoses found in experimental content, to which that form appears intended to draw the reader to complex, *affective*, interaction; to 'authentically' communicate within a space of distancing, suggestive myopic-amnesia and coercive re-narration.

2.2 Communal supplication, individual terraforming

Following this discussion of the state of reality indicated in the experimental novel, reduction and confusion as asserted by dominant cultural symbols is entrenched in the, perhaps as posited, co-opted-co-opting nature of human interrelation; both in social community and in-text synecdoche of this interaction. A position indicated above in the mutual vampiric social re-appropriation of both Charley and Nance in their own post-war normalization, as too Yonnet's 'vengeful Paris'. As Bernard Stiegler writes in *De la misère symbolique* (2013): 'the collective individuation through which a society is made up supposes a *participation* of everyone in the production of the *individual*, as a necessary fantasy and fiction that generates the play-acting of a supposed unity, which one might deign to call *society*'.[139] We are confronted with the imaging of post-war social communities given by Topor:

> Martians – they were all Martians. But they were ashamed of it, and thus tried to conceal it. They had decided, once and for all, that their monstrous disproportions were, in reality, the true proportion, and that their inconceivable ugliness was beauty. They were strangers on this planet, but they refused to admit it. They pretended that they were perfectly at home. He caught a glimpse of his own reflection in a shop window. He was no different. Identical in fact, he looked exactly the same as the monsters. He belonged to their species.[140]

This establishes performative communal participation in the creation and propagation of the post-war false-normal discussed above; a perpetual cycle of mutual self-reduction. And yet, as seen in this performative refusal as an expression of Sorge, as Freud writes this collective incorporation of the individual is not painless: 'human beings, incapable of living in individual isolation, nevertheless find the sacrifices that culture asks of them in order to make human co-existence possible a heavy load to bear'.[141] Again, this process of reduction brings with it a blackness. Thus, content concern here magnifies the dysfunctions of the societal leviathan body; the interconnectivity by which the social grouping itself is relied on to ratify a human status that is malleable, changeable; where the human self is something that is formed, that can be reformed, and indeed rescinded. Established is a prism in which a social whole acts to seemingly self-reduce, self-police within the cult of immersive community that bears the hallmarks of brutalization. And within which quotidian life, the human, would appear, as in Topor's writing according to Calder, linked 'to the world of worms and insects or reptiles'.[142]

Depictions of communal, quotidian life

Echoing that raised by Adorno above, the plotted narrative of Topor's *Le Locataire chimérique* (1964) occurs within the brackets of a perpetual, cyclical 'unbearable scream'.[143] The central conceit of the book around which this scream spirals is its protagonist, Trelkovsky, searching for a new apartment. It is a more or less unremarkable necessity of quotidian life that draws the reader first into the 'objectively' agreed everyday, and then drags them into the wildest magnifications of the subtle horrors of the process of moving house. Again, in Topor's *Joko fête son anniversaire*, Joko has missed his alarm and is running late for work when he is hassled by an apparently psychotic old man in the street who makes him even later. And on, Leonora Carrington's *The Hearing Trumpet* (1974) in which this study is returned again to a retirement home. Léon in Butor's *La Modification* (1957) is on a train on a business trip to Rome. In a vignette within Béalu's *Journal d'un mort* a man enters a photobooth to have his picture taken. In Johnson's *Christie Malry's Own Double-Entry* a young man goes for a job interview. These are not the nowhere-nothings of a Beckettian Malone's room and the broken parables projected across its walls as the inside of a trepanned cranium that does not exist, nor some great Joycean town to be mapped in text. They are very much grounded in a recognizable, identifiable everyday, identifying 'reality', and yet the further extrapolations of the seemingly innocuous conceits that ground the experimental novel holds an inherent sense of this quotidian norm harbouring a very much brutalized-brutalizing engine, that explodes from these reality-rooted unremarkable images. Therefore, quotidian living appears, as will be approached, indeed essentially bracketed too by this articulated unbearable scream.

Characterization of an immersive object space

To refer back to a text with which this study is already acquainted, in Johnson's *House Mother Normal*, the characters appear locked in a cycle of trauma. In the ordinary, quotidian setting of a group of 'inmates' in an evening at an elderly care home the grind of their lives rapidly unravels. What pervades is a swelling background of screaming noise that encircles a silence, that too accompanies Trelkovsky in *Le Locataire chimérique*, of on-going repetitive and cyclical violence. Here resides the slipping concrete marks of an individual systematically dehumanized by interactions with other people, with little input, say, or ability to change their maudlin train track. They have no access to the lever to switch direction, nor a hope of derailing. Sarah Lamson, as seen, trundles on awaiting arrival at an end destination that is entirely absent other than the lexical shrug concluding most of the narrations of the piece; 'never mind'. In her plotted narrative she continues to be maligned by the milieus and environments she is submerged in and yet she pervades; she is still prescient. The train track of her life is not just a fictitious reflex of one committed to by a wider milieu of social subjects who keep-on-keeping-on, but too evokes the train track of narrative Johnson has imprisoned this character in. This is also present in Topor, whose use of nouns like girlfriend, friend, colleague, mother, father slip interchangeably with accusations of the 'enemy'. A fear of those by which the individual would archetypally find solace and support – self-definition – is present also for Johnson when he 'creates' a girlfriend for Christie in *Christie Malry's Own Double-Entry* named 'the Shrike'.[144] Johnson dares the reader to comprehend the reference, 'which will be too obvious to some, too obscure to others'.[145] A challenge here tested.

Jonathan Raban in his review of the book in *Encounter* in 1973 could get little past that Johnson 'makes her do interesting things to his [Christie's] private parts with a vacuum cleaner and some shaving foam'.[146] But there appears a further depth, Johnson's reference is perhaps the 1952 play, the 1955 film *The Shrike* written by Joseph Kramm, in which a man is driven insane by a manipulating and domineering wife. Committed to an insane asylum, the protagonist must completely yield to his wife in order to be passed from institutional incarceration in the asylum to the incarceration of the rest of his life with her. Or, perhaps the 1956 Sylvia Plath poem *The Shrike*, which describes a woman's jealousy of her partner's freedom in dreaming sleep:

> So hungered, she must wait in rage
> Until bird-racketing dawn
> When her shrike-face

Leans to peck open those locked lids, to eat
[…]
Spike and suck out
Last blood-drop of that truant heart.[147]

Both draw comparison of desire to dominate another on the one hand and the enforced yielding of self-sovereignty on the other to the macabre practices of the shrike bird. An animal which lures with a soothing song, then subsequently with its long sharp beak stabs its prey,[148] shakes it to break its neck, then impales it on a long thorn to be eaten at a later date. The killing of more than it can eat a show of personal potency. This interplay of allure, control, malice, insanity, incarceration, killing and blood-drinking as magnified beyond necessity to carnival at the core of such a social institution as marriage, or *love*, displaces the intimacy of connection held high there within a sense of *the beloved*. This reframes love and sex as forms of intimate connection with another as entirely disingenuous modes of humanization, and they take on more a sense of mourning elements indeed stolen from the self.

In this, the reader is led to a textual space pockmarked by the interrelation of people filling virtual roles in which the thefts, the attacks, come from the peopled milieus of the protagonists' interacting textual community that appear as a flock of circling shrikes at their prey. This is a trope common to the peopled environments of the experimental novel, where the protagonist is consistently presented as a consciousness under siege. While in Brophy's *In Transit*, it is a name, a gender, a set of normed behaviours that are imposed on the narrator by interactions with others in the airport departures lounge; the type of drink one must buy at the bar, which toilet to enter, in Figes' *Nelly's Version* (1977) it is the oppressive persistence of a supposed 'son', of a house that is supposedly her own, neighbours who are supposedly her neighbours, who attempt to force the amnesiac international woman of mystery protagonist into the role of housewife 'Mrs Nelly Dean'. As Laing and Cooper write, 'in the atomised, massified, or serialised crowds which enclose us, our reality as subject remains abstract, since our practical impotence paralyses us, and our reality as object resides in the other'.[149] The terror here is not within a 'Kafkaesque' of labyrinthine corridors, and offices, and bureaucrats, and paperwork, it is not the 'horror of a topography of obstacles' that drives narrative and progressively confronts reader,[150] but a turn on the star of the show by the cast and crew. And it is not just the peopled milieus of these fictions that appear as shrikes, but to return to the second iteration of Lamson's train track, Topor's protagonists are also his 'victims' in which both the writer and reader too become an enemy of the protagonist, too further additions to the flock circling. Thus, the book itself, like the camera in the Michael Powell film *Peeping Tom* (1960) singles out one figure in the crowd, and in so doing becomes the weapon of that figure's torture, often their demise. That their amnesiac-myopic drift is momentarily given narrative is enough for the other characters, amidst which they are immersed, to work to not pry them from, but impale them upon, the societal leviathan's 'hallucinatory' social carapace. In this respect, the narrative both opens the scream of individuation, and drives to its inevitable silencing. In this image it is the writer and the reader who, in opening the book, in imposing singularity, open the protagonist up to this attack.

And yet, on Léon's train, everybody has a book in Butor's *La Modification*. As Patricia A. Struebig writes:

> Every passenger on the train, each human being, holds within themselves *their book*; their individuality, their essence, that distinguishes their life. It is Léon's roving gaze, from one passenger to another in this compartment of the train, as he comes to understand, that does this to them, because in describing others, thus writing *their* novel, he writes and constructs his own. The *gaze* always circles back upon Léon and his own unread book, that is, upon his own existence uncomprehending of himself.[151]

To look to the text itself for the repetition of the book image:

> Why haven't you read, this book, which you have bought, who are you perhaps protecting by not reading it? Why, even now that you're sat down, with it in your hands, can you not open it, don't you even want to decrypt the title, while Pierre gets up and leaves, and in the window the moon rises and falls, you only look at the back of this book, of which the cover has become transparent, through which you see the white pages underneath, isn't it almost as though you can read it through its very cover, the lines of letters made of up words you cannot discern?
> And yet, it is in this book, whatever it is, because you haven't opened it, because even now you have no desire to read the title nor the author's name, it is in this book that has not been able to distract you from yourself, you would find help to realise your decision to resist the erosion of your

memories, your apparent resolve against everything that ate away at, denied, your delusions[152]

If the novels on the train, 'because it's a novel',[153] are each and every passenger's story, their self as argued by Struebig,[154] just like the victimization present in the writerly-readerly genesis of the entrapping scream in the act of textual interaction in *Le Locataire chimérique*, this should surely lead to a train-wide murder-suicide. The books tell both the character's own story, and thus the stories of 'people that resemble to some degree those that have successively entered the interior of this compartment throughout the journey'.[155] This mass introspection entailing a train-wide moment of utter individuation, and then its mutually-assured termination. A Kool-Aid moment; Lamson's deathly train tracks. Yet, as Struebig writes, no one on the train, including Léon ever opens their book. They satisfy themselves with staring at one another, out of the window at a warped landscape that passes too quickly, in a sea of memory the more probed the more it dissolves; the more it erodes the pathways of the interior. It is perhaps for this reason that the inhabitants of Butor's train are, by the end of the novel, all apparently allowed to depart their compartments at their destination. Whereas the readers just as the writers, commit the protagonists of other fictions to birth, subsequent myriad modes of torture, and often death, narratives to which they are forever confined. But Butor's figures are locked in confining objectification with one another, and as such their books are never opened; their destination thus forever a simulation of movement and arrival in which they can only ever exist within their compartments; Rome, like Rose, like Yonnet's under-bridge mystic, an erosive fantasy. Léon himself is thus no protagonist, but placed as secondary, as, in Butor's narrating in *you* ('*vous*'), the artificiality, the virtuality, of his interiority is constantly returned to in the second person. This chimes with what Greg Buchanan writes of characterization in Johnson's *The Unfortunates*, the characters of which, he writes, are largely drafted like 'loose leaves in the wind' that threaten to 'blow away'.[156]

> The temporary, provisional, and transitory nature of the resulting draft-like prose is one factor in the apparent lack of concrete reality found in the novel's secondary characters.[157]

To return to Raban, it is, for him, a great failing in Johnson's writing that he 'is always gleefully reminding the reader that this is all a fiction, a card-house of lies,[158] and that he is manipulating his puppet characters'.[159] Again, Raban writes of Johnson as manipulating the milieu of people, he 'makes' the shrike do 'interesting things'; and yet for all this Johnson cannot save he who he invests with interiority, Christie. If these secondary characters are puppets, there appears little of Johnson's omnipotence at their strings, akin to Topor's 'faces that file past in front of him'.[160] This recalls Béalu's *L'Expérience de la nuit* (1945), in which Marcel Adrien horrifyingly discovers that the figures peopling the story around him are, by and large, eyeless puppets created in the factory he is, for a turn, a janitor at.

> Suddenly, it appeared that all these faces were no longer unknown to me, that I had seen them before, on a set of stairs, in a corridor, or passed them in the twilight. Those two there, and those two others, and those there too, all of them, do they not possess exactly, if a bit younger, the same features of the old people at the hotel?[161]

And yet it is not this milieu of puppets that are at odds in the environment, but Marcel running around gazing at the most natural things like a puppet workshop, where people are of course made, with the wild eyes of conspiracy. As, later in the text he undergoes surgery for his eye problems resulting in an ability to see too clearly, which causes his eyes to fire laser beams that evaporate the people around him; he sees too much and must again seek treatment to reverse it. Thus, it is not the puppets, nor the text, that appear here fragile. To return this to Johnson, it is not the shrike, but Christie, like Tony in *The Unfortunates*, dying of cancer. Despite being invested with 'more interiority than other characters',[162] it is the narrating protagonist who, to the reader, appears as leaves blown away. However, the secondary characters in their inhuman 2D appearance slip easily within the bound and/or wrapped and boxed leaves of stacked printed paper. There is a separation at work here. It seems that in opening a book, the reader opens their victim(s), the protagonist(s) – in some instances too narrator(s) (if not combined) – who, thus broken from the confinement of the closed book covers becomes locked in an enforced spiral of interiority borrowed from the spatio-temporal action of a writerly-readerly engagement in textspace. These narrating protagonists are unlike the peripheral characters that amount to interactive objects and mechanisms of the protagonist's immersive environment that would usually act to ratify the individuated character's humanity, yet, conversely here, attack the protagonist's narrated individuation. As, lacking such multivalent interiority, the peripherals' 'books' as such remain closed, and here their drive appears to close the protagonist's book too. Asserted here is a parallel sense of humanity, as defined by communally driven human definition by monadic interrelation; not by a Cartesianesque 'consciousness' (a 'consciousness of consciousness'), nor individuating introspection.

The peripherals assert themselves

To draw out this notion, to look properly to the characters who populate Topor's fiction: in *Le Locataire chimérique* it is the protagonist's enforced interaction with other people in the act of going about his quotidian life that causes the horrors he must endure. If the peripheral characters are leaves, they are such that whip blindingly around the protagonist, which recalls the similar image of shrikes. It is as if these peripheral figures sense that another's book has been opened; the protagonist is victim of an imposed, momentary, erosive hypermnesia. He has, perhaps, remembered his self (or, in being read, is instilled with 'selves'), and thus remembers too much. In this he becomes something of a fugitive in the midst of an attempted prison break within the layered spaces of delimited fictive virtuality; thus, too virtualized social reality. This echoes with what Randall Stevenson writes of Brooke-Rose's *Such* (1966), which 'concerns a psychiatrist's struggle, after his heart has briefly stopped during an operation, to reconstruct some grasp of reality out of the whirling chaos of astronomical fantasies and proliferating imaginings which have invaded his mind'.[163] And yet as these fragments swirl in repetition they are never reconciled, 'the resistance you could call matter melts and mutates into wild energy by a law of conservation that has a perfectly good scientific explanation, so that you give rebirth which hurts to some lost slice of you, a forgotten area of particles that come whirling back to form filaments of gas in violent motion or extragalactic nebulae colliding perhaps on the outer rim, great clusters moving at thousands of miles per second'.[164] A transmutation into the 'unfinished unfinishable story' of post-human continuation,[165] the order of sense is never found and thus remains as an explosive clarity of frittering meanings summing an oblique physics rather than *histoire* and as such perhaps slips from the cultural crossroads that imprison both the protagonist, and the book object, in social interrelation.

To reference Topor as cited below, though not quite so divested of the novel's structural position, it is as if the protagonist's doorway has been momentarily cleared of a muddying excrement. The actions of peripheral characters indeed appear to harbour the motive of pushing a story to its close, in effect *closing* the book; closing this chaotic clarity, and too the protagonist. This process is starkly apparent in *Le Locataire chimérique*: Trelkovsky eventually finds an apartment under lease to a girl called Simone Choule. She is in a coma after attempting suicide, and he horrifically finds himself by her hospital bedside attempting to fathom if she will die soon. Luckily, or unluckily, but fatally (if you will allow the reverberations of fate and fatal) for Trelkovsky she promptly does so and he gets the place. After moving in he slowly becomes convinced his neighbours are breaking him down, disintegrating his self to force him to take on Simone's personality and then complete the cycle by murdering him. There is slippage between Trelkovsky's identity and Simone's that begins with the swapping out of his morning coffee and Gitane with hot chocolate and a Gauloise,[166] until he becomes a cross-dressing simulacrum of her, and is thrown, or jumps, out of his apartment window. The peripheral characters have succeeded in bringing Trelkovsky's narrative to a close, as he wakes from a coma in a hospital bed where he sees himself as at the beginning of the story hoping the girl in the bed will soon die and, realizing Simone always was a simulation to be dissolved to, lets out the 'unbearable scream' that bookends the narrative. Thus ends, and essentially begins again, the puppets' work.

This reassigning of Trelkovsky's interiority is prompted by those around him, but driven by an internal desire for the inside and out to vibrate at the same frequency (the drive of the co-opted-co-opting subject), and seems an attempt by Topor to enter his wartime experience 'hiding in plain-sight'. Trelkovsky is first divorced from figures external to the milieu of the story, his work colleagues and potential pre-novel romantic attachments, by a continual beating at the walls, floor and ceiling signalling disapproval of his housewarming party. Following the break-up of the party:

> For four nights after, his neighbours banged on the walls.
> Now, when Trelkovsky saw his friends, they took the piss out of him. At the office, his colleagues had heard about it, and together laughed at his

panic. [...] at no point during his life in the apartment did he forget that there was precisely one person above, one person below, and others to the sides. If he ever managed to forget it, someone was there to remind him.[167]

It is the beginning of a process in which his neighbours, under the guise of pushing their perceptions of proper conduct, grind away the individuation offered Trelkovsky by narrative; a process of trituration which for all his appeasement or resistance ends, as it begins, within the same screaming confinement in a full-body cast. To follow its beginnings, as referenced above, when a single mother, Mme Gadérian, with a crippled daughter is forced out of the building for her community deficiencies, before promptly being disappeared, she smears her excrement across the building, the landing, across the apartment doors. As Trelkovsky did not sign the petition for her removal she misses his:

> Holding back his nausea, he took from his apartment a piece of card from a box, and with it he collected some of the excrement from the stairs to the next floor. His heart went like the clappers while he went out on his expedition, his skin crawled with fear and disgust. He poured out the contents of the card on his door. After, he got rid of the piece of cardboard in the toilet. He was more dead than alive by the time the job was done.[168]

He struggles to adhere to established concerted normality as subscribed to by his neighbours; a norm, it appears, intended to always place him back in the same hospital bed divorced from both his body and his self; to make of him a shape as 2D as they (the supernumerary Simone), in this ouroboros of recuperation to community he becomes 'the chimerical tenant' of the title in which his torture and demise appear to force upon him the form of an eternally slipping Janus. This theme is also raised within the character of Joko in *Joko fête son anniversaire*, who, when an apparently psychotic old man shouts at him, jumps on his back and offers him gold to be a human-horse, he refuses. However, he is subsequently coerced by friends and colleagues, and to make up for rejecting the task, strives to become the best human-horse in town.

> JOKO (*red with frustration*)
> Carrying people about, it's degrading. Getting a bit of pocket money doesn't really come into it...

> MONSIEUR BAPTISTA (*with kindness*)
>
> That's good, Joko. That's very good. You have a sense of dignity. All the same you know you must serve them. Saint Christopher carried Christ, as I understand, and without shame. Parents carry their children, and bear no disdain for doing so. The strong carry the weak. It's only fair, in fact it's charitable.
>
> JOKO
>
> Yes, but when it's the stronger that the weaker have to carry...
>
> MONSIEUR BAPTISTA (*smiling*)
>
> What advantage would there be in that? The strong can get around much faster on their own, with less tiredness, without useless exertion. On the other hand, a weak person that works will rapidly become strong. He'd find himself stronger, in his flesh and in his soul, because work is a blessing, and I know no work that would bring dishonour. Come on, calm your concerns, Joko, they're unjustified.
>
> A WORKER
>
> As for me, I might as well carry some bloke about, after all I carry around my own shit.
>
> OTHER WORKER
>
> Especially for what they're paying![169]

Here again is this communally defined accepted normal, or 'objectively agreed' reality, to which the individual is coerced, then forced to adhere to; in this instance, the service of a human-horse. This is a process of blocking out or hiding discursive elements in the internal space and accepting a dominant imprint of the external. And yet this obscured violent on-going seeping from an unfathomable violent genesis though hidden, can be found bubbling at its grotesque core. For Joko it is when, in working to become an exemplar of his community, he becomes more and more representative of its willingness to adhere to the new norm, and as such loses all access to what one of his riders Professor Frank refers to as his 'precious little self'.[170]

This process is echoed in Carrington's *The Hearing Trumpet* when Dr Gambit tells Marian: 'every member of this community is closely Watched and Studied in order that they can receive Help. No Help can be of any avail if there is not collaboration and Effort on the part of the individual [...] you cannot overcome so many psychic deformities in a short space of time. You are not alone as victim of your degenerate habits, everyone has faults, here we seek to observe these faults and finally to dissolve them under the light of Objective Observation Consciousness.'[171] By this oblique process of dissolving the self, Marian may potentially achieve an 'Inner Christianity', a 'condition that is apt to open psychic doors for New Truth'.[172] Akin to Trelkovsky and Joko, within Marian is perceived a dirty, revolting, schizoid humanity that first must be cleansed, then replaced making of her a better adherent to the community. To look at what is demonstrated in this coercion, it is not a Sartrean 'hell is *other* people', as goes the maxim, but that hell *is* people, the dynamics of community; the blinkered collective, the confused and docile mob, of which all present in text are very much a part. The social human too inherently carries this hell. Behind this image of malicious human interaction there is a potentiality of individuated humanity present, the sense that, if there is a dirty human entity within, below this communal hell, that people are indeed potentially, disturbingly, *revolting*. But, like Billany's Henry in *The Cage*, as discussed below, it is a quality they deodorize from themselves, and as seen in *The Hearing Trumpet*, from others. The social here is characterized as a field in which the individual strives to be a better subject-adherent to the norms, and to the people of their community; to a numerically identical synchronicity with the others around them, and as such are rewarded for their commitment to a participation already obligatory with acceptance, and the solace of care and support, of some sense of concretely *existing*, offered by that, to take Charley Summers as an example. To look again to *The Hearing Trumpet*: 'the fact that You Have Been Chosen to join this community should give you enough stimulation to face your own vices [seemingly individuated "human" traits] bravely and see to diminish their hold over you'.[173] However, while Marian, in the mouth of the nuclear apocalypse, apparently escapes to Lapland similar to *Such*, in which the psychiatrist finds liberation in his utter loss of cogent centre, Joko is trapped in this cycle of giving himself up to a voided space, prepared for the entrance of the 'New Truth'. And yet whether the protagonist is subdued or achieves victorious isolation, they appear still locked within their own impossible limits.

To look again to Queneau's *Le Vol d'Icare*,[174] in which late-nineteenth century writer Hubert Lubert wakes one day to find his main character Icare has, in the reverberations of '*vol*', 'flown', or been stolen. Icare, it transpires, is living elsewhere in Paris determined to fulfil his own life-drive that raises this problematic of 'literature within life' itself. As Claude Debon writes, 'if Icare lives his life, passes from the fictive to the real, he demonstrates the real character of fiction, or the fictive character of novelesque reality: leaving the manuscript, Icare remains in the book, still locked within manuscript. We too are pitilessly locked within literature and words. The author of the novel Hubert Lubert, for his part is equally nothing but a character in a novel'.[175] As Icare resists a return to fiction to live in 'reality', he has succeeded in slipping the bonds of the fictive horizon present in the manuscript that generated him, however unknown to Icare as to Lubert, this fantastic transcendence of a plane of reality is itself created within a wider plane of virtualized reality. It then stands as farce, as the limits of the paper novel, as with Marian, as with Joko, close upon them as an ultimately unknowable horizon; this then appears a reflexive native societal critique I have herein sought to describe. Thus, it is the process of return to a 'levelled' internal status, rather than escape that becomes the narratable territory of the novel. A process of knowing acceptance or unknowing resistance that both consist of a giving up of something. If the norm to be returned to here is malicious in its agents' acts, as is shown in these examples, precludes a process of reduction that causes such Sorge, such terror and panic, what can be said of the very position of the individual itself in such an environment of extremes of violence and overwriting codification?

To look to Billany, in *The Cage* written in the run up to the fall of Italy while a prisoner-of-war there (1943), Billany takes up the I of a third person character, 'Henry', and foresees future reactions to the book through the machinic id of secondary characterization; deigns to inhabit one, again we are returned to this comparison to insects, within a hive of 'minds without a soul':[176]

> I dislike hearts and souls, they are embarrassing. Dan has a most objectionable habit, now and then, of saying things which are creepily intimate. It's bad enough to blush, but to be told why you blushed is intolerable. People don't want to know what goes on in other people's souls, of which they are rightly shy. I hate to blush for other people: I won't do it, anyway. I shall simply avert my eyes. David is much more in my line [. . .] No morbid introspection, no sense of concealed and perhaps smelly human eccentricities in his heart. Clean-limbed English type. No deviations, no sympathy with nonsense, and not overmuch perception.[177]

Page-Dan (a characterization of the writerly function within the book itself) is creepy, he talks of poetry and senses that have no productive function, are morbid and 'un-English', he is excluded from his home culture and remains there a squatter awaiting repatriation; and then, like Trelkovsky, reprimand and reformation. This poetic reality is rejected as 'absurd', which perhaps indicates, in rejection, a reflexive otherwise. As Otto Gross makes reference to the insanity of the self-legitimizing absurdity of the impossible real-unreal, '*credo, quia absurdum est*',[178] for Billany, this appears a fear of absurd, phantasmagoric belief, there is again this Sorge, that Billany channels through Henry of being, due to his own actions, and his own writing, separated, defined 'not normal'. In the textual contexts of Billany's post-war novels, in *The Cage* and *The Trap* he openly discusses his previously secret homosexuality, and attempts to write fictions that might work to approach that socially disavowed experience, at a time when being gay was illegal in Britain, punished by prison and chemical castration, and being discovered to be gay in the military would result in execution. And as such, for Billany, the stakes were high for committing to such textual project, stakes he was very much cognisant of: 'it was a sort of love which, in the world as we know it, could not be made public. One might rather commit suicide; some have done'.[179] Which raises a seemingly paradoxical assertion: while in prison camp, Billany's characters, as too perhaps himself, are in their remove from British home life, in their resignation to death in prison, to some extent expressively, actionably 'free'. And yet, learning they are to be repatriated, he becomes aware this passing 'freedom' will be used as a petard with which to hoist him. In reaction, Billany wrote in his journal upon realizing he was to be released:

> I'll have to get married. Because what's the good of kidding myself I want to go back. Shops and trams and English voices and money in my pocket. But it needs more than that to make a life...[180]

Here 'normal' appears to performative reduction; a process of *self*-editing necessary to survive within social community. Therefore, the term 'normal' as linked to a misleadingly deigned objective reality, as seen above, seems a warped parody of itself in this sense. This is a point on which Roland Jaccard wrote in *L'Éxil intérieure* in 1975,

> For a long time, psychiatrists have taken normality as synonym for successful adaptability. To be normal is to be well-adapted to those who surround you, to the society in which you live, its mores, its technicalities, its dominant

> ideology. [...] On the other hand, we would qualify mental illness by the incoherent, the illogical, to inappropriate behaviour, maladapted, which reveals a person's *abnormality* [...] in which we see, or at least should see, quite quickly societal limitations: a normal person is he who adapts himself, that is to say he who submits himself to the order, to the rules, to the norms of the society in which he lives.[181]

The implication is that to 'be normal' is to wilfully run at a reduced rate, to be abnormal is the, as Billany worries, communally deigned inability to do so. However, Henry the punctilious Englishman is exactly a caricature of this self-definition by rejection, a 'bishop of Everywhere'.[182] These secondary characters appear, echoing Freud as cited in partition one, according to psychoanalyst and psychotic Gross, to act out a symptomatic behaviour 'of people with senile dementia', which, harking back to that stated by these writers above, can only be 'explained by diminished perception'.[183] What the characters of *Back* wilfully yield to as accepted by-product of the 'blacked out glasses' necessary to keep on keeping on post-war. The unnatural way the human is honed post-war synchronizes with the unnatural way these characters are created as eyeless puppets with a shrike beak on the factory floor. These texts are then describing the enactment of the ouroboros of reduction approached in the previous section. Therefore, to look to the individuated protagonist, it appears what is defined as the normal, the ordered adaptation to community, relies on a huge work of self-imposed delusion; a state of the social subject in a constant dementia. For the individuated protagonist, it is the perpetual act of smearing oneself with excrement like camouflage. And yet when confronted with such a sight, the social community is seemingly prone to attack, or disenfranchise the object that forces the image. This community demanded delusion that is borne out by a disgusted aversion and enforced shared reduction, as seen above, attempts to, or is willed to, fill the cracks in quotidian normalcy. Such a framing then defines the normal by its inhuman work of social life as a weird game of shadow play, a series of adopted tics and obsessively repeated mantras of singular truth that a posteriori moulds objective fact. As such, the definitions of an oppositional sanity and insanity as assigned to normal and abnormal seem utterly reversed. Indeed, labels of sorting by which adherents to reduction, and those that must be forced to adhere, or sacrificed in its name, are separated. The fear that emanates from these narratives appears to come from this separation, and appears reflexive not of alienation, but falsity and inherent brutality within those around the post-war subject individuated in quotidian living itself.

This characterizes the actions of secondary characters in these fictions as both adherers and propagators of, as Gross coins a term in *On the Problem of Insanity* (1920); *thanatophilia*. This is the 'passivity to something that is overpowering, of shutting off all one's resistance to a foreign power'.[184] It is 'the idea of yielding to death',[185] that acts like 'religious insanity' in yielding to an unknowable higher being, a schema here applied to community, to which Trelkovsky in *Le Locataire chimérique* attempts to abide. And yet, as Trelkovsky senses in his act of supplication with the single mother's excrement where he becomes 'more dead than alive', such supplication arrives at 'the symbolic meaning of the idea of being dead', where, 'death plays the exact same role as that of surrender';[186] where 'life' itself becomes 'a region of death'.[187] Trelkovsky is returned to a place akin to that described in Burns' *Europe after the Rain*: 'the white beds and the delicate white curtains, no flowers, no books, no work but mental death'.[188] In this sense, the peripheral characters of these texts are Pinget's decorticated beings, themselves the zombie-like dead actors of conformity to the process of societal normalization. The protagonist is, in being read, perhaps akin to the reader, momentarily separated, then in the closing of the book forcibly returned to the simulation. They labour under the misconception that, as Claude Simon quotes Leonardo Da Vinci in the opening of *La Route des Flandres* (1960): 'I believed I was learning to live' but, 'I was learning to die'.[189] The narrative premises of these texts appear a *trompe l'oeil* spiral prison that forever, locked within its dust cover, picked up by reader after reader, grasps at its own tail. The thematic premise is that of the individual trapped in their generated environment that, though thrown through trials and tribulations mimicking the manifested complexities of life, offers no reward other than the final realization of a silent pause, and then the same violent cycle of reduction they will forever be returned to. In the protagonist's horror at the process of return at the level of a primary reading here, and to the peripheral characters, the protagonist, in its thrashing, appears 'an anti-social individual', that 'is of no use to the community', and so 'must be replaced as soon as possible. He must therefore die as quickly as can be carried out.'[190] The protagonist in this sense is very much a victim of their fiction that can only end in their termination as an 'antisocial', perhaps 'antifictional' element, which Butor's Léon appears quite safe from. If the acceleration of forgetting, of reduced perception, of a silent interlocking of monads in a drifting sea that here appears to describe society, as propagated by a domineering culture of reduction then it appears both the writer and reader are, paradoxically, committed as enemies to the protagonist, and function as allies to the cause of the peopled milieu of the text. Both roles drive, akin to the secondary characters, to the protagonist's end; the protagonist often seemingly a *rückenfigur* projection of a writer's own 'asocial' characteristics and drives, that invite correlation with the reader's own, it is thus too potentially a readerly *rückenfigur* that in both cases appears not a figure to be straightforwardly inhabited, but a strawman to be purged. The writer and reader then both also follow the tenets of cultural defence, as Freud writes, 'culture [...] needs to be defended against the individual, and its arrangements, institutions and decrees all serve that end'.[191] In this sense, in post-war societies the constant self and mutual reduction of perception occurring presents Sorge, yes, however if a subject is to voice this in a scream however masked; it is one that must be silenced. A book that must be closed.

It appears then, that it is not these secondary character's lack of apparent interiority, as Buchanan writes of Johnson above, that makes a concrete real impossible, but reflexively makes such a shared objective concept possible at all. The experimental novel throws the protagonist onto a journey of reduction, rather than a societal katabasis, on which they may perhaps be returned to a voided interior without a writerly or readerly driving force; a death-like stasis. While to the past selves of the I in Heppenstall's *The Connecting Door* the narrator states 'you forget, or rather, you haven't quite realised, that without me you don't exist',[192] it appears quite the other way around; it is the I that stands perilously fragile. In *Erika* (1969) Topor attacks the idea of the independent *cogito*, as he writes: 'the idea of the novel that you're about to read came to be seven years ago. At this time, my principle literary activity consisted in systematically blacking out all the words in whatever book fell into my hands. It is without doubt significant that one of these books was [Descartes'] *Le Discours de la méthode*.'[193] Topor does not erase the words or copy them; he blots them out with pen and ink until the pages of the book run as a series of black non-signifying smears, including the phrase *cogito ergo sum*. He writes of words on a page as a 'mob' that 'bully' one another, that 'it seemed to me that the mob of words, that constitute a book, exert upon each individual word vast pressure, to force each other to the public cause'.[194] In this sense, this study is drawn to the correlative of the human in society to the word on the page, as Johnson states: 'language is the straitjacket in which thoughts have to be communicated'.[195] A word, like a narrated character, like an individual within a social system, is too trapped in its relation to others, just as Trelkovsky fears his neighbours above, below, next to him. The word just as the individual is caught in a rabble of objectification, its meaning extrapolated to this or that dictated by its neighbours, relatives and acquaintances, its 'enemies'. Then to short circuit that 'mob', the narratives of these novels appear to be undergoing a kind of content-form 'epileptic fit',[196] that mimics the 'induced spasms' caused by the process of electro-shock therapy (ECT). The effects of which Carrington compares to 'very much like being dead'.[197] If, for an instant, these individuated characters achieve, in separation, a momentary simulation of being impossibly alive, then they are very quickly, like the reader, in the close of the book, returned to a dead-alive stasis; indeed an open book closed. The experimental novel would then successfully portray a space in which, suspended between projected points of apocalyptic catastrophe, the societal human indeed appears 'zombified' by that experience, and the processes necessary to hide it. A zombification that here appears mutually enforced by communal interaction with other humans in the shared societal space normed, perpetually norming. To refer again to Gross on insanity:

> Striving to control reality is inherent in will to power. Where the flight into the unreal has occurred, where insane formation and distorted perceptions must alter the image of reality, there the attempt will not be given up to bring new impressions into a connection with reality and with each other. Logical intellectual activity continues, it strives to create reality around itself, in which one can orient oneself. Will-power also seeks in psychosis to hold onto achievement that gives the human mind its control over the surroundings: the conception of continuity.[198]

In this, Gross offers a succinct linking of the sections of this partition; from the moment the insane social has willed to design, wend and control reality thus take power of it, it creates a perpetual distorted simulation, that must be constantly worked at to develop the organic-seeming sense of a continuity of before, present, and future. Where the 'crazy-maze' of Davies' utterly distorted spider web would appear to describe both the internal, and external human space.

The representative unstable self

Then, the socio-cultural space is indeed, as held throughout this study, impossible to be separate from, and thus makes of consciousness, of the body, a cage. The sovereignty of the self and the sovereignty of the body are united, and just as the one can be repurposed, as in Burns: 'he allowed her to search the mouths of the dead, the gold in their mouths was increasing in value', [199] it is an object to be mechanically used, static, cut up, diminished, bled, so too can the other, which posits the central concern of both bodily and self use-value of the interlocking monadic unit.

> From what point, Trelkovsky asked himself, is the individual more than what we perceive? I pull off my arm, pull at it hard. I say: me and my arm. I pull off the other, I say: me and my two arms. I remove the legs, I say: me and my limbs. I take out my stomach, my liver, my kidneys, suppose it were possible, I say: me and my viscera. I cut off my head: what do I say? Me and my body, or me, my head? What right does my head, which is nothing more than a member after all, to claim the title of 'me'? Because it contains the brain? But there are larvae, worms, I understand, that do not have a brain. For these beings, is there some group of them that functions like a brain that says: me and my worms?[200]

This first phase of bodily, and self, dismemberment posits that the self, as the body, is open to the same potentials of violent degradation. Just as after the violence of war humans returned home with parts of their body missing, they too returned missing parts of their self, as too during, and assumedly for some time after the war, they washed themselves with soap made of the boiled down fat of victims of the Holocaust. And so, in this confusion of the internal space relying on external narration and order, in this entrapping social interrelation, what delimits the individual? The bodily cage is itself variable, then the broken self is too essentially, potentially, incomplete; in-built with this redundancy. And the directional, active mind, like for Topor's concerted mass of worms, lies somewhere in the ether of mass movement. *Humanity* here, following that raised above, is recentred from self-knowledge, to the unit's ability to act, devoid of individuated choice. This enters the realms of the lecture on man given in Themerson's 1953 novel *Professor Mmaa's Lecture*, in which the eponymous professor, a termite academic, talks on the 'bold ape' homo-sapiens:

> 'Let us imagine,' he said, 'that I am Gulliver. Not any common subterranean Gulliver, but a Homo-Gulliver. Imagine that here, among you, stands not Professor Mmaa, but Homo-Professor Mmaa. ... Listen and smell at me closely! Here is the head of Homo-Gulliver. Here are the arms of Homo-Gulliver!' He exhibited the foremost of his six legs. 'And here should be Homo-Gulliver's cardiac pump'. It's what I called arms are armed with the horny exhibit No. 2. Its head is forested with exhibit No. 1. Its arms are governed by its head. But exhibits No. 1 and 2 and the cardiac pump are not governed by the head. They are individuals in their own right. Therefore I ask: 'Am I Homo-Gulliver, an individual in my own right, or only an aggregation of individuals in their own right? And am I, Homo-Gulliver, an individual in my own right, or only an element in some larger Individual in its own right?'[201]

This extra-species objectification of the human as a bodily sum of machinic parts, some unanswerable as the heart to the brain, reflects too, as Topor's worms, the elements of the brain as machinic parts within a larger creative force; a drifting, quasi-directional 'psychosphere' of mass synchronized unthought. At what point does the culturally formed human unit become discernible from the culturally formed human social milieu? From this psychosphere? If the insanity of the objectively agreed real, and the bizarre shades of established 'normality' within it are forged and maintained by a constant interaction with others undergoing the same dementia, same states of delusion, then at what point of separation does the human become a countable noun? Discernibly, essentially, individual within the social leviathan's carapace? To apply this avenue to Béalu's *Journal d'un mort*:

> On the boulevard, an uneasiness seizes me: how can I prove to these strangers that I exist? I do not have any papers on me or certificate of residence or identity card, nothing. I decide to go to a photographer. Five minutes is enough to obtain self-reproduction in six copies. Reassured I sit in front of the mechanical eye. But this photographer is a joker, the picture he gives me after a quarter of an hour of waiting is that of a former president of the

republic. Without wasting time arguing I run to another photography shop. There, after a good half hour, the operator brings me with compliments the portrait of a little girl with a silly smile. I'm suffocating with fury. Don't you see, it's not me! [...] In succession, twenty photographers have me sit in front of the lens, and successively my figure in the dark room becomes the head of a fat bald man, that of a cavalry officer, a boy at his communion, a cinema actor, then the face of a bulldog, then the image of a fruit bowl![202]

The interior appears fickle, as Joko becomes the eternally decaying tomb of his riders, Béalu's man looking for proof of his interior sovereignty becomes engaged in a bizarre game of pass the *cogito*. As Quin's narrator in *Passages* posits, 'the question then: who is it that inhabits me?'[203] But this questioning arrives nowhere, as, as Béalu's narrator concludes with frustration: 'it goes on like this until, it strikes me, I finally remember that I have no identity anymore and that, moreover, the photograph would only be required by the establishment for a death certificate, the only legal document that anyone is ever likely to ask of me'.[204] Just as in Burns' *Europe After the Rain*, where no one in the novel has a name, and those names that do exist appear not exclusively attached to this or that character: the narrator meets a boy who 'wasn't sure of his name, it had been signed away to someone else'.[205]

This arbitrary sense of identification imposed upon a confused fluidity is raised again and again in Perec's *Quel petit vélo à guidon chromé au fond de la cour?* (1966), which begins by tracing the protagonist as:

> There was this dude, he was called Karamanlis, or something like that: Karawo? Karawasch? Karacouvé? Well anyway, Karawhatever. Whatever it was, a name out of the ordinary, a name that says something, that we wouldn't forget too easily.[206]

And again in Queneau's *Zazie dans le Métro*, where as Anne Clancier writes this ambiguity of self-definition is raised, again, in cross-dressing: 'Gabriel and Marceline who becomes Marcel by the end of the book [...] problems of identity are equally approached, agent Trouscaillon appears in diverse guises to the point where even he does not know who he is.'[207] Here is presented a paradox of the horrors of post-war life, each social individual appears a golem animated by community, to whose mouth an order, a formed identity, is inserted. If the golem threatens to deviate from this order it will be brought to heel, broken down and with the same parts rendered anew, there appears no individual privilege to self-access, nor self-knowledge. Just like Béalu's man, when Trelkovsky tries to demarcate his self, the more he grasps for it the more it eludes him: 'I have to find myself again! What was it that made him him, uniquely him? What was it that differentiated him from others? What was his reference number, his type? What was it that made him say: that's so me, or that's not me at all? [...] he remembered it as if from some dream'.[208] And again, in Quin's *Tripticks*: 'a fluid dance, and all our limbs flowing into, out, through, until I had no idea whose hands, breast, leg I touched. Or was touched by. Time seemed no longer time of real life but a hugely amplified present. When fantasy has the weight of fact; and fact has the metaphoric potential of fantasy.'[209] It indeed appears that the confused exterior labyrinth of Davies' broken spider web, for the character experiencing in-text, 'has become the interior'.[210]

To the extent that, as Quin's narrator-protagonist in *Tripticks* must commit to a daily 'thinking period' to poll, attempt to re-form, a sense of self, placing an 'X' on a scale from 'good', to 'bad', 'pleasant' to 'unpleasant', 'heavy' to 'light', of his character of the day before, to try to edify a shifting sense of stable self-understanding.[211] Therefore, in defence of community's violently guarded shared delusions such an openly broken figure must be reduced, re-appropriated; made again an objectifying-objectified object. This continues the question of external terraforming of the internal space. As too, Vian states in contrast to his parody character 'Jean-Sol Partre': behind the veil of the eyes 'there is no essence'.[212] Of a divine-prayer-path or meditative internal insight there is nothing to speak of one individual as differentiated from the others of the leviathan's body. Similarly, Billany writes, 'most people are really praying to their Unconscious when they think they're praying to God. But it makes no odds, there's never any answer'.[213] For Billany 'the Unconscious, like God, is deaf'.[214] In these texts there appears little presence of authentic individual self, no universal access to a soul-based freedom of action or privilege of a divine higher being's ear, only a dead-end premise built as the unachievable end-game of a life that demands perpetual meaningless degradation in motion.

As such, the external social artifice appears to drown the individual, forces it to communal drive of 'levelling' by incite or threat of both physical violence upon the body and symbolic violence upon internal sovereignty,[215] and this subsuming by calm unnatural forgetfulness is craved; they are already defeated in the personal sense of unreconciled trauma, violently reformed into a blank receptacle readied for use. The moment of comprehension again slips and disappears at the precipice of realization. They are, like Rosetta Stanton who stands as a kind of Rosetta Stone in *House Mother Normal*, already helplessly drowning:

> Let me out, or I shall die
>
> No, I do
> not get any
> l i g h t e r,   I v y,
>   I   I n -
>   tend
>   n o t
> t   o   g   e   t
>   a   n   y -
> t   h   i   n   g
>   a   n   y
> m   o   r   e
>
>   n   o
> m   o   r[216]

The text, as her ability to think, dismembering itself, drifting down the page to the blank depths of unthought. This passage is followed by six entirely silent pages implying Rosetta has drifted off into an unnarratable territory of 'undeath', an unthinking, self-less state; an utter lack of individuation. As Ivy Nicholls asks without response: '*all right, Mrs Stanton? Yes, she's all right.*'[217]

To follow the thread of an insane norm

As an antisocial entity, figures like Trelkovsky indeed appear, in diverging from the unnatural norm, quite mad, to look back across the demonic scenes described by Béalu and Topor. And as such, as Salim Jay writes of Trelkovsky in *Merci, Roland Topor* (2014):

> The hallucinating man fearfully asks himself what is standing in front of him. For a moment, the reader would believe himself imprisoned within a nightmare.[218]

However, if the genesis of this reality too imprisons, passingly, the reader it is perhaps evident that the definition of insanity here is indeed, as discussed, quite the inverse. The madness descended into is not Trelkovsky's attempts at suicide, but his becoming Simone. It is his insane attempts to live by the milieu's abnormal codification of expected normality, which too draws parallels with the sovereignty of self present both intra and extra text here. The story, it appears, itself describes not a protagonist's life, but the defence of agreed reality in society around it committed by the writer and the reader figures' textual allies. The same processes by which interiority may be terraformed and locked in synchronicity with the environment and milieu around it allows for a catching of the discursiveness present in primary characterization in fiction. Trelkovsky's abnormality is potentially contagious, and thus these peripherals appear to work to close the book in the interests of the writer and the reader.

In *Rat* (2006), Jonathan Burt writes in reference to Davies' rat catcher and scientist Andrew Melmoth's obsession: 'Bourdon de Sigrais noted in the eighteenth century the expression "to have the rats" ("*avoir des rats*") is a sign of madness and yet, at the same time, the history of rats is inextricably connected to human nature.'[219] There is a slippage between the concept of being mad and being human which lies at the centre of post-war, post-Hiroshima/Nagasaki, society for Melmoth. It speaks of the difficulty in differentiating the natures of sanity and insanity present here, and thus too the problem of *who*, or even *what*, is delusional, as Burt writes:

> Melmoth, a scientist who works on rats, eventually disappears into the sewers, apparently to live among them, having become convinced that rats are capable of some sort of sign language. Haunted by the possibility of nuclear annihilation Sykes Davies comments that rats 'may be at the beginning of all that will survive of any organisation on this planet'. The rat is figured as a creature free from affection, duty, conscience, disgust and, importantly, kindness and cruelty. The sole mainspring of its social organisation is a single-minded force and cunning. However, the human drive towards the nuclear apocalypse can equally be seen as singleminded, involving actions beyond affection and conscience and pathologically motivated by a power-driven and suicidal self-interest. At the apocalypse human and rat swap identities.[220]

The question raised is whether Melmoth 'has the rats', or the social community around him does. The implication in these texts is that, like Billany's character projection 'Dan', like Trelkovsky, Melmoth, singled out, is socially perceived as 'having the rats' in his realization that those around him are the very rats themselves. And yet 'having the rats' doesn't seem quite so singular, as Davies supposedly finds in Melmoth's notebook there is no need for war to bring about the impending nuclear apocalypse, simply the continuation of accelerating nuclear tests that whittle down the clock to doomsday:

> One of the more probable results of genetic damage will be a sharp rise in mental disease. It's an exponential process. Every 'test' made is an act of insanity, and it increases the amount of insanity in the future, thus ensuring that more 'tests' will be made, producing still more insanity, and so on.[221]

If a collective insanity which pushes adaptation to reduction, in an amnesiac, myopic march from Holocaust to apocalypse is the order of the day then in their momentary awareness of the absurdity of this reduction, these protagonists indeed appear abnormal, but in their sense of horror very much sane. The nuclear apocalypse is, for Melmoth, an unseen endgame which will cause such genetic damage that 'some may actually be born without faces', but if they were to desecrate the tombs of those who caused the catastrophe they would only 'find their occupants as faceless as their victims'.[222] This recalls a number of images already mustered, of myopia, of eyeless puppets, and finds grounding in Derrida's development of Benjaminian *gewalt* that entails a phantasmagoric policing, 'a formless violence (*gestaltlos*) [...] there is a spirit, both in the sense of the spectre and the sense of life that is raised, precisely through death, by the possibility of the punishment of death'.[223] This policing is the invasive homogenizer of the social that has 'become so hallucinatory and spectral because they haunt everything; they are everywhere, even where they are not'.[224] Derrida here appears to describe the insanity of the communal shrikes of the social; its co-opted-co-opting subjects, where Walter Benjamin would perhaps place a sense of 'rottenness'. Through Melmoth, Davies describes a perpetually accelerating collective insanity as the chief motion of unnatural post-war societies made up of inhuman, faceless people; Topor's demonic lacunae, Béalu's eyeless puppets, Billany's 'minds without a soul'. This places the stability of reduced world-meaning fed by a cultural evasion of trauma, inducing dementia on the unstable precipice of apocalypse, driven by a communally enforced inhuman grouping of rats, or puppets, or shrikes, or leaves, or spiders, or Martians etc.; a continuation of the endemic de-anthropomorphia of the Second World War. A constant pushing of imagery of parasitic, endosymbiotic entities that reinforces that they live off and are subsumed by a systemic environment to which they have become estranged; 'alien'. And as such, it seems from within an insane holographic reality policed by community, in a space where the human is arbitrarily humanized by dehumanizing interrelation, as Billany writes in *The Cage* 'freedom is a hypothesis, prison a fact'.[225]

PARTITION THREE

Treatment: Breaking Down Within the Horizon of the Real

3.1 Creating space in text

If what is diagnosed by the experimental novel in the previous partition is a reduction that amounts to a veneer of objective meaning, and an *anabasis* into the interior of this redefinition, then as raised in a sense of formal treatment, there may exist the potential for a *katabasis* critical approach to this veneer; a push against an anabasis of damaging reductive truth. The potential of which lies in the essential element of *thanatophilic* contagion in human interrelation. In this third partition I intend to follow the pathways, or those at least apparent in this study, of this synchronic unit contagion. If partition one allowed a space in which literary, cultural and socio-historical dysfunction could be observed, partition two has allowed for a space in which, far from 'the ivory tower', these societal issues have been textually raised as a staging-ground of confrontations and destabilizations, and as such, in a sense, indeed 'diagnosed'. But this partition three does not endeavour to offer a cure, or a way out. I look for more an antibiotic that might work with the organism of the socially immersed, formed, reader towards a modicum of communicative clarity, and attempt at real-access, which perhaps too is bound to some sense of self-access, a fleeting individuation.

To establish some clarity in contrast: early twentieth-century Russian Zaum would appear to display formal aim correspondences with the efforts of the post-war experimental novel in this sense of treatment. Where 'the focus is on innovation rather than destruction',[1] similar to Sarraute's perception of 'innovation' harbouring the potential to 'uncover the new'. However, Zaum figures' modernistic belief that by the very act of innovating they, as Kazimir Malevich wrote, 'have destroyed the ring of the horizon and escaped from out of the circle of [referential] things',[2] appears in our contexts, and indeed the societal contexts of twentieth-century Russia within which Malevich would later undergo trials, imprisonment, suppression and an early death, a fallacious supposition. And yet the very idea that in reading Zaum, as Craig Dworkin posits, a text may cause the reader 'to slip out of the referential noose' is an interesting potentiality in which novelistic aesthetic might indeed be demonstrably 'affective'.[3] It may indeed indicate that impossible living has the potential to be in some way a viable *demi-monde*. I posit that the referential horizon is maintained in the texts here approached, to repeat an assertion previously made: like Icare in Queneau's *Le Vol d'Icare*, whether the pretence is offered or not, there is no societal katabasis available here. Indeed, this horizon presents itself in the words of Ludwig Wittgenstein as 'a halo' that 'thought is surrounded by';[4] Johnson's 'straitjacket of language'. Therefore, here this study looks primarily for the potential for 'empathetic' communication between monadic individuals frozen in a shared space; whereby Perec's 'refusal, pure and simple' might be by-passed by hypertrophied novelesque formal mechanics, where this *aesthetic affectivity* would indeed function as an analytical uncovering of those limits.

And despite its own limitations, Zaum might offer something of an opening: the idea that at the lingual core of writing, its language physiognomy, there is the potential to be *za* 'across; beyond; to the other side of', *um* the 'mind; intellect; head' runs a path by which that raised in the preceding partition can be communicated, as raised.[5] In *Metafiction* (1984), Patricia Waugh citing Hayden White argues 'literary change of a generic nature reflects change in the general social-linguistic codes and that these reflect changes in the historico-cultural context'.[6] If the tenets of the post-war experimental novel have been described in the previous partitions as exclusive to their spatio-temporal contexts as, not a (re)genrification of the novel, but a destabilizing of the novel definition and its dominant consensus-making role, then the historico-cultural contexts of these novels begets this destabilization. It inhabits, creates; allows (perhaps) this practice, and as such the socio-linguistic codes of the experimental novel become the medium of communication of the violent socio-cultural milieus of partition two beyond, potentially, the removal of potency found there inherent in the falsities of inadequate storification of *histoir*ically stabilized social reality. Then, while in our context it appears the 'referential noose' cannot be textually slipped, it can perhaps through *gaming* the variables within the generative staging ground of the novel (that is, to clarify gaming, to apply these tenets in modes for which they are not *dominantly* coded to be so), gaming language, momentarily break the reader's *agnosia*; to make them feel this referential noose about their neck, if you will. As Céline writes in *Entretiens avec le professeur Y* (1955): 'the scaffold, so to speak, awaits the artist'.[7] but too the reader; that may perhaps leave a mark. Thus, it may allow a lingering grasp of the broken field of the real beyond the holographic monolithic delimitation of post-war normative reality.

I will first turn then to this linguistic rupture, a contagion base of pluralistic 'unmeaning', or rather 'sur-meaning', or 'infra-meaning' or perhaps 'plu-meaning' (or however we wish to designate it). A gaming with linguistic multivalency played by these writers which perhaps begins a process of fracture that ripples *za – um*. Here I will address the, perhaps revealing, correspondences between the use of language in the experimental novel and that of the 'schizophrenic' asylum inmates of Dubuffet's collection of *écrits bruts*, which, though separated both temporally and by social access synchronize with the writerly methods of these texts, and thus act as uncanny key. I will then follow to address this seepage in the physical environments of the text, the materiality of text: how objects themselves become unreliable; a reverberating dreamscape, that perhaps creates a weird sense of lucid dreaming. In this, I aim to follow the contagion of pluralistic unmeaning (or 'whatever-meaning'), in a space of attempted utter phantasmagoric quantification, to its perhaps transitory, emancipatory (to some extent) potentiality.

Za – Um

To return to a text briefly lit upon in partition two, Topor's *Erika*, within which is found a relatively succinct – and, integrally, frustrated – delineation on the use of written language in the experimental novel. Topor writes:

> By dint of fighting words, I soon came to understand them. It appeared to me that the mob of words, which constitutes a book, exerts on each unit considerable pressure, in order to bend each to the public cause. A word, as soon as it is in a group, is entrapped by multiple laws, diminished by the idea of which it must transmit. It is not entitled to a chapter, even less a contents page.

'Why, I asked myself, don't I isolate every word on its own page, like so many Robinsons on their beach?'

[...] I believe my creature functions. For me, that's most important of all. Is it enough? Should a good novel always be adaptable to cinema? Well, in that case it's not a good novel. Is it literature? How can I defend the few words scattered without forethought on the surface of this white paper?[8]

Here, Topor describes his attempts to break with what Wittgenstein calls 'a *picture* [that] held us captive. And we could not get outside of it [look to horizon above]. For it lay in our language and our language seemed to repeat it to us inexorably.'[9] In his attempt to address this, Topor introduces a novel in which every page houses a single word, other than the first and last page which include a bracketed opening and closing phrase, akin to Johnson's first and last sections in his book in a box of loose sections, *The Unfortunates*. Here this gives a context of the opening and closing of a romance with 'Erika' in the past tense. In the contextualizing brackets of this first and last, as with *The Unfortunates*, *Erika* is perhaps, in the words of Sebastien Jenner in reference to Johnson, an 'aleatoric novel'.[10]

> *Alea* derives from the Latin for die or dice, an etymological link that reinforces the fact that the aleatoric novel's enactment of chance is always controlled and bordered by prescribed boundaries; only one of six surfaces can land face up when the die is cast. Aleatoric art therefore always enacts a conscious engagement with the concept of chance, and often means an 'open work,' or one that invites the audience to become the instigator of the chance procedure, but contained within a discernible composed logic.[11]

This speaks against the ultimate politically revolutionary potentiality of such writing given by Malevich above; that the effect of the inarticulate scream is *articulated*, a creature designed for this *affective* purpose. Topor appears rather to be answering the call of Samuel Beckett from 1937, who wrote in the infamous 'German letter' to Axel Kaun: 'more and more my own language appears to me like a veil that must be torn apart in order to get at the things (or nothingness) behind it [...] to bore one hole after another in it, until what lurks behind it – be it something or nothing – begins to seep through [...] is there any reason why that terrible materiality of the word surface should not be capable of being dissolved?'[12] Synchronizing with Beckett's rather more

Fabian, cultural concern,[13] Topor asserts both the fragility of the single unit, echoing that of the individual figure in community in the previous partition, and the freer potential of the open signifier. In the act of reading, from one page, '*Americano*',[14] to the next '*bas*',[15] the referentiality of these words are imposed largely on the part of the reader. They lack punctuation, a grammatical connection, prepositions, verb-noun meetings on the page; they are all *proposition* thus the blank pages fill with ambiguous connections, and wider extrapolations based within the readerly pause of page-turning (kept not on a train track of referential narrative, but an individuated space of experiential reference – there is an imbalance of power in the writerly-readerly here, that would centralize a readerly role of decoding). In this the blank pages themselves, almost devoid of words, flood with meaning; a man, at a café. He orders a coffee, no, an Americano, that is an espresso with added water. He is calm, or low, or stockings, or hose. The waiter brings the coffee, the narrator (or rather, barely present reporting spectral figure) notices a girl, or rather her stockings, perhaps. *Or*, the narrator enters a café, he sees a girl, Erika, across the room. *She is drinking an Americano and wearing stockings. Or* the narrator is buying stockings in a shop called Americano. *Or* the narrator orders an Americano *cocktail*, which in the context of Paris would be more likely, though this context is not apparent, and the waiter who delivers it is wearing stockings. Perhaps on his head, in preparation from a robbery. *Or* is it simply a love letter to a broken-down beloved 'Erika' brand typewriter? *Or* . . .

It would appear that Topor quite successfully pushes against the reduction of meaning that Ferdinand de Saussure refers to as the 'tyranny of letters',[16] that perhaps goes some way to throwing off the written 'disguise', behind which 'there remains nothing but the image of language'.[17] He creates a literary mechanism that gives credence to Wittgenstein's statement 'language is a labyrinth of paths',[18] that though readers approach the same object, it is constelled by the myriad of footings that lead there. This does not speak of a non-linear narrative, as addressed in partition two in reference to parallel and back and forth reading. As each reading, just as those two modes, here represents, in an instance of reading, a single *pathway* to the ends of the book. It is that this narrative motion is confused, a tumbling that to some extent breaks with predictability of textual movement and Genette's 'logical paradox' of generation of meaning.

Ergodic engagement

As Georges Charbonnier states in discussion with Queneau, 'language is temporal, it is linear. It goes from one side to the other; words go one after the other, even more so in writing rather than speech,' but 'one can put together different pathways, and for the most part propositions can potentially be preserved, reversed or modified.'[19] This potential plurality, just as Robinson Crusoe had to return – that is as Defoe pretended Crusoe was a real person – to *become* Crusoe, so these words connect in the aleatoric space of this beach due to the gaze across the black objects stuck in the white sand by a readerly eye – a readerly connectivity of these floating signs. As Topor concludes his introduction 'might the slightest critical wind blow them away? Or perhaps they might take root, and flower in the imagination of the readers?'[20] This does not take this study to the seeming utter capitulation of Aram Saroyan's untitled packaged ream of typewriter paper (1968),[21] or Isidore Isou's *Œuvre infinitésimale ou esthapéïriste* (1956), but acts as an attempted answer to Topor's years of seeing no potential but the blotting out of words as seen in his novel *Souvenir*. With *Erika* Topor lays a challenge at the reader's feet, he attempts to force them to textually interact, to break with their passivity, a gauntlet thrown down he signs off in the Diogenean spirit of Johnson's 'never mind': 'whatever ... it's all the same ...'[22] Topor here forms a moment of embrace or aversion in the creation of what Espen Aarseth refers to as an *ergodic* literature (which has itself become a bizarre literary genre, perhaps a repackaging of the apparently very unsalable descriptive 'a challenging text'):

> the user will have effectuated a semiotic sequence, and this selective movement is a work of physical construction that the various concepts of 'reading' do not account for. This phenomenon I call ergodic, using a term appropriated from physics that derives from the Greek words ergon and hodus, meaning 'work' and 'path.' In ergodic literature, nontrivial effort is required to allow the reader to traverse the text. If ergodic literature is to make sense as a concept, there must also be nonergodic literature, where the effort to traverse the text is trivial, with no extranoematic responsibilities placed on the reader except (for example) eye movement and periodic or arbitrary turning of pages.[23]

Though Aarseth might like to make such a black and white distinction, I would argue that a novel, by its experimental romantics as I have taken to calling its intra and extra world mechanisms, passes to a greater or lesser extent in and out of a number of *scales* of ergodic states. There is no monopoly here on the 'challenging text' (challenges of which are potentially so diverse, and so reliant on reader-context for whether a certain mode would be 'trivial' or not, a binary opposition cannot be defended on the ground of an objectively deigned triviality/nontriviality). But, to apply this ergodic concept as a more *open* textual potentiality, in Johnson's book box of loose sections *The Unfortunates* he utilises spaces in sentences, missing words to too, as Topor, create a kind of build your own adventure book in this ergodic sense.[24]

In the assigned first section Johnson writes 'how did I not realise when he said, Go and do City this week, that it was this city?   Tony.   [...].'[25] These silences around Tony mean: Johnson has asked a question and received no response, he nudges Tony to respond and the silence pertains. Then he has lost his friend; Tony who he would usually find clarity with is dead. Or, standing alone in the centre of the page, that Tony is the topic of this discussion. Or, a rupture in thought that has just dredged, caused by his travel to 'do City', from the depths of memory the realization that he once had a friend called Tony; who is dead – a shard of memory stabbed in from the margins upon the amnesiac orderly *tabula rasa* of the page, of the silenced internal human space. To look again to Wittgenstein, detaching words, or strings of letters from a sentence 'introduces a new unit of linguistic spacing which takes precedent over that of the word'.[26] It would appear then, to quote John Cage, in these texts 'there is no such thing as silence'.[27] These spaces are again, as seen in *Erika*, an extra-textual entity used to elicit a scale of ergodic investment. To look again to Cage, 'there is no such thing as an empty space or an empty time. There is always something to hear, something to see. In fact, try as we might to make a silence, we cannot.'[28] They are harnessed as a communicating zero to signify, akin to one of Céline's uses of ellipsis in his post-war novels, a break in narrative trajectory. As Johnson writes 'yes how the mind arranges itself, tries to sort things into orders, is perturbed if things are not sorted, are not in the right order, nags away   Southwell   [...].'[29] Here he both decries the reductions necessary for ordered thought, then gratuitously throws the reader through space to a change in narrative signified by 'Southwell', another space and then the new trajectory begins. In these instances, Johnson pushes the reader from the stable footing he offered them in allowing them to shuffle the story as they like (other than the aleatoric bracketing sections first and last); he removes the assured reader's calm within *their* created singularity of text within the aleatoric safety of that book gamed.

Elsewhere, Johnson uses this as a pause to correct his memories made inaccessible by the long drawn out trauma of Tony's death: 'I cannot think that either Tony or I went prepared to play garden cricket on this occasion. Tony did come to lunch, yes that was I think sure.'[30] While Coe writes that it is the remembering of Tony that was 'interrupted at random by the action on the pitch and his attempts to start writing a match report,'[31] these spaces appear more pauses in quotidian living. They prevent him from writing to word count for his report, from properly watching the game, from his pint, from his walking in the street, as if in grief at the most ordinary things his body calcifies and drags him with it to a trawl of the internal space, a process that brings him to the brink of pain. Then the engine kicks back in again, pulls him back to perpetual motion. This appears evermore apparent in a further use of these spaces within the text:

> The pitch worn, the worn patches like   There might be an image there, I could use an image there, if I can think of one.[32]

This example appears to show, against Coe's statement, the way this insistent remembering has shaken Johnson's thoughts to misstep, to misremembering, and as such makes difficult his attempts to formulate his match report; that is here he is writing about the difficulty of scripting an event at all. But this impossibility of writing spreads.

> It begins to rain, the rain thin like   Images for rain are common, I cannot think of one, I do not need to think of one, really, for what purpose?[33]

Here it is not the match report that has lost meaning, but the writing of *The Unfortunates* itself, the contagion has spread through the layers of writing from reported experience, to the experience itself, and shaken loose its attempts at orderly formulation.

Guignery notes this constant attempt and failure to hold on to memory, and too a thread of the book itself, also in interjecting phrases: 'note the recurrence of expressions such as "if I remember", "I do not remember", and hypothetical phrases like "it must have been" or "perhaps it was".'[34] As with the constant whirl of return created by the shuffling of the loose sections that re-regiment the piece reader by reader Johnson creates an 'audacious mimetic solution' to this issue of ambiguous repetition and loss of thread, according to Guignery.[35] A mimesis that causes, as discussed in partition two, a constant tripping return at the doorstep of traumatic memory. But this is not what Kermode criticises as a disengaged 'mimesis of pure contingency'.[36] As seen, it is locked in referentiality, but it does indicate multiplicity; the *incompleteness* of fictive world. In its ergodic reliance on the reader, it too perhaps spreads this contagion of floating meaning in its obsessive return to an internal absence, the *tabula rasa*, the blanked-out space as established in partition two as present within the social subject. A contagion Saussure appears to agree with: 'in English *the man [ ] I have seen* ("*l'homme que j'ai vu*") demonstrates a syntactic element that seems to be represented by zero. Which in French we would fill with *that*. But it is precisely the comparison with French syntax that produces this illusion that nothingness can express something; in reality, material units, aligned in a certain order, generate this value themselves. [...] a meaning and a function exist only through the support of some material form [...] it is because we are inclined to see immaterial abstractions hovering above the units in the sentence.'[37] These ergodic spaces are indeed aleatory, akin to *Erika*, their meanings are not hovering immaterial abstractions, but form the space in which the reader throws the dice. As in Perec's *La Disparition* (1968) in which the communicating zero of both language and character are hidden in lipogrammatic elision, A. Voyl is missing.[38] The partial structures are there, and by which their incomplete liminality indicates absences the reader must act to fill: *unE voyEllE*. Thus, there appears evident a contagious praxis of detachment and colocation present within these texts that pushes for a referential plural textual interaction; a motivation caused perhaps by the suspicious synchronized feeling something is indeed missing, obscured, has been made inaccessible.

Spatial multiplicity

A further use of communicating absence in *The Unfortunates* is evident in Johnson's recitation of a match report over the phone to the copy desk:

> The remaining eight minutes   were played out to the continuing
> sound   of the City supporters s apostrophe delight at the goal

comma   and perhaps at the discomfiture of Mull   and
the pain that Edsons apostrophe s   last effort had apparently cost
him full point   For they are that kind if crowd comma   and
this was indeed their kind of match full point.³⁹

This telegrammatic speech is a rendering of written language in spoken language in written language which posits a weird flipping of Saussurean language masks that works to emphasize the inadequacy of the constraints of written language as a mode of communication; in a parody of exactness the copy desk can't quite get exact. Prefiguring text-speak, Billany too uses the flippant reductions of telegrammatic speech to introduce the utter devastation of his family after their house was bombed back in Hull:

****

TELEGRAM
LIEUT MICHAEL CARRTHE ---- SHIRES PWLLHELI NORTH WALES
BOMBED OUT MOTHER AND DAD IN HOSPITAL DAVID DEAD
COME QUICKLY ELIZABETH

****40

From the horror of the Blitz to the boredom of a bus journey, this mode is also appropriated in one of Queneau's quotidian permutations in *Exercices de style* (1947):

Telegraphic
BUS PACKED STOP YNGMAN LONG NECK HAT BRAIDED BAND
SHOUTING UNKNOWN PASSENGER WITHOUT CLEAR REASON
STOP PERHAPS TOES HEEL TROD SUPPOSED PURPOSEFUL
STOP...⁴¹

Further, these generative reductions align with Jean-François Bory's parodic hypertrophy of what Saussure calls 'literary language' in *Post-scriptum* (1970):

> And after the subject the verb followed by a qualifying adjective in accordance with the gender and number of the subject. The same subject, an adverbial pronoun, an auxiliary verb, an article, a substantive, a complementary attribute, an indefinite pronoun and a verb in the infinitive. An adverbial preposition, a prefix, a verb in the third person future of the singular indicative, a comparative adjective, a subordinate conjunctive proposition with a spatial adverb and a determining substantive.⁴²

Here the written structure, the disguise as Saussure calls it, by which meaning is both locked and conferred is perfectly rendered and yet the meaning which it obscures has been utterly overrun by order. And yet, to actually address the text, in an extreme ergodic form; *someone is something*, etc. A narrative here can be followed and thus the very exactness of ordered written language, that Johnson scoffs at with his report of the football match, the inadequacy of the announcement of an annihilated family in Billany, that Queneau opens up in reduction, has been usurped, employed to generate multivalent vagueness. An example to give to Wittgenstein's assertion 'where there is sense there must be perfect order – so there must be perfect order even in the vaguest sentence'.[43]

Open signifiers

Approaching this same point from a different pathway, we may look to Themerson's *Bayamus*, in which 'the author replaces certain words with their dictionary definitions'.[44] A process which again corresponds with the experiments of Queneau, who adopted the mode from Themerson as 'definitional literature' and applied it in *Oulipo : la littérature potentielle* (1973) as noted in partition one.[45]

> The cat HAS DRUNK the milk.
> The domesticated digitigrade carnivorous mammal HAS AVAILED ITSELF of a white liquid with a sweet taste, produced by female mammals.[46]

Queneau here demonstrates an opening in meaning by direct comparison of script, however to look to his inspiration in Themerson without this key to meaning:

> There were four openings: three of them serving as entrances with wooden structures moving on hinges for closing them, and one, not very large, filled with panes of glass fixed in a movable frame.[47]

Raphael Rubinstein helpfully explains, 'in other words, the room had three doors and one window'.[48] Like Johnson's copy desk, the reader first receives language through the inadequate medium of writing, akin to receiving written language over the phone, and then must decipher some logic of sense there. The reader is forced not to skate across the text, but to go back across it, not to decipher it as hieroglyphs, as these are perfectly familiar signifiers, indeed they have been appropriated from a dictionary, but decrypt a vague sense of intra-text referential linear meaning. The other pathways here are not bricked off, but hang about the sentences not as immaterial abstractions, but alternative cognitions. There are wider images not offered by Rubinstein's explanation, that are summoned by connection to the reader's experiential reference. This indicates the potentialities of the polysemic aspects of words and plurality of communicated object. To look again to Billany, and his narrator's efforts at learning Italian:

> The dictionary gives the following:
>
> > Domani = tomorrow
> >
> > Dopo = after
>
> These may be combined in the phrase 'dopo domani', which is said to mean 'the day after tomorrow'. The word 'oggi', according to the dictionaries, means 'today'. As a result of our residence in Italy – during which we have made frequent use of these words in inquiries as to *when* certain amenities would be granted, *when* there would be cakes or peaches in the canteen, *when* the new compound would be ready, we are able to correct the dictionaries as follows:
>
> > Oggi = tomorrow
> >
> > Domani = next week
> >
> > Dopo domani = never[49]

Here the readjustment of language, the attack on the straitjacket, on a quotidian basis presents a pluralizing of meaning, a frenetic liminal space akin to Queneau's opener for *Zazie dans le métro* 'wezzatstinkcumfrum ["*doukipudonktan*"]',[50] which is at first a nonsense word, and yet verbally renders something like 'where is that stink coming from? ["*d'où qu'il pue donc tant?*"]' with some probing (which, in both French and English, has been rendered in varied transcriptions, altering meaning). As Albert Doppagne writes: '*doukipudonktan*' for Queneau is 'a manifestation of the phatic function in language: he shakes his reader by periodically presenting them with a kind of rebus, that is more or less straightforward or more or less obscure'.[51] With '*doukipudonktan*' Queneau unleashes this destabilizing of the flowing act of reading '*ex abrupto*',[52] in a challenge to the socially held concepts of a genred novel the reader brings to *Zazie dans le métro*.

This bears parallel with the breakdown of sense, meaning and nature of language for the protagonists described as incarcerated fugitives in partition two, just as the prisoners in Billany's *The Cage* after years away in North Africa and Italy. In a moment of fervour in anticipation of finally moving to a new camp the mass mocking chant of 'the feelthy breeteesh!' breaks down into 'oriental' chants that hold within them the experience of war:[53]

'Yah! Wah! Yah! Wah! Yah!'
'Yahwahyahwahyah!'
'Backsheesh Backsheesh Allala!'
'Eggs-a-bread. Shoeshine?'
'Backsheesh. *Feelthy* postcards.'
'Yah! Wah! Yah!'[54]

Language here communicates a mixture of bastardized Arabic, bastardized Italian and bastardized English set in the mimicking of the calls to prayer heard while stationed in North Africa. This breakdown of meaning carries within it years of collective experience of extraction from British quotidian social norms and linguistic identity. If, according to Derrida, *Communication* is enacted when 'it gives passage to, transports, transmits something, gives access to something', this 'field of equivocacy within the word "communication" is massively reduced by the limits of what we call context'.[55] Here the context is the novel, or the state of an element of its experimental romantics, it is the prisoner of war, living in Britain, fighting in North Africa, imprisoned in Italy. And yet this is not a concretely singular, objectively communicated experience. The writer has both built and broken down the novel as a 'transmitting tunnel', creating a productive and active ambiguity in communication by which a meaning-object may be transmitted, but it is mimetically incoherent, broken; confused. What is reduced here by historical context from its linguistic fractals like white light through a prism, through native and historical opacity, a pluralistic schema of reading is achieved. There is then the possibility for a schema of open involvement beyond reductive interpretation, that maintains a primacy of textual meanings whilst including the plurality of conveyed meaning invested by reader; whatever those meanings might be.

This perhaps infers a 'darkening' of the sample in the name of enlightenment of perception and extrapolative recall. For example, for Topor's burglar waiter in *Erika*, it is assuredly Themerson's three boarded up exterior windows that would indeed act as entrances, rather than the interior door with inset panes of glass. Here, despite Rick Altman's insistence that we must critically perform 'resistant reading',[56] I may perhaps be accused of purposeful 'aberrant decoding'.[57] And yet I would counter that as rather attempting to inhabit the open referentiality of these connecting signs; for the purposes of these texts there appears little such thing as 'misreading'. The traits of these texts speak of a disintegration of inadequate orderliness which harbours a sense of falseness, and generation of a mimetic vagueness for a disavowed vague world. This formal suspending of the veil then appears an attempt to authentically communicate with the reader in a dismemberment of the falsities of a singular truth frozen by a singular reality as vampirically reduced by a false singular communication locked by a dominant novel 'disguised'. And yet, it is an *attempt*.[58]

3.2 Babel, babble, xenoglossia and private language

                Galluog

Lwcus

                  ynad[59]

As seen in the apparently nonsensical quote given by Rosetta Stanton here, the communicating absences present in Johnson's *The Unfortunates* are not confined to that text. In *House Mother Normal* 'three pages of George's monologue are blank white rectangles; as in *Travelling People*, printed words give way to visual representations of states that seem to be beyond language'.[60] In the previous partition I referred to Stanton, who narrates an odd jumble of nonsense letters strewn across pages, surfacing through the sand of the page before being again covered as by a shifting dune, as a kind of Rosetta Stone in this archaeological sense, in that her babbling nonsense words are anything but. To refer again to Nicholas Tredell, 'Rosetta has become a stone occasionally inscribed with strange fragments', which though appear to the reader as utterly non-signifying are in fact 'isolated Welsh words'.[61] In the example given above, *galluog*: able; clever; gifted, *lwcus*: lucky, *ynad*: magistrate; justice. What appears to be utterly decodified rambling is revealed to be the floating signifiers of an internal prefiguring and parallel to Anglo-Saxon culture, a marginalized, internal minor language; hidden layers opened more or less by a dictionary or

Google Translate. Here, Stanton attempts, and fails, to communicate in the language of her childhood, which her 'sense' has degraded to.

This offers a primal challenge to communication, against both the anachronisms of national language as unnatural, unstable, in an age of xenoglossia in the 'brief American century', and the building of language as a constricting cage within it, that creates the sense of the reader discovering bizarre 'fragments of some lost epic',[62] to approach as a primordial cultural echo. This invokes a primacy of language that straddles both the marginal implications of both these words as an actual language, and the attempted decryptions of a reader who, by and large, would have no idea that it is such. To read this without access to Welsh creates a sense of what Wittgenstein refers to as the human reading, 'perhaps drugged', which creates the feel of recitation of incantations rather than reading of orders of language:

> Suppose he has in this way read (or interpreted) a set of five marks as A B O V E – and now we shew him the same marks in the reverse order and he reads E V O B A; and in further tests he always retains the same interpretation of the marks: here we should certainly be inclined to say that he was making up an alphabet for himself *ad hoc* and then reading accordingly.[63]

Again, we are presented with an *affective* slippage in reality; just as Billany's soldiers generate a nonsense chant instilled with experiential meaning. Language here is not adrift in *no sense*, but fully locked in tumbling reference in which a coda of comprehension is generated 'ad hoc', what is created is a divergent codification of linguistic communication. Welsh becomes the babbled snippets of some ancient epic, Queneau's Zazie elides language to an invoking of the country girl, a football ground style chant is a call to prayer; the reader is struck by the generative potential of 'speaking in tongues' in which there is generated the sense of a beyond societies' fossilized 'fixed system'.[64]

Glossolalia

Michel de Certeau designates this linguistic interaction as 'glossolalia'.[65]

> 'Glossolalia' means 'to babble,' see stutter, stammer (*lalein*) in language, 'to speak in tongues' (*glôssa*).[66]

Allen S. Weiss refers to this as 'the enunciation of the pure signifier, the refusal of meaning, and the reduction of speech to the pure voice, of language to the body'.[67] An *attempt*, however, as Certeau relates the strange episode of Saussure transcribing the 'Sanskritoid' of a medium, Mlle Hélène Smith, after it was decided her 'tongues' warranted decoding. And after much study, Saussure found

> 1. The speech 'resembles' Sanskrit, it 'recalls' the words and bears 'fragments' that have some meaning; 2. The rest of it is unintelligible, but does not have an 'anti-Sanskrit character,' that is, it does not present 'groups materially contrary or in opposition to the words of Sanskrit' [...] there is a syntactic 'thread' of French words that, for these semantic units, the medium has looked for other sounds to 'substitute to give it an exotic aspect' of heteroclite origin (English, German, etc.). The speech as a whole obeys an essential rule: 'it must above all and only function, to not appear to be French.'[68]

That Mlle Smith's attempts at invoking the exotic are tied to an inescapable linguistic base, for her French, shows the entrapping referentiality of 'nonsense' that it is not nonsense at all, but a meaningful push of ambiguity against that which is asphyxiated in reductive order, echoes the concerns of Beckett raised above. As Certeau continues: 'ordinarily, in a society, its institutions found, guarantee, maintain the space of speech. [...] it organises the chessboard of positions that both authorises and limits verbal circulation, division and control [...] the foundation of speech is found therefore treated as a mode of spatial distribution.'[69] Language and the tenets of its use are an ordering base of Bourdieu's violent symbolic monolith discussed in earlier partitions, it usurps communication and cohesion with division and reduction akin to the no-variance of what Saussure calls a 'literary language'.

This is what Certeau calls, harking back to the minoring of the experimental novel in partition one, 'the major voice', where 'the fragility of language is disappeared. Occasional mispronunciations are effaced, as too hesitations and audible tics, slips of the tongue or derivational sounds coincides with the distancing found in the transformation of the interlocutor into a public.'[70] As Gilles Deleuze writes in *Logique du sens* (1969) such reduction of language, such 'proper' 'sense is therefore: the affirmation of a singular direction; [...] the orientation of time's arrow, of the past to the future, and following this determination; the directional role of the present in this orientation; this future projection therefore makes possible; a kind of sedentary order.'[71] It is then this ultimate base of reductive process that the experimental novel's treatment of language, as demonstrated here, attempts to destabilize; it attempts to reimpose fragility of meaning, the potential of not a breakdown in communication, but a failure of agreed objectivity; of that fixed in sedentary order. It attempts to reassert the 'rupture of language' from within its horizon, as Dubuffet argues, 'because the accent, the intonation, is the vehicle of meaning itself. Are more significant perhaps than what is said. And the movement of thought is more important than its content, and the movement of speaking more important than its content.'[72] Where this formal treatment is raised paramount to the function of the post-war experimental novel project.

Écrits bruts and the experimental novel

To align this discussion with a revealing synchronicity, Dubuffet's 1945 onward collection of *écrits bruts*. A critical pivot whereby a social process of this disintegratory and dismembered treatment of language might be better edified. Michel Thévoz describes the collection thus:

> One might say that it consciously engages the network of social communication in the most alien ways. This is mainly due to these authors' distaste for vocabulary and syntactic and orthographic rules, and their inclination to change the language system to fit the ways they think. Yet they bear no notion of reformation (as in the case of professional writers who dream of seeing their neologisms or their coined phrases consecrated by popular usage): they seem to insist on the contrary on the character of transgression and aberration of their linguistic singularities and put all their energy into disrupting communication.[73]

Écrits bruts then demonstrates corresponding concerns with the post-war experimental novel, and yet they are not 'professionally written' texts, and though as a developed concept and use application they are, their generation itself cannot be ascribed post-war; they have no assigned place in the field of literature. The term refers primarily to the collection of works spanning 200 years collected by Dubuffet, akin to their better-known visual counterpart, *art brut*. They are an array of texts that look a lot like letters, poems, novels, encyclopaedias, epics, scraps of aphorisms that Dubuffet procured from the archives of psychiatric hospitals across France, Belgium and Switzerland. They are not the product of creative psychiatric treatment, but fragmented outpourings beyond, according to Dubuffet, the aping traits of literature,[74] of subjects with varied assigned mental pathologies. Removed from the socio-cultural field to the confines of a cell, 'their authors are, socially and mentally, marginalised',[75] 'in short, their production does not pay heed to the institution of literature'.[76]

These figures generated vast tracts of writing on napkins, cheque books, toilet paper: diaries of fictional families, living war heroes recounting 200 years of battle experience, letters from fictional, and fictionalized real, ambassadors to fictional, and fictionalized real, heads of state, fantastical accounts of the grand palaces of France rendered in copia to the most minute detail. The realities of which their writers are utterly convinced; a 200-year long life, a love affair with Kaiser Wilhelm *is* their reality. This is a familiar usurping of reality as concretized norm. The texts are designated in English by the term 'outsider' – the implication is that utterly removed from the socio-cultural field, the intense break down of writerly convention inherent in the texts is the product of total social extraction; the deluded ravings of the insane never intended to be read by other than a prescriptive doctor, let alone published. What is found here is a binary opposition of on the one hand, the experimental novel as a symbolic social artefact at the razor's edge of the liminal slippage of the rational real, and an utterly socially excluded irrational *écrits bruts* essentially fished from a bin, a writing assured in its solipsistic isolation. And yet they vibrate within similar frequencies that cannot be reconciled by cultural status of artefact. Just as the experimental writer fights a resistant uphill insurgency not against social reality, but literary and cultural strata as discussed in partition one in reference to Johnson, Heppenstall, Butor and Robbe-Grillet, the *écrits bruts* writer simply is not allowed to that space of contention. The correspondence in this is if 'the depths of mental illness reveal the extreme possibilities of the human condition: horrendous psychic pain, radical isolation, total depersonalisation, fragmented perceptions, distorted concepts, obsessive activities, theological catastrophes, and mystical bliss of the highest order',[77] what does it mean when these elements bleed into the socio-cultural field from this utterly marginalized extraction? Where the asylum cell becomes synecdoche of social life, it appears, as Octave Mannoni writes 'the asylums materially and actually isolate what cannot [in society] be denied'.⁷⁸

Qonestsans

To place here a demonstrative comparison, the *écrits bruts* figure Annette's *La Feuilleton de la Qonestsans*, and in the title may be noticed the beginnings of this textual correspondence – Qonestsans ('*Connaissance*': 'Nolij', 'Knowledge')? Abused as a child, then separated from her abuser by the First World War, Annette saw his face in men in the street incessantly. Between the wars she was shuttled between asylums in Belgium and Northern France, harbouring an intense fear he would return to kill her, she was preoccupied with the fear of poison in her food. Her speech is described by doctors as 'electric', jumping between French and a Flemish inflection. Writing down her experiences in 1942, this electricity is too orthographically rendered. Below first the original, followed by Anne Beyer's effort of transcription, and then a rough rendering of that transcription in English:

> je qou je fezest ici a la dat du katre le kalendriee l'entre tiin la nestsans de ma volonté je swi libre Ann ette le trestfle s'est t'en vole le lo de la fé notre bon l'est pour festr du feu évapo rasion vint sis trent sis piestr trent rente poul estqsestlent je t'enten au pluma je magnifiq la chestr les e pour te mang sen songé j'atan de minme qe twa⁷⁹

> *je couds je fais ici à la date du quatre le calendrier l'entretien la naissance de ma volonté je suis libre Annette le trèfle s'est envolé le lot de la fée notre bon lait pour faire du feu évaporation vingt-six trente-six pierres trente rente poule excellente je t'entends au plumage magnifique la chair les ai pour te manger sans songer j'attends de même que toi*⁸⁰

> I sew I do here on the fourth date of the schedule the upkeep the birth of my will I am free Annette the clover that flew the fate of the fairy our good milk to make fire evaporation twenty-six thirty-six stones thirty salary excellent chicken I get you with your beautiful plumage the flesh they have to eat you without thinking I await the same fate as you

This sense of the text demanding an immediate decoding recalls that above in Queneau and Themerson, but what is immediately brought to mind looking across the symbols is correspondence with Perec's *Les Revenentes* (1972).⁸¹ The lipogrammatic conceptual sequel to *La Disparition* in which shifting from the novel that searches for what is missing, the letter 'e', the sequel has lost 'a', 'i', 'o' and 'u', using only one vowel, the rediscovered 'e'. At the beginning of Perec's text some uniform rules are explained, for example 'Qu' is rendered 'Q',[82] just as, appearing before Annette's *Qonestsans*, Thévoz explains similar apparent rules. For example, the sound 'ou' will be represented by 'W'.[83] This raises a pertinent question, are these the 'utterly meaningless' babblings of Mlle Smith, that too inherently betray an orthologically-grounded system, or short circuiting inflections of a rupturing literature; or in this post-war space of reflexive societal madness, have these elements indeed as questioned above, been brought to shared ground? An unreconciled traumatic event for Annette, that is on-going, has shaken her writing to homophonic rendering, has thrust communication into a falsity that must be usurped. Is this not a process that has been described in the preceding two partitions as a driving engine of the post-war experimental novel, which for the refusal it underwent, is still 'literature'; is published? As Weiss similarly asks, 'are not these "disorders" indeed characteristic of certain stylistic features of modern poetry?'[84] Where, in the face of violence, the bonded limits of the novel genre slipped, became fluid, became itself, as has been described in this study, to some extent, too a poetry, a music; an artistic plasticity.

Annette's themes too appear familiar, in the quote above she cycles through images of the strict quotidian rigours of the routine of her incarceration, to a freedom of thought and expression alien to the environment, to the thirty-six, perhaps stones, of a sense of depression – a seeming link to the French idea of being 'thirty-six under' linked to salaried cannibalistic figures around her, a distinction between orderlies and inmates, to whom both her and her magnificent chicken reader await the same cannibalization despite, or perhaps because of, their beauty which though hidden is coveted. Akin to Trelkovsky in Topor's *Le Locataire chimérique* amongst the other harried figures of the previous partition, they are menaced not by some Kafkaesque internal crisis, but because of it, via the imposition upon them of singularity by a cannibalistic crowd of people in which they are immersed. In common, these figures appear incarcerated, and like the chicken, are on that evening's menu. When both the individuated protagonist, just as Annette in life is deemed reprehensibly mad, ripe for 'curing', it must be asked how much of this is the effect of irreconcilable trauma, 'and how much to what would be a normal reaction to the severe conditions of [...] incarceration.'[85] What a traumatic event has seeded, imprisonment perhaps warps in magnification.

The manner in which Annette writes speaks of a resistance to the strict linguistic orders around her that brings to mind the 'Foucauldian' pathological definitions, brought up by Connolly in partition two in relation to Johnson's *House Mother Normal*, or capitalized jargon of Carrington's *The Hearing Trumpet*. The subjugation without trial or charge empowered by the alien and formulaic language of doctors defining existence by listing illness, of strict schedules that order sleep, meals, leisure. Through these limits Annette is remoulded, reformed; again like Trelkovsky whose process of dehumanization is begun with his manipulation into replacing his routine morning espresso and Gitane with hot chocolate and Gaulloise. And again, in the rejection of grammatical structures also witnessed in these writers, who use disintegration of the tenets of written language to break its ordered distancing, and approach some sense, or façade, of unburdened communication, of immediacy. This formation of Annette's writing appears exclusively generative of a function, she diagnoses her situation in her own recodified language, 'the schedule the upkeep the birth of my will', the utter rejection of the four walls of the cell around her, the eventual concession that the flight of fancy will always end consumed in reduced objectification, incarceration. It is an edification of the imposition of strict exterior social structures upon an internal space beyond the frantic desperation described in partition two. It is not a confused unknowing mad dash, but a self-conscious attempt to evade, or attack, the colonization, the terraforming of the willed internal self; to, against the quantifying language of her doctors, and reductions of her carceral surroundings, keep the Gitanes. This describes a footing for that set out above; the communicating object drops from primary intent, and the rupture itself, the communicating break, becomes essential as communicating zero. As Danièle André-Carraz writes of the engine within Antonin Artaud's post-war writing: language itself becomes 'a medium of insanity, rupture, the labyrinth of unreason [...] because there is no panacea, no logic, no signification. There is only rupture.'[86] André-Carraz here evokes the Billany-like primordial chants of *Artaud, le Mômo* (1947):

ge re ghi
reg heghi
g ehena
e reghena
a gegha
riri[87]

Artaud however takes these plu-meaning signs further than Billany, he here chimes with the weird inflections of H.P. Lovecraft's Cthulhu that recall a primordial, pre-established-meaning system of communication that beckons the apocalypse: 'Ph'nglui mglw'nafh Cthulhu R'lyeh wgah'nagl fhtagn!' As André-Carraz writes this is a language of 'glossolalia, echolalia ....'[88] It presents, as too perhaps Artaud straddled his own shifting moments of sanity and insanity, the terrifying proximity of concrete realities and truths beyond-within our accepted holographic singular own, recalling discussion of the electroshock jerks of writerly response to social *thanatophilia* in the previous partition. In *Momo*, Artaud perhaps scripts the horror of passing through the Beckettean delimited veil of reality, as he handwrote in the margins of the galley: 'I am sorry to have met the dead under electroshock therapy that I hadn't wanted to see.'[89] Through the holes in the monolithic veil of normed reality Artaud has perhaps viewed the field in which that virtuality unhinges, and falls apart. Thus, when Weiss asks 'does this unique language evince a certain insufficiency, or rather a hyperreal grasp of the tortured depths of the psyche and the terrifying expanses of the cosmos?'[90] We might answer, both, as the structures of language, as too its cultural superstructure, *is* inadequate, a toxic reduction of experience that leaves space only for this ambiguous signalling of inadequacy as communicative of social Sorge.

What seems apparent in these texts is the inadequacy of novelistic processes, existing within the constructs of wider social reality, the generative aspect is never *constructed*, but forever half made. Just as disintegratory technique can never achieve the impassive state of void, but is left with the fragmented remains of its disintegration. Both processes are locked within the reductive and creative paradox of post-war experience, a book-world complete, a world-meaning complete. And yet the scream caused by this frustration trawls a space of this forever rupturing incompleteness that is here clearly prescient in this socio-historical moment. As Weiss writes, 'here, the sublime unites with the banal, the catastrophic with the monumental, the imaginary with the nonsensical [...] which all create a disturbing aesthetic interference with our standard modes of everyday expression'.[91] Just as the plotted conceits of the experimental novel spiral *trompe-l'oeil* from quotidian living, to confusion, to a book closed.

Language as structural reality referent

This moment of realized confusion, perhaps conveyed in this Adorno-Jabès-Topor-Artaud scream, this decentring of communicated meaning as approached in textual space and object above, approaches the space of the real that crumbles at the foot of delimitation, and is thus realigned. The delimited real falls from veil to hyperfield shifting sea, not oscillating but tumbling; tidal. The individual in the field of the real as such itself appears as a *cypher* immersed, but in tumbling referential connectivity, not a 2D referential stasis. This is described in J.M.G. Le Clézio's 1970 novel *La Guerre* as the reader plunges with M. X:

> In a sea full of signs
> Full of letters
> Lost in the middle of constellations of signs.
> Where can I go?
> Where can I go?
> Up? But there are signs there.
> Left? But there are signs there.
> Forward? But there are signs there.
> Leave, and finally forget, but dreams are signs too.[92]

This is the real field of relation between forgetting and realization described in partition two that gives a mimetic aspect to the communicative potentials of the experimental novel described in this study, where the experimental novel here not only indicates the obscured horrors of reality, but further, potentially indicates the realization of the damaging, reductive, supposedly protective, communal limits and thus potentially expands perception to the inundation of realities in which the subject-individual is awash; to doubt, to self-doubt. As Topor similarly writes:

> If I put a hand in place of a head, some people will say 'That's horrible, how disgusting!' But such a reaction is pathological. By putting the liver where the brain is, and the brain in place of the feet, I don't feel like I'm trampling on values or contributing to the collapse of society. I seek to enlarge the field of play and speculation a little, by disrupting things that appear too stable, or immutable. Personally, I don't believe in this stability. We tend all too easily to fix things in permanence.[93]

The language base of writing here has chipped away the artifice of regimented text on the page, and too signs in structure, which has the effect of creating, according to David Toop, 'a soporific dissociative [of the written word] state of mind that can lead to psychosomatic changes'.[94] And this does not posit a contagious schizophrenia, but, akin to Gustav Metzger's *nouveau réalisme* derived principles of 'auto-destructive art', 'an attempt to deal rationally with a society that appears to be lunatic'.[95]

To draw back from the pretence of the brink of utter dissolution of communicable immediate meaning, from the 'literature' of Artaud's *Momo* writings (published by Gallimard) to Annette's archived explosions of 'madness'.[96] Both texts, against Weiss, *are* intrinsically referential. Just as Artaud's 'screams that come from the delicateness of the marrow' are 'intellectual screams'.[97] Like Mlle Smith, as he attempts to throw himself through the holes bored in the veil, his foot becomes lodged. With knowledge of the intrinsic failure of this leap, in Annette, in Billany, in Queneau, as Toop writes 'when common language is manipulated like this so as to elevate it onto the plane of the uncommon, it becomes processable to decompose and reintegrate the world',[98] and it is there perhaps a communicable shift, rather than averted electric shock, may lie. Toop here argues that, like Certeau's glossolalia, on the primordial level of language these forms have the potential to pull apart and reform the socio-culturally defined, reduced, world and uncover something further. While Toop perhaps overstates this effect within the reader, as Beckett wrote in a letter to Mary Manning Howe two days after the Kaun letter: 'I am starting a logoclasts' league [...] I am the only member at present. The idea is ruptured writing, so that the void may protrude like a hernia.'[99] It would appear in the post-war that this league has come into its own, as the horizon cannot be breached, its chaos is invited to morph into the plastic limits of normalized reality.

There is then indeed, from the language base of communication, to the textual field of the novel-object and its tenets, the potential to push against the raised spectre of the socio-cultural colonization of thought, expression and communication to a state of language one adheres to. What is a nullifying of the internal space by a terraforming dominant language, dominant culture, *histoire*, social reality, a domineering communal milieu; the strong arm of dominant entities within the socius that bring the asphyxiating walls of violent normalcy together. As Félix Guatarri presented in *Notes on Power and Meaning* at the Schizoculture conference in 1975,

> the phonological, syntactic, and semantic components of language. The primacy of the formations of power over the unconscious [...] [is] semiotic subjugation on all levels: – body – socius – gestures – mimicry – speech – attitudes – glances – dance – tears – organs – a license to drive – a license to fuck – watch what you're saying.[100]

It would appear in this sense that Jean Baudrillard, when speaking of Saussure's binaries, is wrong to state that 'there is no "affluence" in language'.[101] As Guattari writes, 'the unconscious is structured like a language to the extent, and only to the extent, that it falls into the clutches of a formation of power'.[102] An internal, what I have called socio-cultural terraforming, that here appears resisted, where a grounded 'nonsense' of meaningful confusion creates a malformed bulge mimetic of the wider tenets of reality; that there is an 'outside'. Guattari here linking to Artaud, to Beckett, to Dubuffet, to the novelists of this study, a resistance that perhaps may only achieve the most fleeting 'escape from meaning', that lies within the rupture of language here described, as presented in Annette's *Qonestsans*.

Slang, idiom, argotique

This synchronizes with the similar use of what Gilbert Adair calls 'phonetic-cum-demotic' language in Queneau's *Zazie dans le métro* as met above,[103] which begins with this startling phrase '*doukipudonktan*', before rolling out coincidentally with similar oral tics and lapses as a, perhaps, socially digestible form of Annette's 'rebus' disintegrations. In very similar fashion this is also present in Johnson's *Albert Angelo*: framed as statements written by Albert

Angelo's students about their teacher, the language lays closer to that spoken: 'evry time he gets on the scals the scals say one at a time. or no elephant alowd. THAT IS THE END OF GOLDY-LOX'.[104] This phonetic-demotic language, akin to further use of slang, or argot in both texts – 'YOU ARE A FAT FOMF OXEN NIT LOLOP RABBI FART-FACE',[105] – as in this framing 'rationed', is certainly a distinction Céline would make. To look to his page manifestation in *Entretiens avec le professeur Y*:

> ah well! colonel, you'd better remember this: *argot* [idiomatic slang] is an admirable spice!... but an entire meal of spice would make a terrible dinner! your reader would murder us! he'll trash your kitchen! with his gob burning like that! he'll go back to comics, your reader will! and how! ... *argot* is alluring but it doesn't go down so well...[106]

Sparingly, perhaps 'professionally', it becomes, in the words of Céline, a tool of 'emotion in written language!... written language is petrified [...] to rediscover the emotion of "speech" in writing! it's not nothing! ... it's small but it's something! ...'[107] Akin to Johnson's disintegratory sections in *Albert Angelo*, there is an utter lack of grammatical punctuation in the statements' formulation; no capital letters, full stops. Here the vocal rendering of language, akin to thieves' cant, or *argot*, becomes a code that is resistant in its obscurity, challenging in its crumpling together of differing orders of signs, indeed an 'emotive' window of communication. Used sparingly it is perhaps more subtly received, rather than averted from by 'the public',[108] which 'is animal, mentally deficient, etc.' for the vitriolic Céline.[109]

In contrast, according to Michel Bigot in Zazie's 'childhood' she passes for the reader acceptably 'at once both true and entirely unreal' and thus 'appears as the medium of an iconoclast language'.[110] Just as in *Albert Angelo* Albert's students, as children not yet socially expected to be able to fully form written language, prefigure in section 'Development' what is to formally come to the novel itself in section 'Disintegration'. This iconoclasm is the upending of the coda of communication, in which the casual drop in and out of Latin and Greek that is common to the canon of dominant written cultural discourse (*viz.* Eliot's *The Wasteland* (1922)) in a time in which access to these dead languages was increasingly uncommon, and too exclusory akin to the psychiatric doctors' notepad. This writing thus recentres access to meaning: it is not the knowledge stashed away, dictated by the symbolic structures of social order, to refer back to Bourdieu, but 'nolij', to refer to Annette's *Qonestsans*. By which these texts reach to an adjacent, experiential quotidian, order of social reality to that established as normalized referent of literature. As Doppagne writes, akin to Céline, Queneau falls through argot and neologism to create a living language 'between the dead French language and *néo-français*'.[111] A written language closer that spoken, rather than the ancient Greek 'dead French' is institutionally tied to. This Saussure, through Certeau above, suggests is a more immediate, perhaps more 'human',[112] mode of communication. Then, at post-war a new socio-cultural environment has spurred new attempts to approach itself. And it is from within this order that Queneau's Zazie made such an approachable figure for the post-war French social conscious, selling well over a million copies. Again, this cutting through the distancing of formal language constraints; the rendering of a human voice and tone in text being received as a sign of communicable authenticity. And this fundamentally reframes the experimental novel, there is at play within it structures of rationality and irrationality, that clearly do not make it exclusively socially unapproachable as, as has been discussed, it has been lambasted since its immediate contemporary. The experimental novel would appear to inhabit the precipice of accepted meaning, non-meaning and plu-meaning that lies at the centre of human communication, of post-war socii, of the post-war individual-cum-social subject. As seen in this phrase '*doukipudonktan*', there appears the intention to impose ambiguity of language at the crux of the harnessing of this rupture, the paradox, not of clarity in singular reduction, but the clarity of communicative multiplicity, confusion and ulterior; an opening of meaning rather than a closing off.

Synchronicities in the published/unpublished work

What is then found here is an environmental bleeding of these two forms of the experimental novel and *écrits bruts*. The *écrits bruts* writers' experiential scripting of trauma, illness and incarceration displays a great synchronicity with the post-war experimental novel writers, novel-object itself, projected reader, and thus betrays a coincidence of environmental conditions, therefore a correspondence of textual treatment. And yet, Annette is perceived irredeemably disconnected from social reality, but Artaud is an 'anticultural' visionary; Queneau a breaking through to a more authentic rendering of reality, Johnson an accumulation of masking lies rejected by printers. Here lies a tacit paradox passingly stated above, where the definition of socially immersive and socially excluded lies not on the frontier of rationality and irrationality as, in the field of swapped accusations of madness these blur within one another in a social space that demands delusion based in the field of fantastically delimited reality norm, but on the edifying printing presses of Gallimard and Penguin. There is a separation there, according to Jean Charles Chabanne:

> These *fous littéraires*, in particular the delirious linguists, I tend to see as distant doubles of Queneau, brothers in that they both pursue to the point of insanity the quest for Truth in language. They give abrupt answers to the Fundamental questions that drive all linguistic curiosity: what is Meaning, and which Meaning is legitimate? [...] Is it possible to abolish the mediation of language and rediscover below the form of the Mother Tongue or Language Preserved, a language without these defects and inadequacies?[113]

Yet, Weiss writes, the works of *écrits bruts* 'are expressions of pain, attempts at communication, cries of recognition – as well as productions of art [...] pain, the memories of pain, or the overcoming of pain is transformed into meaningful signs of the relation of the creator's body to the socius',[114] which makes of them doubles perhaps not as 'distant' as Chabanne states. It entails that both have some notion of their own traumatic pain and, in their attempts to communicate it, that it is to an extent a *shared* traumatic pain.

As Wittgenstein writes 'imagine a person whose memory could not retain *what* the word "pain" meant – so that he constantly called different things by that name', and thus in communicating language the elucidation of 'pain' is dropped from the circuit of cognition. If here the communicable lexicon of 'pain' has been communally scrubbed, or experientially shaken to silence, or as one begetting the other, both, it is perhaps 'a wheel that can be turned though nothing else moves with it, it is not part of the mechanism'.[115] In a space of lexical lack these writers appear to be attempting to add new wheels to the mechanism, to create a short-circuit, or malform those that lock communication; are attempting to re-found the presence of unnameable experience. In their novels as critique they appear to reject the renewing concepts of tradition, and attempt to create modes of communication, critically, altogether new, though entombed in societal interrelation, thus perhaps perpetually unsuccessful as an immediate communicability.

Then the functioning engines of both these entities here rest in the same place, both of which appear to drive the reader to, rather than reduce their perception, reinforce a struggle for the empirical rational. They appear to empower a reconciliation with the very irrationality of meaning of the real field, in rejection of a socius enforced reductive faux-rational, these projects emanating from the same ruptured, traumatized, centre. It is in the very recodified building blocks of the writing itself. To look again to '*doukipudonktan*', which I rendered 'wezzatstinkcumfrum', it has in translation been represented by 'howcanaystinksotho', 'holifart watastink' and 'whozit who stinks?' Whereas my own maintains the ambiguity of the source of the stink, be that the character thinking it, Gabriel (to which it transpires it is), the place, a specific other, or just the crowd in general, the other renderings pinball between these designations in separation. This too is present in the *Qonestsans*, where Beyer's transcription gives *pierres*, and *ai, avoir*, they too have the potential to represent *piestres*, an old currency, or *pieces*, a current term for currency, and *ai, oeuf*, eggs, amongst other calibrations. In Queneau this here represents a slippage of characterization, is Gabriel the source of sensory imposition, or is he just another stinking body in a crowd? For Annette it is the difference between digging through the ground to a depressive low and being surrounded by doctors and orderlies, being offered the chicken's own offspring for food rather than potentially being offered as it; cannibal and cannibalized.

And yet both appear to slip within, in the words of Daniel Delbreil 'a lexical codification by unstable approximation [...] it therefore generates a "noise" that mimics the noise of the exterior'.[116] Where 'the universe of these noises and screams becomes [...] a domaine of [relative] freedom in language'.[117] Thus, these points of contention of meaning decentre meaning itself in echoing, accessing, approaching, the occluded noise of the exterior, in the mode of Beckett, Artaud and Guattari's rupture, thus indeed achieving, perhaps, a moment of beyond-normative human cognition. It then perhaps achieves a discernible break down of externally imposed reliable 'objective' truth, the fleeting presence of personal will; a realization of the unhinged confusion that surrounds the post-war communally subjectified individual. There is present a realization, that the post-war is a knee-jerk sum rather than a hopeful *histoire*; that indeed something has been removed from the circuit. This harbours, however, like Albert Camus' absurd moment, nothing more than a passing edification of '*Qonestsans*'. As, for all her likability, Annette and her chicken are to consume or be consumed, Zazie and her reader never do get to go on the metro, nor do Albert's students get to continue their torture as he is summarily thrown off a bridge to his death; incomplete though it may be, the covers of the book close for text-figures, just as they do for writer and reader. They are returned to their respective incarcerations; a cell with no sky, a town with no metro, and perhaps a more competent teacher. This moment of ambiguity slips back into its order, just as these characters, these phrases of contention are supplicate to their context from which they have, in writing, to some extent been unroped and as texts drift, bumping against other contexts; a context discussed below in reference to books in boxes, possible to reshuffle, to pass on for the reader long after their moment of textually induced torpor has closed; thus reset. Then, to return to Beckett's letter 'the fabric of the language has at least become porous',[118] thus too a sense of cognition of the world hidden within disavowed memory and delimited perception.

3.3 Cut, shuffle, re-align, re-define

To push this attempt to usurp the *trompe-l'oeil* the protagonists of partition two are locked within further, it is perhaps given a wider reaching praxis in cut-up. An approach adopted by a number of post-war figures, one strain was developed by Burroughs and artist Brion Gysin after 'Gysin discovered the process while cutting a mount for a drawing, having sliced through the layers of periodicals that were protecting the table from his Stanley blade.'[119] In doing so, Gysin inadvertently 'realised that printed language had a materiality like paint and canvas or sculpture'.[120] This is contested by Burns, who argues 'I insist I invented [cut-up] because I used it before I'd heard of Burroughs.... I create a sea of images and disconnected phrases in which I find stories.'[121] A similar physical process may be ascribed to Raymond Hains and Jacques Villeglé's treatment of Camille Bryen's *Hepérile* (1949), *Hepérile éclaté* (1953), as too Queneau's *Cent mille milliards de poèmes* (1961) as a number of bound poems, cut into strips of paper to be aligned in *cent mille milliards* different ways, a process too carried out elsewhere by Perec. As Queneau writes in the preliminary '*Mode d'emploi*', the book is 'a sort of machine for fabricating poems, but in limited number', it 'will keep the reader busy for nearly two hundred million years'.[122] Thus, as Queneau quotes Alan Turing: 'only a machine can appreciate a sonnet written by another machine'.[123] This essentially inhabits the realms beyond 'historical death', in which the discontinuity of the reader is toyed with by an impossible text that rests complete, but can never be actualized as a full text in readerly praxis. It too corresponds with the readerly potentialities of cut-up discussed below, and pushes Burns' contest of originality through another prism of perception. The varied application of knives and scissors to text thus demonstrates more than Burns' writerly ego, the disagreement describes a synchronicity of environmentally generated concern in the period that can be ascribed to the wider correspondences of approach throughout the texts observed in this study. Burns' statement too further opens up the potentials of the method beyond scissors and newspaper.

No lie junk

To first follow the environmental concerns, according to Carl Darryl Malmgren cut-up is a creation of perception familiar to that already described: 'Burroughs' revelation consists in the realisation that what we accept as "reality" has been imposed upon us by an infernal and clandestine group of "control addicts," bent on feeding their habit by extending their control.'[124] Again, the presence of this phantasmagoric, seeping mutual self-control harboured within the communal base of human interaction. Again, literature-at-large is a tool of vampiric reduction as 'conventional narrative is merely one more form of control [...] conventional narrative acts as a tranquiliser prescribed to render readers "Gentle."'[125] If the content of a cut-up book 'diagnoses the "virus" that has infected all of America [for Burroughs, for us it appears a more aspirationally global infection] and reduced the entire populace to junkies', the experiential process of cut-up itself is 'designed specifically to counteract that sedative'.[126] It pushes a process of 'rehabilitation of the reader',[127] that is, a treatment of a societal, human illness. For Burroughs and Gysin a treatment consisting of, as delineated in *The Exterminator* in 1960, performing 'violence upon the "word lines"'.[128]

By such a method they attempted to deal 'no lie junk' to their 'Addict Reader';[129] to ground an understanding that, 'NOTHING IS TRUE? EVERYTHING IS PERMITTED'.[130] The supposedly chance placement of the unsure question mark being operative in this statement: they are on the 'lie junk' too. This grounds the mimetic gaming of language described here solidly within a perception of a treatment; what is committed through variable language, space, and glossolalia above, is here first achieved with a knife, or scissors, or folding the page. To look to Gysin's 'first cut ups':

> A huge wave rolled in from the wake of Hurricane Gracie and bowled a married couple off a jetty. The wife's body was found – the husband was missing, presumed drowned.
> Tomorrow the moon will be 228,400 miles from the earth and the sun almost 93,000,000 miles away.[131]

The piece was concocted of 'sample articles and advertisements from the *Daily Mail*, *Herald Tribune*, *Life Magazine*, and the *London Observer*'.[132] It creates a sense of the reported real to be cut at, dissolved and reformed. The morbid and fantastic slip of imagery a subluxation of its original intended use-value. Gysin brings the language of reduction into the realm of ergodic-aleatoric writing, and instils there an ambiguous sense of critique, an indicated beyond, thus indicated limitation. Hurricane Gracie has resulted in a tragic scenario, presumably a reported truth, of a couple drowning, and yet it is a quotidian tragedy that, beyond a sense of immediate compassion, pales in the profound scale of a universe of violent processes in which these events amount to yet another example of cyclical, and perpetual, violence. To look to Burns' *Babel* for a development of the presence of this critique:

> In his cellar the rich alcoholic attempted to rebuild society. His consultants corresponded with government officials in each case and concluded that the H-bomb would not be a catastrophe for the chiefs of staff. A system of H-bombs attached to boot straps would restore a nation's dynamism, a rigidly programmed computer might emerge as a great power, Russia would lose her credibility, German humans would be used as slaves, Kennedy would withdraw from the United States, the world would decline into crazy history.[133]

Burns' cut-up treatment jumbles the narrated strains of *histoire* generated in newspaper and overheard gossip and presents these building blocks of 'worldly' 'what's going on' as dramatic farce, an inconsequential rambling with the potential to result in a very much definitive *ending*, an H-bomb dynamism at the beck of a drunk hermit. As the back cover of the Calder edition attests, Babel is an 'original treatment of our contemporary confusion of tongues [...] compounded of aphorisms, newspaper clichés, poems, snatches of conversation and anecdote [...] world events are constantly fragmented and reset into patterns which reveal the Babel myth as the tragedy of all attempts to construct a secular Utopia.'[134] Burns' book presents a 'panoply' of 'voices and characters', listed in the back, who, along with their own twisted contexts, surface into view and descend back again into the fragmental milieu of the text in a 'cacophony of confusion' in the same way the familiar characters of whatever current newspaper dramas draw up and let drop this or that president,[135] or contextualizing political spat that appears forever on-going, too perpetual to consistently follow with quite the initial front-page viscerality at the beginning of whatever scenario. They pass from whatever depth of page depending on how engaging their actions have been the day before, or that morning, for the evening edition. Further, as Madden writes '*Babel* abounds with sentences that not only challenge perception but that disrupt the expectations of syntax.'[136] I would argue that these elements are not dual, but one begets the other; the disruption of language is linked, allows, opens the disruptive challenge to received perception.

Liberating the page

In this the project of cut-up aligns with those above, and also with that of Metzger's auto-destructive art, who as cited above demonstrates shared concerns with the experimental novel. In the same correspondence of time, in the words of Metzger: 'starting in January 1945, I asked myself how art can contribute to saving society, to changing society.'[137] To do so, Metzger states that auto-destructive art approaches the nothing behind meaning, yet for Lucio Fontana, according to Metzger, it is a 'constructive process where I liberate space behind the cut. In and behind the cut there is space which I liberate.'[138] Here again there is a veil, or a mechanism, or a circuit beyond which is a further, or a something else, or a liberating, thus productive rather than reductive, absolute silence. Applying this to Johnson's use of scissors, through a hole cut in pages 147 to 150 of *Albert Angelo* the reader is promised a future murder:

> struggled to take back his knife, and inflicted on him a
> mortal wound above his right eye (the blade penetrating
> to a depth of two inches) from which he died instantly.[139]

The murder a prefiguring scene of Albert or, by that stage perhaps, page-projection of Johnson, thus his own death, in the book's coda, but in a progressive context a tangential discussion of Kit Marlowe's death in Deptford. The cut here has misled the reader and accessed an adjacent sense of textual ambience and generation of linear meaning, the readying for tragedy builds for what is not there. The spaces cut, then, have liberated this short three lines from the book itself, and created, fleetingly, an entirely otherly meaning, it has split, briefly, the *pathway* of the book; a space has been liberated, and then upon arrival at page 151, is closed down. This frenetic dualism then creates a fleeting liberating space that is an active element in the wider application of scissors; it is Chekhov's gun misfiring.

Indeed, this extends somewhat to an entire novel in Burns' *The Angry Brigade: A Documentary Novel* (1973),[140] which purports to answer the calls of the newspapers, seemingly included as cut-outs in the front of the book, of 'who are the Angry Brigade?' by relating a series of interviews with Maoist terrorist cells in Britain. In preface Burns writes, 'there are three groups in London, and at the time of writing (Spring 1973) at least two outside [...] in the course of writing this book I made contact with two groups: a gang of London street kids living virtually as outlaws, squatting in derelict houses; and a small group of intellectuals who combined a "straight" life with intermittent urban guerrilla activity.'[141] However, as expressed in the newspaper cutting, the Angry Brigade was something of a spectre in Britain at the time, and as Burns related in conversation with Sugnet in 1981:

> I purported to have discovered them and the book contained what seemed to be a series of tape-recorded interviews with them. Needless to say it was a fiction and those 'interviews' were mainly conducted with my friends on topics quite other than those discussed by the characters in the book.[142]

The 'documentary' element of the subtitle subsumes the 'novel' element, creating at first read, accompanied by the coercion of the author in preface, an entirely factual reading of the book, which would not be revealed until nearly a decade later as a fiction, or perhaps not the documentary it was taken to be. A reading of 'documentary novel' Burns would appear to invite from the very cover, despite it being a reference rather to how the novel was composed. Linking closer gamed language and cut-up here, Burns used tape-recordings to generate the novel, as he states: 'the recorder was a godsend to me. I cut out the cut-up and found this other way of creating the "ocean of raw material" I have always needed, so that I could "find" the good stuff among the debris – to mix my metaphors. I also discovered the wonderful music and subtlety of people's speech, and there was a bit of politics in *that* also.'[143] In Burns' use of a tape-recorder, in his positioning of a novelistic cut-up, derived from the selection of *spoken* segments from recordings of conversations with friends, façading as documentary reportage of a quasi-mythical terrorist group living under the radar in Britain, Burns achieves something of a reversal of reportage, turns it in upon itself. If the source material used by the varying approaches of cut-up and auto-destructive art harness a cultural mainstay, the process cuts up 'culture [that] was an attempt to escape from the realisation that we're infinite; culture was the idea that we would have these monuments forever'.[144] As Johnson misleads the reader into a false knowing, scissor text formulation therefore aspires to cut the eternalizing, stabilizing 'illusion of infinity'.[145]

Like Johnson's use of holes, Metzger's most lauded piece *Acid Nylon Paintings*, at the South Bank Demonstration, 1961, consisted of spraying three screens with hydrochloric acid in public thus creating an artwork of what is not there. Or perhaps, revealing the Palace of Westminster and the various civil service and armed forces headquarters across the river; the proper veil, for Metzger, 'revealed'. This recalls again Beckett's logoclast desires for writing, the holes themselves viewable, the canvas in tatters. As Metzger states 'in the end all you had was some strips left. It was never frozen in time, and it was never meant to be.'[146] In doing so Metzger, akin to the drive in cut-up, dissolves the held premise of a gradual achievement of utopia which he finds a term 'rather disturbing' and creates dynamic 'Pharaonic monuments to man's capacity to destroy'.[147] Using auto-destructive art to unlock the experimental novel then, in their shared concerns and approach both projects described here are inherently *logoclast*; at essence the artwork, the novel created, is mimetic not as monument of a utopian illusory infinity or 'crazy history', described in partitions one and two as a holographic reality, but are presented already 'obliterated'; and thus are the already-ruined artefacts of the always-already ruined realities behind the holographic veil of world delimitation.

Hysterical mimesis

Beyond the use of scissors, Perec states that 'you could compare my own work to Burroughs' technique because it's a kind of biographical cut-off [assumedly, sic – *cut-up*]'.[148] A mode of reminiscence that creates a memory-work 'close to our own, and that we find almost the same as our own history'.[149] This Perec ascribes to a praxis behind the forms of much of his work, prevalent in *Je me souviens*, *W ou le souvenir d'enfance*, and the cycle of *tableaux vivants* that structures *La Vie mode d'emploi* (1978). In application, memory becomes dislodged, slips into a confused, fantastic reflexion of itself; a socio-cultural dreamwork of inaccessible personal experience that generates a sense of Freudian 'hysterical identification'.[150] That is where the 'patient' is 'enabled to express in their symptoms not merely their own experiences, but the experiences of quite a number of other persons; they can suffer, as it were, for a whole mass of people'.[151] For Freud this extends to a schizophrenic inhabiting of these personalities, but here it is not a 'patient' which appears to demonstrate these symptoms, but the novel itself which exhibits a kind of 'hysterical' mimesis in which snippets of global experience fall as fragments through it, and thus their status as universal is split into the personal as viewed by the extra-textual figures present in the novelistic staging ground. As Perec writes of *Je me souviens*:

> I'm not the only one remembering myself. I could call it a 'sympathetic' book, it's in sympathy with the readers, the readers will easily find themselves within it. It functions as a kind of call to memory because memory is a thing that is shared. It's completely different to autobiography, to the exploration of one's personal memories, marked out, occulted. It's a work of communal memory, of collective memory.[152]

'In sympathy with the reader', Perec's staging of the text makes attempts at a sympathizing, or perhaps rather, empathizing textual field and thus aligns with

Burroughs' cut-up in mashing together these formally established, thus understood, signs in grotesquely, sympathetically, emphasized patterns. The form perhaps then succeeds in that empathetic work of the experimental novel; to 'establish new connections between images, and one's range of vision consequently expands'.[153] Because, as Eagleton is quoted in partition two, the reader of a text is, paradoxically, 'reading themselves', here too it seems potentially 'composing themselves'.

As Burroughs states: 'any narrative passage or any passage, say, of poetic images is subject to any number of variations, all of which may be interesting and valid in their own right. A page of Rimbaud cut up and rearranged will give you quite new images. Rimbaud images—real Rimbaud images—but new ones'.[154] Again, this paradox of readerly participation in a textspace they did not, initially, compose; Harris' 'second death'. For Robin Lydenberg this 'world of violence' in cut-up indicates the limitations of the reader's diseased perception and offers them a 'panorama of *delusions*' that seems to describe the spiralling horrors discussed in partition two.[155] The language schema approached here in their indication of a 'wheel somewhere spinning' throw into relief the normative societal world for what it is; a phantasm; a fantastic, horrifying delusion of relativized, irrationalized ruination akin to Freud's 'rebus house'.

> A house, upon whose roof there is a boat; then a single letter; then a running figure, whose head has been omitted, and so on.[156]

In viewing such a rebus-reality, as grotesque as found earlier in this study, as presented in the rebus-house cut-up and gamed language above, as Freud states, 'I might be tempted to judge this composition and its elements to be nonsensical. A boat is out of place on the roof of a house, and a headless man cannot run; the man, too, is larger than the house, and if the whole thing is meant to represent a landscape the single letters of the alphabet have no right in it, since they do not occur in nature.'[157] But, while Freud's dream-reader must apply a rigorous interpretation to decrypt such imagery, while the reader may 'avert their gaze', the oblique act of generative reading musters meaning in the physical linearity of text-reading; the broken house shifts into culturally contextualized, thus perhaps reified, observability.

If cut-up 'attempts to destroy the power of that world and its arsenal of images by a method of cure in which the reader is immunised by exposure', freedom of access appears still curtailed.[158] As discussed above, the act of reading always falls within a 'consecutiveness, "logic," continuity, connections, or common sense' as 'any act of semiosis, taken on faith and meant to be deciphered, reveals itself as a reifiable truth system'.[159] Then experimental treatment of the novel potentially betrays its own experimental potential by its a priori intention to ameliorate, treat or rehabilitate: it walks a trembling tightrope above externally imposing culturally immersed truth, and perhaps there slips. It is for this reason the problematic of communication, the reader and the success or failure of the experimental novel has followed this argument from the beginning of this study. And yet here can be grounded as a violently born *fata morgana* in text;[160] that this mode of reader sourced text meaning is a definitive element of the experimental novel and integral to the text as a cultural treatment of a societal disease.

The response-ible reader

In cut-up the writer 'implicitly demands that readers cut up his texts as well as the texts of others [thus he] instigates a process',[161] what at first appears an essentially writerly praxis, cutting, folding, arranging, transcribing, is repositioned as too a readerly praxis. This creates what Malmgren refers to as the '*response*-ible reader',[162] immersed in what was discussed above as an aleatoric-ergodic literature. As Burroughs states:

> Cut-ups are for everyone. Anybody can make cut ups. It is experimental in the sense of being something to do. Right here write now. Not something to talk and argue about. Greek philosophers assumed logically that an object twice as heavy as another object would fall twice as fast. It did not occur to them to push the two objects off the table and see how they fall. Cut the words and see how they fall.[163]

Therefore, Malmgren argues that indeed, 'the space of the reader changes ontologically from HERMENEUTIC to COMPOSITIONAL'; normative societal reality is after all the rebus-house in which both writer and reader live, the use of a pen is not a hierarchical distinction of enhanced perception, nor lack of blindness. And, in that the reader role would indeed appear compositional, rather than hermeneutic. The text-in-disarray, the 'DIY' text proffers a textual interaction not of truth-statement, reality-statement (hermeneutic interaction), but an experiential, mimetic indication of truth-predicament, reality-predicament (compositional interaction). Thus, the staging-ground of the text becomes an uncovering praxis for figures involved in the generative textscape. To refer to the closing pages of Burns' *Babel*, on the precipice of failure:

> the experiment succeeded, obviously, suited by complexity, a colourful thing, it is sensational, the pattern within, the individual, worth examining, it has character, if you look, you will find Him, it is no accident, this is where you belong[164]

The experiment potentially succeeds in that both the writer and reader create their own text, and 'if one literally make's one's own text, one can be sure that the "truths" discovered therein are not imposed from without but come from within'.[165] If in writing the writer is offered an indication of limitation, of a disease that must be treated, then the reader too must also be to some extent 'free to chart his own course through the inexhaustible network of textual associations and digressions' present in the aleatoric-ergodic novel.[166] The process of textual realization, confusion, sense, critique and conclusion here has the potential to be recentred away from external dictation, and within the generative staging ground of the novel give indication of the wheel removed from the mechanism. As such the experimental potentiality of the novel hinges on the variable potency of Blanchot's spatio-temporal void of genesis within text, and of those texts here described, within the predicament of meaning, within the predicament of reality, within this space it appears 'the reader is everywhere present'.[167]

Shuffle

To return to Johnson, his use of this opening up of space in *The Unfortunates* appears with a closing down in its tail that perhaps leads that text to slip the tightrope of readerly textual involvement; he attempts to load the dice and thus appears to renege on the potentialities of his own text's formal projects. His use of space in *The Unfortunates* described above, at turns begins to become suspiciously stylistic in pauses less in the name of accessing some sense of actual memory, or its impossibility: 'I could see he was very   ill at ease in his mind.'[168] Johnson seems to be encroaching upon this elegy, to have shifted to the use of this silence as a writerly tic to ingratiate himself into Tony's story; as Coe comments it appears a rather 'egocentric response' to a promise to record his friend's death.[169] It too seems to renege on the promises of the form of the novel itself, and as such appears a begrudgingly carried out task. Johnson seems to prefer that these memories stayed buried, and as he speaks in partition two of 'exorcising his memories' and burying them in books in discussion with Burns, in Johnson's own failure of katabasis, a tripping return to traumatic absence, it speaks too of a readerly opening, and thus essentially, burying. But the essentially transitory nature of the successful opening itself is indeed what I am here attempting to demonstrate, as too a failure to achieve this. Johnson's insistence of himself while attempting to bring singular clarity to this vagueness inescapably defeats either textual project. As Buchanan writes it is 'a doomed and unstable attempt to depict the particularity of events, and in the end underline[s] the narrative's inability to present the material it addresses'.[170]

To look to the spatial readerly praxis of interacting with *The Unfortunates*, akin to Marc Saporta's *Composition no. 1* (1962) as Tom Uglow writes in introduction to the English language textual-digital 're-imagining', the loose pages for Saporta each consist of 'a strand of self-sufficient narrative which, when "shuffled" by the reader, forms the story'.[171] In an explanatory note preceding the French text not included in the English version (which of the two versions is most accessible), Saporta writes 'the reader is asked to shuffle these pages like a pack of cards. To deal them, if the reader so wishes, with the left hand, like a fortune-teller. The order in which the pages leave the deck will orient the destinies of X.'[172] The compositional element of the text itself is again placed firmly in the hands of the reader, in which it is they who decide the travails of the elusive protagonist, X. Such an insistence on the reader's compositional *responsibility* is paramount to text here, and can too be found in Topor's *Psychotopor* (1966). A further book in a box, in which the pages make up pieces to a sort of game of *Cluedo*, through which the reader-player would discover, by the ends of variable narrative, a self-diagnosis of their pathological dysfunction; cannibal, necrophiliac etc.

However, this open reliance on readerly responsibility isn't exactly accurate in Johnson, whose *The Unfortunates* is made up of a number of sections with a more rigid contextualizing interdependence upon one another. But, still for each of these box-books, the relation of page to page as the reader turns them is again a space of genesis, as demonstrated in Topor's *Erika*. This aleatoric-ergodic element that appears a physical imposition of the ambiguity of space, though this in *The Unfortunates* seems perhaps a largely redundant practice. This point is to some extent supported by Kaye Mitchell who writes 'does the ending of *The Unfortunates* confer this plenitude of meaning or does the disruption of the central space of the narrative render the whole less determinate, leaving us in a state of perpetual suspense?'[173] For the purposes of this study, this perhaps opens up to the question of whether the indeterminacy of readerly composition creates an extra-textual treatment, or if it falls into the same traps of confusion it endeavours to employ in order to attempt to induce a destabilization of reduction. While the sections do succeed in a sense of 'the trivial and the important', 'our life with his dying', running together as 'chance' it has a much reduced potential to vary the temper, plot or further multiplicities of the story(-ies).[174] It is perhaps mimetic in the very limited modicum of chance offered as too chance is dictated within life.[175] Perhaps, but the imposed reductions of Johnson's need for control over the fiction constantly pulls away the wider ergodic tendencies of the attempt at an open schema, that removes even the more or less limited implications of the dice throw (from a concrete *cent mille milliards* to a vaguely variating *one*). Though, in my reading taken to write this section I was left with perhaps the most poignant tract 'by chance' (second to) last:

> He was deteriorating, disintegrating, so the last thing I said to him, all I had to give him, alone with him, with my coat on, about to go, the car waiting outside to run us to the station, staring down at him, facing those eyes, he staring back all the time now, it must have been a great effort for him, yes, and I said, it was all I had, what else could I do, I said, I'll get it down, mate.   It'll be very little, he said, after a while, slowly, still those eyes.   That's all anyone has done, very little, I said.[176]

And thus 'chance' gave me Johnson's promise, and final words to Tony last. This created a post-textual sense of Johnson's pain beyond what would have been elicited by a more innocuous chance ending that would perhaps infer a bathos rather than pathos. This implies a degree of potential multiplicity, seemingly despite Johnson.

To follow this coincidence of the last page somewhat independent of the flawed aleatoric encroachment of Johnson, to the coincidence of the first page of Saporta's *Composition no. 1*. From the first time I opened Saporta's box I have found the challenge of the text my own, readerly, sense of aversion. The chance first page contained a comparatively full exposition on the theme of rape in war-time:

> Revolver in hand, the men of the third section are already in the street, and searching the villas. We'd better hurry before he snags all the prettiest girls [...] here is indeed a good catch. A young woman took refuge in the cellar with two little girls of ten and twelve years old. The girls are obviously too young, although the Moroccans would not see them so, but the company is composed of civilised men [...] women are taken to the requisitioned houses and used immediately, right there on the floor. They offer no resistance.[177]

And yet while this stark revelation that that coded as the moral liberation of Europe entailed the violent mass rape of hundreds of thousands of women across the continent, not only, as commonly held, by those otherly, dastardly, 'Nazis' and 'Soviets', but too the British, French and Americans;[178] by our field representatives, is startling, it is what this chance placement does to the further narrative that makes this text specifically so difficult to read.[179] The following page, again by chance, began 'Helga started getting hot under the collar',[180] and follows to describe the character Helga 'enjoying' a rough sexual encounter. Without reference to the page before this would not harbour the same meaning created by this paginated colocation, which creates a grotesquely misogynistic legitimization of the soldiers' acts. Further, the other strands of narrative pale, and fade and I, here as reader representative, feel little energy to understand Marianne, nor discover the elusive X, as I dig through the pages as banal interruptions in a constant return to Helga's rape characterized in different fashions. Five pages later, 'Helga offered no resistance',[181] seven pages after that 'Helga with a bat in her hand like a Bengali prisoner. She tries in vain to use it. Her wrists are tied tightly to the bed,'[182] and on. *Composition no. 1* becomes a cycle of violent rape, in which Helga is locked in traumatic return to the instance, locked in a cycle of repeated and perpetual violence that perhaps pushes past the cyclical trip before the source of trauma.

The dominant artifice of the Good War is brutally and cyclically broken down around the reader in this linearity of the text, forces the reader to bear witness to the violence perpetrated by 'our boys' over and over and over again; in this sense it is the reader who commits this, the reader who, then, is after all X. And as such, through the praxis of the text the reader does indeed, not interpret, nor decode, but composes themselves. And any amount of shuffling does not dispel these markers now they have been set. Johanna Drucker writes, supporting points I have previously argued, 'in denial, the citizenry pulls their shades against the reality of violence that runs through the very fibre of daily life, the warp and woof of contemporary existence in even the safest-seeming neighbourhood'.[183] Shades that are farcical, and terrifying, in their inadequacy. To look to Billany's *The Cage*, as it begins with a letter from the home front. The letter is full of ellipses, dashes, spaces, blacked out sequences of words as a strange observable historical external imposition on the text which renders the letter farcically unintelligible, other than the morbid simplicity by which, ascribed co-author, David Dowie's aunt and uncle transform interminable internment in a prison camp into a jaunt at a Roman themed Butlin's.

> Your uncle says ... most beautiful country, beautiful climate ... envies your opportunity [...] see all those beautiful cathedrals and Roman ruins ... beautiful ... Regard it as a Heaven-sent opportunity rather than a ... Your uncle has joined the ---- ----- -----. Last week we went to ----- and saw ----- . But Italy will soon -----. Keep your pecker up and think of the -----.
>
> Your loving Aunt,
'   _____.'[184]

How many times has this letter been censored? To assume an Allied censor, perhaps an Axis censor, both Billany and Dowie's editing, the editing of the respective families before publication, the publisher's edit, my own for want of space. And yet this fragmentation has not made the text incomprehensible, the very opposition posited itself, the outward folding frame of the censor's black pen, dots, dashes and voids, and the impotent, distant words of consolation speak of an utter and irredeemable cleaving of reality. The aunt and uncle appear locked in a *mélange* of don't know, don't want to know, and actively ignore the stark realities as an impenetrably horrifying truth which embodies a bizarre cognitive dissonance discussed in partition two between two irreconcilable states of things, tourism through barbed wire. But viewing the letter itself as embedded in text demands of the reader the ergodic decryption of these erasures and ellipses that draws this realization from within them, they therefore instil, within themselves, a grotesqueness to the unnatural and unknowing banal utterances of a standard communication with those around the social subject that would usually seem so very normal.

This returns us to the concerns of back and forth reading discussed in partition two and reasserts the primacy of a physical interaction with text. As Dworkin writes of Man Ray's erased poem *Lautgedicht* (1924), 'visual prosody interact[s] with the syntactic and denotative meanings of textual reference, and their formation can underscore those references [...] or contradict them [...] the visual text also encodes more specific information about the material production of its language.'[185] Man Ray's poem prefigures Topor's erased novel, where the run of black smudges generate all meaning from the readerly reference to the single word associated with it, its title, *Souvenir*, written on a slip of paper to be slid off the book before reading. A book in which the non-signifying smears on the page, framed by this slip of paper, take on progressively generated meaning. This obscuring pushes the equation of Butlin's and prison camp in Billany, communication and erasure, and makes of this closing off of written communication a generative opener of meaning beyond the falsities originally intended by the aunt. Just as in Saporta, the chance placement of those first two pages, and the synchronizing repetition of this event breaks the reader's own distanced 'sweet dream' of reality, creates of it a nightmare, caused by the 'transgressive ends' of some corners of contemporary American cinema for Drucker,[186] here for us, Saporta, and wider, the post-war experimental novel. If I had read Topor's *Erika* following Saporta's text it too holds this potential meaning, it would be drawn into its wake, from romance to violence that shows an extra-textual passing of this contagion of perception. And yet, like the violent genesis of the truth and truthfulness discussed in relation to Žižek in partition two, does this readerly reaction embody realization, or aversion? It is a problematic raised by Perec in his essay *Robert Antelme, ou la verité de la littérature* (1962):

> Micheline Maurel, in *Un camp très ordinaire*, tells us that the question people asked her most often upon her return [from the concentration camps] was: 'did anyone violate you?' It was the only question that truly interested people,

the only thing that entered their heads when they tried to think of terror. Other than that, there was nothing, they didn't understand, they couldn't comprehend. Just a shrugging compassion.[187]

Is my reaction that of interaction with the text, or a mask of understanding in this sense. As Žižek posits in similar terms, can reactions to attempts to report the sheer violence of that war and its fallout, in its myriad violent modes, plethora of 'nightmarishness', be anything other than averted or stupefied by 'anesthetising horror'?[188] It would appear difficult to state the reader has the clear capacity to move beyond 'a falsifying pity that is a refusal, pure and simple'.[189] What perhaps allays this problematic is the sense that the reader, in being able to shuffle these episodes to whatever greater or lesser sense comes to the back or fore within the narrative tableau of Saporta's text, has a hand in this repeated violence; the reader is made, makes themselves complicit in this cyclical violence, and in refusing to put down the book, given the potential by Saporta, reveal the violence in benign and distanced constructs that encircle the societal human. That indeed forged, and maintain the distancing remove from the real. As stated above, in reading, the reader becomes X, forges 'their own textual destiny'.[190] Following that discussed above concerning cut-up, these truths are synchronic with an interior, a connection internally generated, not externally imposed, it then here dissolves this quotidian disguise of 'shrugging compassion'.[191]

Yet, as seen, to turn away, to censor the genesis of this horror is still a potential inherent in both writerly and readerly praxis, which connects two elements that culturally inhabit entirely separate scales, would be to refuse that they, factually, inhabit one and the same. This again shows a pushing of textual responsibility upon the reader, further, an approximation of proper historical responsibility upon the individuated subject extra-text. Whether they like it or not the textual contagion spreads, as it is irreducibly carried with the same 'virus' of community that allows for the usurping of a social desire for 'a simplicity, a quotidianity, to the unidentifiable'.[192] If there is a falsity in this 'simple everydayness', it is because, for Perec, it 'betrays "reality", to explain it in a clearer way, it blocks us from being able to perceive the "unbearable"',[193] as has been discussed at length. And yet within the texts herein discussed, there is an active and to some degree successful process of subluxation of what Perec fears has whitewashed perception, rendered it stupefied.[194] As Jean-Yves Pouilloux writes:

> To seek to escape the trompe-l'oeil by reference to the real would be to submit even more to it. [...] To write [and to read], is therefore to recompose the 'verbal trompe-l'oeil' thanks to which we are able to traverse the paths of unknowing, the forgetfulness, the disappearance, the misdirection, and put them to the test, and in so doing, we gain a chance to open our eyes.[195]

These texts have invoked the vague, and as such problematize the received simplicity of the veneer. To take this effect a step further, there is present a further extra-textual potential praxis to this sorting noted above.

To look, anachronistically, to the strange phenomenon surrounding *Arrested Development*, a cancelled TV show brought back in 2014 by Netflix. Free of studio pressure, the producers decided to employ a similar technique to Johnson's *House Mother Normal*, in which each episode follows a character's perception of the series long plotted arc to which they are more or less present or relevant. Bizarre things occur, screams, shouts, actions, dialogue that appear to have little to do with the story of that episode, and lay unexplained until given a wider sense of meaning by a viewing of the full series where these snippets of meaning may be ambiguously connected. Of course, unlike *House Mother Normal*, it is not quite so present to the video medium to flick back and forth between episodes as it is with book sections to clarify the perceptions of multiple narrators. These moments are not bookmarked by page number. Thus, the viewers, frustrated by the ergodic challenge of the format of the series, in a kind of cut-up of reversal, re-edited it into a straight-line linear narrative, which has proven widely more acclaimed than the original series itself. Here the viewers have rejected the experimental ambiguity of the fiction's generative format, even more so, they erased it. To apply this to the books in boxes, as Uglow writes in his introduction to *Composition no. 1*:

> Most often, it is the previous reader who has decided the order you read it in, as the instinct not to manipulate the 'deck' is almost overwhelming.[196]

Both books were bought second-hand, and in reading both I succumbed to the apparent chance of the order they fell to me. If there is a contagious potential of realization of collective trauma, of guilt, of reduction and effacement and its accompanying pain or Sorge within experimental novel content, this fellow-reader formatting of the text creates the ergodic potential to formally spread the contagion not just writer > text > writer, writer > text > reader, to some extent here also reader x > text > reader x;[197] but also reader x > text > reader y. Unlike the letter in Billany, which has been tampered with by readers prior to writerly use and framed as such by the text,[198] the readerly impositions of Johnson and Saporta describe a multiplicity of potentially empathetic interactions occurring within the text between ergodically invoked cognitive referents. Like the potential of the recut-up cut-up, it constellates the potentiality of what Joanna Gavins calls the 'discourse world' of text, and makes of it a world of simultaneous *discourses*.[199] Whereas the previous reader could have, like the viewers of *Arrested Development*, done away with the more challenging recurrences in their aversion, thrown away the pages, or assembled them in less potent order, it is indeed possible that these pages were placed specifically to propagate a spread of the previous reader's own destabilized sense of horror created by *their* reading of the text.

This also opens up a wider understanding of Perec's 'memory cut-up' *Je me souviens*, which includes a handful of blank pages at the end, where Perec invites the reader to add their own remembrances. The copy I have has been added to by two different readers, an 'A. Buffard', and a 'CEF'.

> A. Buffard
> I remember my eco teacher had no teeth because he smashed his face on the floor leaving school one time.
> I remember the first jazz record I ever bought: Greatest Hits/Fats Waller RCA.
> I remember my first cigarette and everyone laughing at me.
> CEF
> I remember Manhattan Transfer.
> I remember my lieutenant at Satory. He said that I was not resourceful! . . .
> I remember also stealing a combat JACKET, for his girlfriend . . .[200]

If Perec's project in his contribution to the text is to offer some concrete documentation of fleeting human experience in the process of disappearing, to create a relic by which it may be returned to again, an object to which it may be moored, he invites the readers, plural, to participate in an attempt to remember, both the worn and demolished landmarks of a shared cultural past, and the flowing and disappearing touchpoints of individual human experience as generated by his preceding missive notations of loss.

If the writer here appears a sort of Victor Frankenstein at his creature, it appears so too is the reader, their monster, or rather monsters, the language physiognomy of communicated reality; thus, perhaps perception of reality itself. As Green states it is within the reader, 'in the spell of his own imagination the characters and story come alive'.[201] This adds a curiously social aspect to reading, that may, to a certain degree like marginalia in second-hand books, the busy termites scrawled in the leading of Themerson's *Professor Mmaa's Lecture* or the comic book marginalia asides in Quin's *Tripticks*, and conversely the generative erasures of the many hands on Billany's letter, draw from beyond the standardized singular relation of writer, and text, and reader, thus sublimate the process of confined reading itself. And as such, would appear to form a potential for the transitory breakdown in objective meaning and reduction created in-text to slip its jacketed, or boxed, bonds. These readings formulated by writers, readers create; in Billany, a misalignment with reality so wild the reader is forced, in a book about inevitable death in a fascist prison camp, to laugh; in Perec, a sense of shared loss; in Topor a horrific *debanalization* of the everyday; in Johnson, a pain the reader is forced to try not to embrace; in Saporta, a violence the reader is forced to try not to reject. If for Saporta this has achieved one of myriad unknown results of his experiment, in relation to Johnson, it appears despite his best efforts, he has created a hydra he cannot bring to heel. To refer back to the Kaun letter 'in this dissonance of instrument and usage perhaps one will already be able to sense a whispering of the end-music or of the silence underlying it all'.[202] But, as we have seen, these silences are perhaps the unrecognized windows into a field of the horrifying noise of the post-war. Moving from a focus upon the beach of the page and its structure, to the signs speared through it, Beckett's holes here appear bored, and realization of a removed beyond begins to seep through them.

Notes

Preface

1. Claude Bernard, *Introduction à l'étude de la médecine expérimentale* (1865) (Paris: Flammarion, 2010), pp. 15–16.
2. Fredric Jameson, *The Political Unconscious: Narrative as a Socially Symbolic Act* (New York: Cornell University Press, 1981), p. 10.
3. Conroy Maddox, "Poem" (written 1941; exhibited 1986), *The Thirteenth Stroke of Midnight* (Manchester: Carcanet, 2013), p. 125.

Partition One

1. Depending on the critical, cultural tradition, or a specific critic's perspective, as an epistemic epoch this might be clarified to the 'late-modern', or 'mid-modern', for the particular vaguely nineteenth century to vaguely twentieth century period of time that is 'artistically' here described in active 'modernity' (not to speak of the current critical turn towards the prefixing of 'long'). And yet these ism constructs appear to dominate any and all of these epochal 'literary modern(/ity)' constructs.
2. James Clements, *Mysticism and the Mid-Century Novel* (London: Palgrave MacMillan, 2011), p 1.
3. Ibid.
4. Peter Brooker, 'Introduction: Reconstructions', *Modernism/Postmodernism* (London: Longman, 1992), pp. 1–33. p. 4.
5. Ibid.
6. Ibid.
7. Fredric Jameson, *The Modernist Papers* (London: Verso, 2007), pp. 48–9.
8. Frank Kermode, 'Modernisms', *Continuities* (London: Routledge & Kegan Paul, 1968), pp. 1–32. p. 28.
9. The new scholarly designation of a 'modernist' as a researcher of a specific field of, assumedly, 'modernism', would appear to favour a 1920ish classification.
10. Brian McHale, *Postmodernist Fiction* (London: Routledge, 1991), pp. 10–11.
11. Brooker, p. 4.

12 David Harvey, *The Condition of Postmodernity: An Enquiry into the Origins of Cultural Change* (London: Blackwell, 1991), p. ii.
13 Ibid., p. iii.
14 Ibid., p. 3.
15 Ibid., p. 10.
16 Ibid., p. 9.
17 Ihab Hassan, 'The Culture of Postmodernism', *Theory, Culture and Society*, 2, 3, Fall 1985, pp. 119–31. p. 123.
18 Brooker, p. 11.
19 Ibid., p. 14.
20 Gérard Genette, *Palimpsestes: la littérature au second dégre* (Paris: Seuil, 1982), p. 290.
21 Harvey, p. 356.
22 Jago Morrison, *Contemporary Fiction* (New York: Routledge, 2003), p 3.
23 Members of the Oulipo at large, and in particular Georges Perec regularly denounced Robbe-Grillet as narcissistic or obscurant. Roland Topor writes of Robbe-Grillet's *'nouveaux romans'* as 'a complaisant self-portrait of the artist': Roland Topor, 'Preface' (1990), in Daniel Spoerri, *Topographie anécdotée* du hasard* (1962) (Paris: Centre Georges Pompidou, 1990), pp. i–ii.
24 Fredric Jameson, *Postmodernism, or the Cultural Logic of Late Capitalism* (London: Verso, 1992), p. xx.
25 In speaking of Dostoevsky and Kafka, Sarraute highlights the inadequacies of such a 'baton-passing' image of literary history; counter to Johnson's application.
26 B.S. Johnson, *Aren't You Rather Young to be Writing Your Memoirs?* in *Well Done God! Selected Prose and Drama of B.S. Johnson*, eds. Philip Tew, Julia Jordan, Jonathan Coe (London: Picador, 2013), pp. 1–140. p. 30.
27 Genette, *Palimpsestes*, p. 291.
28 Clements, p. 1.
29 Ibid.
30 Ibid.
31 Alain Badiou, 'The Three Negations', *Cardozo Law Review*, vol. 29:5, 2008, pp. 1877–83. p. 1880.
32 Marshall Berman, 'The Twentieth Century: The Halo and the Highway', *Modernism/Postmodernism*, ed. Peter Brooker (London: Longman, 1992), pp. 74–81. p. 80.
33 Helena Bassil-Morozow, 'On the Reality of the Shadow', The IAJS Shadow Online Seminar http://jungstudies.net/wp-content/uploads/2012/06/IAJS-Online-Discussion-Shadow-seminar.pdf (accessed 20 December 2015).
34 Béatrice Joyaux-Prunel, *Les Avant-gardes artistiques. Une histoire transnationale 1848–1918* (Paris: Folio, 2017), p. 66.

35 Roland Topor, 'Préface', in Daniel Spoerri, *Topographie anécdotée* du hasard (1962)* (Paris: Centre Georges Pompidou, 1990), p. ii.
36 Jean-Paul Sartre, *Qu'est-ce que la littérature?* (Paris: Gallimard, 1948), p. 15.
37 Clements, p. 1.
38 Kristin Bluemel, *Intermodernism: Literary Culture in Mid-Century Britain* (Edinburgh: Edinburgh University Press, 2009).
39 Marina Mackay and Lyndsey Stonebridge, *British Fiction After Modernism: The Novel at Mid-Century* (London: Palgrave, 2007).
40 Gabriel Josipovici, *Whatever Happened to Modernism?* (New Haven: Yale University Press, 2011).
41 Raymond Williams, 'When Was Modernism?', *New Left Review*, 175, May/June 1989, p. 49.
42 Mackay and Stonebridge, pp. 1–2.
43 Perhaps if Aristotle's rumoured *Poetics II* on comedy had survived, the writer might have equally argued a state of perpetual bathos.
44 Williams, 'When Was Modernism?', pp. 49–50.
45 Patrick Lacoste, *L'étrange cas du Professeur M.: Psychanalyse à l'écran* (Paris: Gallimard, 1990), p. 60.
46 Joyeaux-Prunel, p. 37.
47 Jameson, *The Modernist Papers*, p. xi.
48 Christine Brooke-Rose, *Invisible Author: Last Essays* (Columbus: Ohio State University, 2002), p. 35.
49 Tzvetan Todorov, *La Littérature en péril* (Paris: Flammarion, 2007), pp. 18–19.
50 Ibid., p. 17.
51 Brooke-Rose at time of publication in 2002 was seventy-nine and died in 2012 aged eighty-nine; Todorov at time of publication in 2007 was sixty-eight and died in 2017 aged seventy-seven.
52 Also met in Williams, 'When Was Modernism?', p. 49: '"avant-garde" may be indifferently used to refer to Dadaism seventy years after the event or to recent fringe theatre'. As a 'singular' and seemingly 'perpetual' entity, it carries with it the implication of anachronism or spatio-temporal indifference.
53 Jacques Rancière, *Les Temps modernes* (Paris: La Fabrique Éditions, 2018), p. 10.
54 Jean Dubuffet, *Asphyxiante culture* (Paris: Éditions de Minuit, 1968), p. 9.
55 Rancière, p. 53.
56 Fredric Jameson, *The Political Unconscious: Narrative as a Socially Symbolic Act*, p. 10.
57 Wolfgang Iser, *The Implied Reader: Patterns of Communication in Prose Fiction from Bunyan to Beckett* [*Der Implizite Leser: Kommunikationsformen des Romans von Bunyan bis Beckett*, 1972], (Baltimore: John Hopkins University Press, 1974), p. xii.

58 Philippe Sollers, *Logiques* (Paris: Éditions du Séuil, 1968), p. 229.

59 Craig Dworkin, *No Medium* (Cambridge: MIT Press, 2013), p. 9.

60 Theodor Adorno, 'Letters to Walter Benjamin', *Aesthetics and Politics*, trans. Harry Zohn (London: Verso, 2007), pp. 110–33. pp. 115–16.

61 Tzvetan Todorov, 'Présentation', *Littérature et réalité*, eds. Gérard Genette and Tzvetan Todorov (Paris: Éditions du Séuil, 1982), pp. 7–10. p. 8.

62 Jameson, *Postmodernism, or, the Cultural Logic of Late Capitalism*, p. xx.

63 Peter Osbourne and Éric Alliez, *Spheres of Action: Art and Politics*, ed. Éric Alliez and Peter Osbourne (London: Tate Publishing, 2013), p.7.

64 Rayner Heppenstall, *The Fourfold Tradition* (London: Barrie and Rockliff, 1961), p. 178.

65 George Watson, 'Remembering Prufrock: Hugh Sykes Davies 1909–1984', *Jacket* 2001, http://jacketmagazine.com/20/hsd-watson.html (accessed 3 June 2016).

66 Much to the annoyance of Joyceans on tour, I would assume, James Joyce's plaque at 71 rue de Cardinal Lemoine reads 'British writer'; so, I suppose such classifications are always up for debate.

67 This position developed from R.A. Bentley, A. Acerbi, P. Ormerod, V. Lampos, 'Books Average Previous Decade of Economic Misery', *PLoS ONE* 9(1) 2014: e83147. <10.1371/journal.pone.0083147> (accessed 14 August 2014).

68 B.S. Johnson, *The Evacuees* (London: Victor Gollancz, 1968), p. 18.

69 Eva Tucker, 'Eva Figes Obituary', *The Guardian*, https://www.theguardian.com/books/2012/sep/07/eva-figes (accessed 14 July 2015).

70 Roland Topor, *Un Beau soir, je suis né en face de l'abattoir* (Paris: Denoël, 2000).

71 Roland Topor, *Pense-bêtes* (Paris: Les Cherches-midi, 1992), p. 2.

72 Georges Perec, *W ou le souvenir d'enfance* (1975) (Paris: Gallimard, 2006), p. 11.

73 The sample taken for this book was largely established during the B.S. Johnson 'one man avant-garde' era of criticism of the post-war experimental novel – he is, for example, the only British figure to, albeit briefly, appear in the apparently exhaustive *The Routledge Companion to Experimental Literature* (2012). In its original iteration at over twice the length of that which now appears in print, a central aim of *The Post-War Experimental Novel* was to meet and reroute that critical over-investment in the figure of Johnson into a wider field of figures, texts, contexts and indicative openings into myriad potential spaces for discussion of the experimental novel. That field itself is now in the process of opening up well beyond Johnson, and I hope this book might now participate in that process of exploration and reassessment. In terms of my own work, building a groundwork for continued explorations elsewhere further pursuing the representational backgrounds and aesthetic potentialities here indicated, that demand far more attention and space than this short book is able offer.

74 Brooke-Rose, *Invisible Author*, p. 35.

75 A tendency that would appear to have been established as effective framework of reappraisal by Jonathan Coe's extensive figure-study of Johnson, *Like A Fiery Elephant* (2004).
76 Michel Butor, *Butor*, ed. Georges Raillard (Paris: Gallimard, 1968), p. 257.
77 As will be seen below, the synonymous treatment of the words 'reductive' and 'cinematic' relates here to the formulaic romances of post-war 'Hollywood' cinema and the perceived imposing of this 'formulaicness' onto the novel genre-at-large. This is a position highlighted by many of the writers of this study, not least Brigid Brophy who refers to reality itself as 'the perpetual cinema show'.
78 Georges Perec's *La Disparition* (1969), and the hunt for A. Voyl.
79 Roland Topor's *Le Locataire chimérique* (1964), and the twisting realities around Trelkovsky.
80 Ann Quin's *Tripticks* (1972), and the incorporation of comic book cells into the pages of text.
81 David Lodge, for example, who in *The Art of Fiction* (Harmondsworth: Penguin Books, 1992; 2011) writes disparagingly of the *genre* of the experimental novel as 'more fun to read about than read' (p. 108), as ultimately a game which sets an 'arbitrary, artificial obstacle between the language of prose and its normal [social] function' (p. 107), obstacles set for 'the writer's satisfaction of his own ingenuity' (p. 108), which 'resemble the very ordinary features of poetry' (p. 108) and in which 'constitute a deliberate transgression of the boundary that normally separates these two forms of discourse, and, astonishingly clever as they are, to be "marginal" to fiction' (p. 108). This marginality, used here by Lodge with the intention of disparaging 'experimental writing' as a blanket term for 'too clever' writing, elitist, self-reflective, a leftover of its 'heyday' in the 1920s and 1930s, a misguided appropriation of rudimentary laws of poetics, or socially moribund are precisely the terms of assumption I here counter.
82 Nathalie Sarraute, *L'Ère du soupçon* (Paris: Éditions de Minuit, 1956), p. 73. It is in the 1963 English translation that Maria Jolas chose to give to the word *'recherche'* the inferred synonym of 'experimental'; 'investigative' or 'analytical' would perhaps work closer the original, but as here demonstrated, these words appear somewhat linked. This collection of essays is heavily cited by the British writers of this study, notably Johnson, Heppenstall and Brooke-Rose. It can therefore be regarded as a consequential point of crossover.
83 Iser, *The Implied Reader*, p. xi.
84 Alain Robbe-Grillet, *Pour un nouveau roman* (Paris: Éditions de Minuit, 1963), p. 14.
85 Zulfikar Ghose, *The Contradictions* (London: Macmillan, 1966), pp. 109–10.
86 Georges Perec, *Entretiens et conférences I: 1965–1978*, eds. Dominique Bertelli and Mireille Ribière (Paris: Joseph K, 2003), p. 80.

87 Raymond Williams, 'Realism and the Contemporary Novel', *Universities and Left Review*, vol. 4, Summer 1958, pp. 22–5. p. 25.
88 Sartre, p. 303.
89 Perec, *Entretiens et conférences I*, p. 247.
90 Sartre, p. 301.
91 Sarraute's *L'Ère du soupçon* collection of essays, many of which appearing in Sartre and Simone de Beauvoir's *Les Temps modernes* can be regarded to a great degree as attempts to answer this question.
92 Émile Zola, *Le Roman expérimental* (Paris: G. Charpenter, 1880).
93 Sartre, p. 301.
94 Ibid., p. 303.
95 Jean-Michel Ganteau, 'L'Expérimental comme fidélité au spectre: *Quilt* de Nicholas Royle', *Miranda* 16: 2018, p. 7.
96 While clarity might be sought in France in terms of conceptualization, again, this is not to argue that the experimental novel of the post-war era is a simply French construct which the British writers, and those of other cultures somehow 'followed' – but rather a transnational interaction. As will be seen, not only were the forms of writing dubbed generic descriptor 'nouveau roman' traced by French figures to a British source (in Heppenstall), but foundational tenets of the more clearly technically structured works by the writers of the Oulipo pay precedent to that literature also (in Themerson).
97 This is particularly frustrating in Sartre's *Qu'est-ce que la littérature?*, where this conceptual splitting is essential to the fundaments of the text, and yet is not present, and more so, Philippe Sollers' *L'Écriture et l'expérience des limites*; the translator cannot quite decide whether Sollers is talking about experimenting with literary reduction, or experiencing it (in the English sense), and so freely flips between the two.
98 Colette Becker, 'Introduction', in Émile Zola, *Les Rougon-Macquart* (Paris: Bouquin, 2002), p. vii.
99 Zola, *Le Roman expérimental*, p. 26.
100 Becker, p. xxv.
101 Ibid.
102 Ibid., p. xii.
103 Ibid., p. xiii.
104 Ibid., p. xiv.
105 Butor, *Butor*, p. 258.
106 Brigid Brophy, *In Transit* (London: Penguin, 1969), p. 27.
107 Maurice Blanchot, *L'Espace littéraire* (Paris: Gallimard, 1955), p. 212.
108 Sarraute, p. 73.

109 Wilson Harris, 'Introduction', *The Guyana Quartet* (London: Faber, 1985), p. 7.
110 Raymond Williams, *The Long Revolution* (London: Penguin, 1961), p. 300.
111 Ibid., p. 301.
112 Sollers, *Logiques*, p. 228.
113 Philippe Sollers, 'Préface' in Maurice Roche, *Compact* (Paris: Éditions du Séuil, 1966), pp. 9–12. p. 10.
114 Vanessa Guignery, *Ceci n'est pas une fiction: les romans vraies de B.S. Johnson* (Paris: Presses Universitaires de la Sorbonne, 2009), p. 203.
115 André Breton, "Du Surréalisme en ses œuvres vives" (1953); *Manifestes du surréalisme* (Paris: Gallimard, 1995), pp. 163–73. p. 167.
116 Maurice Roche, *Compact* (Paris: Éditions du Séuil, 1966), p. 96.
117 Roche, *Compact*, p. 107.
118 Rick Altman, *Film/Genre* (London: British Film Institute, 1999), p. 85.
119 Eugene Thacker, 'The Sight of a Mangled Corpse, An Interview with Eugene Thacker', *Scapegoat Journal 05 'Excess'* September 2013, pp. 379–86. p. 385.
120 Alexandre Devaux in Roland Topor, *Théâtre Panique Tome 2* (Paris: Wombat, 2016), pp. 210–11.
121 Perec, *Entretiens et conférences I*, p. 85.
122 Ibid., pp. 87–8.
123 Ibid., pp. 86–7.
124 Rayner Heppenstall, *Imaginary Conversations* (London: Secker & Warburg, 1948), p. 8.
125 Jean Tortel in Noël Arnaud, Francis Lacassin, Jean Tortel, *La Paralittérature* (1967) (Paris: Hermann, 2012), pp. 74–5.
126 Counter to this opposition, as is demonstrated, that Robbe-Grillet's translator Richard Howard terms in English as the 'literary caste system' judging Robbe-Grillet's 'revolutionary new novel' (Alain Robbe-Grillet, *For a New Novel*, trans. Richard Howard (Evanston: Northwestern University Press, 1989), p. 17.). A collection of qualifiers prefixed I am uncomfortable with, but the described conservative reaction to his *revolution* appears familiar: 'by no means, should one have any illusions about the difficulties in attempting to renew this genre. They are considerable. The entirety of the established literary world (from the publishers to the most modest of reader, from the bookshop to critique) fights against unestablished forms that try to participate,' *Pour un nouveau roman*, p. 19. A struggle with 'literary life' Johnson, for example, fought head-on, as told by the back and forth of letters with the entire strata of what Robbe-Grillet's 'caste system' included in Coe, *Like a Fiery Elephant*, chiefly pp. 168–74.
127 Jameson, *The Modernist Papers*, p. xi.

128 For example: Kaye Mitchell, 'Post-War Fiction: Realism and Experimentalism', *The History of British Women's Writing, 1945-1975*, eds. C. Hanson and S. Watkins (London: Palgrave, 2017), pp. 19-36.
129 Johnson, *Aren't You Rather Young to be Writing Your Memoirs?*, p. 15.
130 B.S. Johnson in Jonathan Coe, *Like a Fiery Elephant: The Story of B.S. Johnson* (London: Picador, 2004), p. 366.
131 Cyril Connolly, *Enemies of Promise* (1938) (Chicago: The University of Chicago Press, 2008), p. 82.
132 Heppenstall, *Imaginary Conversations*, p. 8.
133 Stefan Themerson, *A Few Letters from the 1950s* (Wisconsin: Obscure Publications, 2009), p. 16.
134 Bertrand Russell quoted in Keith Waldrop, 'Introduction' in Stefan Themerson, *Bayamus* [1949] *and Cardinal Pölätüo* [1961] (Boston: Exact Change, 2004), pp. vii-x. p. viii.
135 Hélène Cixous, 'Langage et regard dans le roman expérimental: Grand-Bretagne', *Le Monde*, 6959. viia (18 May 1967), p. 16.
136 Raymond Queneau, 'La Littérature définitionnelle', *Oulipo: la littérature potentielle* (Paris: Gallimard, 1973), pp. 119-22. p. 119.
137 Andrew Murray Scott, *Alexander Trocchi: The Making of the Monster* (Edinburgh: Polygon, 1992), p. 108.
138 Scott, *Alexander Trocchi*, p. 108.
139 Rayner Heppenstall, *The Master Eccentric: The Journals of Rayner Heppenstall, 1969-81*, ed. Jonathan Goodman (London: Allison & Busby, 1986), p. 219.
140 Johnson in Coe, p. 151.
141 James Campbell, 'Alexander Trocchi: The Biggest Fiend of All', *The Antioch Review* vol. 50, No. 3, *Thinking: Books or Movies?* (Summer, 1992), pp. 458-71. p. 458.
142 John Calder, 'Obituary: Roland Topor', *The Independent*, 18 April 1997 http://www.independent.co.uk/news/people/obituary-roland-topor-1268000.html (accessed 3 May 2013).
143 To context, the same year of this staging, 1977, in cinema is the year of release of *Eraserhead*, *The Exorcist II: The Heretic* and *The Many Adventures of Winnie the Pooh*.
144 Henri Peyre, 'Trends in the contemporary French novel', *New French Writing*, ed. Georges Borchardt (New York: Grove Press, 1961), pp 73-87. p. 73.
145 Heppenstall, *The Fourfold Tradition*, p. 251.
146 Samuel Johnson in Cedric Watts, 'Introduction' in Laurence Sterne *The Life and Opinions of Tristram Shandy, Gentleman* (1759) (London: Wordsworth Editions, 2009), pp. v-xxi. p. xvi.

147 William Cooper, 'Reflections on some aspects of the Experimental Novel', *International Literary Review* no. 2, ed. John Wain (London: John Calder, 1959), pp. 29–36. p. 29.
148 Morton Levitt, *The Rhetoric of Modernist Fiction: From a New Point of View* (Lebanon NH: The University of New England Press, 2006), pp. 124–6.
149 A list predominantly made up of public school, Oxford old boys, this is perhaps some intimation of what 'social' they were 'realing' in the post-war. From their position of benefit from the preservational continuation of pre-war societal structures, however broken, it is difficult to see why they would 'rock the boat'.
150 James Jack Gindin, *Post War British Fiction: New Accents and Attitudes* (Berkeley: University of California Press, 1962), p. 257.
151 Mackay and Stonebridge, p. 5.
152 Brooker, p. 9.
153 Pierre Bourdieu, 'Sur le pouvoir symbolique', *Annales. Histoire, Sciences Sociales*, 32nd year, No. 3, May–June 1977, pp. 405–11. p. 407.
154 Ibid., p. 408.
155 B.S. Johnson in Alan Burns and B.S. Johnson, 'B. S. Johnson', *Imagination on Trial*, eds. Alan Burns and Charles Sugnet (London: Allison & Busby, 1981), pp. 83–94. p. 93.
156 Dan Billany, *The Trap* (1950) (London: Readers Union, Faber and Faber, 1952), p. 89.
157 Sigmund Freud, 'The Future of an Illusion' [*Die Zukunft einer Illusion*, 1927], *The Future of an Illusion* trans. J. A. Underwood and Shaun Whiteside (London: Penguin, 2008), pp. 1–72. p. 13.
158 Ibid., p. 12.
159 Ibid., p. 12.
160 Ibid., p. 12.
161 Dubuffet, *Asphyxiante culture*, pp. 15–16.
162 Ibid., p. 38.
163 Henry Green, 'Unloving', *The Times* (1961), in *Surviving: The Uncollected Writing of Henry Green*, pp. 280–3. p. 282.
164 David Bellos, *Georges Perec: A Life in Words* (London: Harvill Press, 1993), p. 284.
165 Cixous, p. 16.
166 Eva Figes, 'B.S. Johnson', *Review of Contemporary Fiction*, 5:2 (1985), pp. 70–1. p. 70.
167 Roland Barthes in Todorov and Genette, *La Littérature et la réalité*, p. 89.
168 Robbe-Grillet, p. 7.
169 Sartre, p. 293.
170 Ibid., p. 171.

171 Green, 'Unloving', p. 282.
172 Perec, *Entretiens et conférences I*, p. 78.
173 Michel Butor, 'Balzac et la réalité' (1959), *Répertoire I* (Paris: Éditions de Minuit, 1960), pp. 79–93. p. 79.
174 Sarraute, pp. 77–9.
175 Raymond Queneau, 'Préface', *Anthologie des jeunes auteurs* (Patis: Editions J.A.R.,1955), pp. 9–33. p. 32.
176 Arnaud in *La Paralittérature*, p. 394.
177 Sollers, *Logiques*, p. 50.
178 Nick Bentley, *Radical Fictions: The English Novel in the 1950s* (Bern: Peter Lang, 2007), p. 158.
179 Peyre, p. 73.
180 And appears to act as a faux cultural high-water mark, by which 'innovation' in Britain in the post-war period can easily be reduced to non-existent fugue. Beyond the experimental novel I here observe, there are further questions to be raised regarding obscured presences in Britain like the 'post-cubist' neo-romantic painters of the 1940s and 1950s; the neo- or post-surrealism movement 1967–79; The Liverpool Poets, British 'Pataphysics' and on – this 'dead' period of non-engagement in Britain appears actually, very much alive.
181 Even during the trial Vian did the saloning too, though it sounds now bizarrely archaic.
182 Noël Arnaud, *Dossier de l'affaire 'J'irai cracher sur vos tombes'* (Paris: Christian Bourgois, 1974), p. 107.
183 Ibid., pp. 10–11.
184 Ibid., back cover.
185 For example, throughout Louis-Ferdinand Céline, *D'un château l'autre* (Paris:Gallimard, 1957).
186 Céline has a stake in such a critique; to displace his own personal guilt onto a populace that has castigated him. However, as will be seen, the French communal refusal of the years 1940–4 in the period following docs prove problematic.
187 Topor, *Pense-bêtes*, p. 2.
188 Genaert in Topor, *Théâtre Panique Tome 1*, p. xii.
189 Ibid. p. xii.
190 Josef Joffe, 'America's Secret Weapon' http://www.nytimes.com/books/00/04/23/reviews/000423.23joffet.html (accessed 16 April 2014).
191 The Louis Malle film version of Queneau's *Zazie dans le Métro* (1960), Michel Gondry's film based on Vian's *L'Écume des jours* (2013), the romantic de-aestheticizing process perhaps best demonstrated by the employment of many 'experimental' literary tropes in *Le Fabuleux destin d'Amélie Poulain* (2001).

192 Christine Brooke-Rose, *A Rhetoric of the Unreal* (Cambridge: Cambridge University Press, 1981), p. 311.
193 Sollers, *Logiques*, p. 50-1.
194 Ibid.
195 Gisèle Sapiro, *La Guerre des écrivains* (Paris: Fayard, 1999), p. 697.
196 Mark Fisher, *The Weird and the Eerie* (London: Repeater, 2016), p. 48.
197 Ibid.
198 Michel Butor, 'Le Roman comme recherche' (1955), *Essais sur le roman* (Paris: Gallimard, 1969), pp. 7-14. p. 14.
199 Fisher, p. 87.
200 Charles Sugnet, 'Introduction', *Imagination on Trial* (London: Allison & Busby, 1981), pp. 2-13. p. 4.
201 Anaïk Hechiche, *La Violence dans les romans de Boris Vian* (Paris: Éditions Publisud, 1986), p. 7.
202 Christopher Nash, *World Postmodern Fiction: A Guide* (London: Longman Publishing, 1993), p. 49.
203 Ibid., p. 49.
204 Johnson, for example, refers to James Joyce's *Ulysses* (1922) as 'the starting point', which implies not only the potential for new birth, but also a discontinuity, a death in *Aren't You Rather Young to be Writing Your Memoirs?* (1973), in *Well Done God! Selected Prose and Drama of B.S. Johnson*, eds. Philip Tew, Julia Jordan, Jonathan Coe (London: Picador, 2013), pp. 1-140. p. 13.
205 Henry Green and Terry Southern, 'Paris Review Interview', *Surviving: The Uncollected Writing of Henry Green*, ed. Matthew Yorke (London: Chatto & Windus, 1992), pp. 234-50. pp. 247-8.
206 Badiou, p. 1878.
207 Harvey, p. 13.
208 Sartre, p. 201.
209 E.L.T. Mesens and Roland Penrose, *Declaration of the Surrealist Group in England* (1947), *On the Thirteenth Stroke of Midnight: Surrealist poetry in Britain*, ed. Michel Remy (London: Carcanet Press, 2013), pp. 38-40.
210 'Meagre' is the word opted for by translator Bernard Frechtman in 1950, but in direct translation: 'a pretty candy so quickly sucked', Sartre, p. 298.
211 Sartre, p. 201.
212 Marc Alyn, *Marcel Béalu, ou le fantastique est une réalité* (Rodez: Éditions Subervie, 1956), p. 7.
213 Victor Gollancz, *Our Threatened Values* (London: Gollancz, 1946), p. 14.
214 Sartre, p. 231.
215 Pierre de Boisdeffre, *Où va le roman?* (Paris: C. Del Duca, 1972), p. 76.

216 James Knowlson, *Damned to Fame: The Life of Samuel Beckett* (London: Bloomsbury, 1996), p. 353.
217 Mackay and Stonebridge, p. 2. Also, Sapiro, p. 40.
218 Lyndsey Stonebridge, *The Writing of Anxiety: Imagining Wartime in Mid-Century British Culture* (London: Palgrave, 2007), p. 1.
219 James Joll, *Europe Since 1870: An International History* (London: Penguin, 1990), p. 422.
220 Hechiche, p. 8.
221 Gollancz, p. 16.
222 Joll, p. 422.
223 Ibid., p. 432.
224 Ibid., p. 431.
225 Gollancz, p. 103.
226 Ibid., p. 15.
227 Max Horkheimer, *Eclipse of Reason* (1947) (London: Continuum Press, 2004), p. vii.
228 We will probably agree that putting a halt to Nazi marshal law and the Holocaust are utterly agreeable aims for violent action, and yet if this action had failed, the common comprehension of justness might be assigned to a different scale entirely.
229 Themerson, *Bayamus*, pp. 74–5.
230 Fisher, p. 22.
231 Gollancz, p. 7.
232 Sartre, *Qu'est-ce que la littérature ?*, p. 213.
233 Ibid., pp. 213–14.
234 Brigid Brophy, *Black Ship to Hell* (London: Secker & Warburg, 1962), p. 41.
235 Anna Kavan, *Ice* (1967) (London: Peter Owen, 2006), p. 122.
236 Brophy, *Black Ship to Hell*, p. 13.
237 Sollers, 'Préface', p. 10.
238 Barry Eichengreen, 'Mainsprings of Economic Recovery in Post-War Europe', *Europe's Post-War Recovery*, ed. Barry Eichengreen (Cambridge: Cambridge University Press, 1995), pp. 3–35. p. 'Avant Propos'.
239 Mackay and Stonebridge, p. 2.
240 Kristin Ross, *Fast Cars, Clean Bodies: Decolonisation and the Reordering of French Culture* (Cambridge: MIT Press, 1996), p. 4.
241 Perec, *Entretiens et conférences I*, p. 125.
242 Mackay and Stonebridge, p. 2.
243 Amongst other discussions, notably in 1940: Dominic Tierney, 'When Britain and France Almost Merged into One Country', *The Atlantic*, 8 August 2017, https://www.theatlantic.com/international/archive/2017/08/dunkirk-

brexit/536106/ (accessed 21 January 2018). And again in 1956: Mike Thomson, 'When Britain and France Nearly Married', *BBC Online*, 15 January 2007, http://news.bbc.co.uk/2/hi/6261885.stm (accessed 21 January 2018).
244 Mackay and Stonebridge, p. 3.
245 Ibid.
246 Stated in his talk 'The British Experimental Novelists of the 1960s: A Forgotten Avant-Garde', given for 'Ragged University' in April, 2015, https://www.youtube.com/watch?v=YPrwtO813eg (accessed 15 September 2015).
247 Benjamin Noys, *The Persistence of the Negative: A critique of contemporary continental philosophy* (Edinburgh: Edinburgh University Press, 2012), p. 70.
248 Perec, *Entretiens et conférences I*, p. 109.
249 Ibid., p. 82.
250 B. S. Johnson, *You're Human Like the Rest of Them* in *Well Done God! Selected Prose and Drama of B. S. Johnson*, p. 153.
251 Philippe Sollers, *L'Écriture et l'éxpérience des limites* (Paris: Éditions du Séuil, 1968), p. 109.
252 Brophy, *Black Ship to Hell*, p 86.
253 Jean Dubuffet, 'Désaimantation des Cervelles', *L'Homme du commun à l'ouvrage* (Paris: Gallimard, 1973), pp. 321–98. p. 389.
254 Paul Virilio, in Perec, *Entretiens et conférences I*, p. 126.
255 Fisher, p. 101.
256 This framing is common. To refer again to that used in Joseph Darlington's talk, or perhaps most shoehorned, in Jeremy Reed's biography of Anna Kavan, in which Reed positions a hermit, ill, heroin addict, elderly-before-her-years Kavan as a part of the '68 movement' despite her death that year: 'London exploded into cool. Youth had gone chemical. No matter how indistinctly the revolution filtered through to Anna, in her overheated apartment with its Burmese gong acting as a coffee-table and her mother's gilded lamp, she was living in a city that was the epicentre of cataclysmic social unrest': Jeremy Reed, *A Stranger on Earth: The Life and Work of Anna Kavan* (London: Peter Owen, 2006), pp. 137–8.
257 Kavan, p. 117.
258 Horkheimer, p. vii.
259 Stefan Themerson, *Special Branch* (London: Gaberbocchus, 1972) p. 9.
260 Sigmund Freud, 'Mourning and Melancholy' [*Trauer und Melancholie*, 1917], *The Future of an Illusion*, trans. J.A. Underwood and Shaun Whiteside (London: Penguin, 2008), pp. 73–112. p. 87.
261 Benjamin Noys, *The Culture of Death* (Oxford: Berg, 2005), pp. 3, 12.
262 Jameson, *The Political Unconscious: Narrative as a Socially Symbolic Act*, p. 287.

263 Alyn, p. 20.
264 Ibid., p. 21.
265 Fisher, p. 97.
266 Jameson, *The Political Unconscious: Narrative as a Socially Symbolic Act*, p. 287.
267 Tacitus, *Agricola* trans. H. Mattingly (London: Penguin, 1954), p. 21.
268 Kavan, p. 153.
269 Brooke-Rose, *A Rhetoric of the Unreal*, p. 10.
270 Ibid., p. 10.
271 Brophy, *Black Ship to Hell*, p. 451.
272 Ibid.
273 Ghose, p. 111.
274 Bruno Latour, *Nous n'avons jamais été modernes; essai d'anthropologie symétrique* (Paris: Éditions la Découverte, 1991), p. 6.
275 Perec, *Entrétiens et conferences I*, p. 124.
276 Mackay and Stonebridge, p. 2.
277 Jean Duvignaud in Perec, *Entrétiens et conferences I*, p. 128.
278 Ibid., p. 126.
279 Perec, *Entrétiens et conferences I*, p. 127.
280 Paul Virilio in Perec, *Entrétiens et conferences I*, p. 128.
281 Raymond Queneau, *Une Histoire modèle* (Paris: Gallimard, 1966), p. 10.
282 Michel Foucault, *Histoire de la folie* (Paris: Gallimard, 1962), p. 11.
283 Pol Bury, *Cinétisations* (Brussels: Daily Bul, 1960), p. 1.
284 Salim Jay, *Merci, Roland Topor* (Paris: Fayard, 2014), p. 67.
285 Gilles Deleuze and Félix Guatarri, *Kafka, pour une littérature mineure* (Paris: Les Éditions de Minuit, 1975), p. 52.
286 Gilles Deleuze and Félix Guatarri, *L'Anti-Œdipe* (Paris: Les Éditions de Minuit, 1972), p. 165.
287 Walter Benjamin, 'Critique of violence' [*Zur Kritik der Gewalt*, 1921], *One Way Street and Other Writings*, trans. J.A. Underwood (London: Verso, 1979), pp. 277–300. p. 286.

Partition Two

1 To be grossly poetic a moment: as viewing the skies some stars shine brighter than others, too this study is peopled by both dilated textual observation and quieter textual imposition, as, through research, these texts made themselves apparent.

2   Including his stories *The Wall* in *Modern Choice 1* (1965) and *The Girl on the Bus* in *Modern Choice 2* (1966), curated collections of 'modern' short stories within which only Sansom is a returning figure.
3   William Sansom, 'Fireman Flower', *Fireman Flower and Other Stories* (1944) (London: Hogarth Press, 1966), pp. 123–63. p. 132.
4   Georges Perec, 'Robert Antelme, ou la verité de la littérature' (1962), *L.G.: une aventure des années soixante* (Paris: Éditions Seuil, 1992), pp. 87–114. p. 93.
5   Ibid., p. 91.
6   Butor, 'Le Roman comme recherche', p. 10.
7   Theodor Adorno, 'Cultural Criticism and Society' (*Kulturkritik und Gesellschaft*, 1949), *Prisms*, trans. Samuel and Sherry Weber (Cambridge: The MIT Press, 1983), pp. 17–35. p. 34.
8   *Viz*. Gollancz.
9   'France did not participate in the Holocaust', British violent action, i.e. Dresden, was blanket 'necessitated'; the horrors were caused and acted out by a primordial inhuman '*Nazi*' entity that was arbitrarily discontinued in 1945.
10 John Lyle et al., 'Lot 175' seen on Chiswick Auctions website https://chiswickauctions.co.uk/lot/160720-lot-175/ (accessed 17 July 2016) – the only publicly accessible documentation of the 1967 Exeter Festival of Modern Arts.
11 Perec, 'Robert Antelme, ou la verité de la littérature', p. 95.
12 Raymond Queneau, *Bâtons, chiffres et lettres* (1950) (Paris: Gallimard, 1965), pp. 178–9.
13 Fisher, p. 86.
14 Sartre, p. 302.
15 Slavoj Žižek, *Violence* (New York: Picador, 2008), p. 4.
16 Themerson, *Bayamus*, p. 21.
17 Ibid., p. 25.
18 Adorno here appears to amend something he is popularly believed to have said, as repeated by Žižek below, viz. 'impossible'. However, as translated above, the sentence written speaks rather of 'barbarism', rather than 'impossibility'.
19 Theodor Adorno, *Negative Dialectics* [*Negative Dialektik*, 1966], trans. E.B. Ashton (London: Routledge and Kegan, 1973), p. 362.
20 Žižek, p. 5.
21 Robert Pinget, *Passacaille* (Paris: Les Éditions de Minuit, 1969).
22 Žižek, p. 5.
23 Edmond Jabès, *Le Livre des questions* (1963) (Paris: Gallimard, 1988), p. 18.
24 Ibid., p. 17.

25 Octavio Paz, *The Labyrinth of Solitude* (1961) [*El laberinto de la soledad*, 1950], trans. Lysander Kemp, Yara Milos and Rachel Phillips Belash (New York: Grove Press, 1985), p. 52.
26 Edmond Jabès, *L'Enfer de Dante* (Paris: Fata Morgana, 1991), p. 14.
27 A Freudian nod more fully developed in partition three.
28 Alan Burns, *Europe after the Rain* (1965) (New York: The John Day Company, 1970).
29 'I met the commander walking along, I never showed my face, he did not know I had passed. I noted the shape of the commander's thin fingers, felt the texture of his palm. His palm smelled of sweet gas. I knew the time for his death': Burns, *Europe after the Rain*, p. 65.
30 Alan Burns, in David W. Madden, 'Alan Burns: An Introduction', *The Review of Contemporary Fiction* 17:02 Summer 1997 *Wilson Harris/Alan Burns* (Champagne: Dalkey Archive Press, 1997), pp. 108–21. p. 111.
31 Burns, *Europe after the Rain*, p. 35.
32 Burns and Madden, 'Alan Burns: An Introduction', p. 111.
33 Alan Burns, Charles Sugnet and Alan Burns, 'Alan Burns', *Imagination on Trial*, eds. Alan Burns and Charles Sugnet (London: Allison & Busby, 1981), pp. 161–8. p. 166.
34 Žižek, p. 4.
35 R.D. Laing and D.G. Cooper, *Reason & Violence: A Decade of Sartre's Philosophy* (London: Tavistick, 1964), p. 40.
36 Themerson, *Bayamus*, pp. 74–5.
37 Peter Krapp, *Déjà Vu: Aberrations of Cultural Memory* (Minneapolis: University of Minnesota Press, 2004), p. 4.
38 Alan Burns, in David W. Madden and Alan Burns, 'In Conversation with Alan Burns', *The Review of Contemporary Fiction* 17:02 Summer 1997 *Wilson Harris/ Alan Burns* (Champagne: Dalkey Archive Press, 1997), http://www.dalkeyarchive. com/a-conversation-with-alan-burns-by-david-w-madden/ (accessed 15 April 2014).
39 Jean Tardieu, 'Dix variations sur une ligne', *Le Professeur Froeppel* (1951) (Paris: Gallimard, 2003), pp. 179–88. p. 188.
40 B.S. Johnson, *Trawl* (1966), in *Omnibus: Albert Angelo, House Mother Normal, Trawl* (London: Picador, 2004), p. 17.
41 Carol Watts, '"The Mind Has Fuses": Detonating B.S. Johnson', *Re-Reading B.S. Johnson* (London: Palgrave, 2007), pp. 80–93. p. 80.
42 Guignery, p. 168.
43 Watts, p. 80.
44 Eva Figes, *B* (London: Faber, 1972), p. 107.
45 Fisher, p. 123.

46 Georges Perec, *Je me souviens* (Paris: Hachette, 1978), p. 119.
47 Perec, *W ou le souvenir d'enfance* (1975), pp. 97–8.
48 Georges Perec, Franck Venaille and Georges Perec, 'Le Travail de la mémoire' (*Perec, le contraire de l'oubli*, 1979), *En dialogue avec l'époque 1965–1981*, eds. Dominique Bertelli and Mireille Ribiére (Paris: Joseph K., 2011), pp. 96–104. p. 98.
49 Perec, *W, ou le souvenir d'enfance*, p. 98.
50 Robert Pinget, *Cette voix* (Paris: Éditions de Minuit, 1975), p. 214.
51 Maurice Roche, *Codex* (Paris: Seuil, 1974), p. 8.
52 Johnson, Alan Burns and B. S. Johnson, 'B.S. Johnson', p. 85.
53 Teresa Bridgeman, *Negotiating the New in the French Novel: Building Contexts for Fictional Worlds* (London: Routledge, 2005), p. 182.
54 Which Butor writes, a novel *always essentially* is: 'the novel is a particular form of *récit*', Butor, 'Le Roman comme recherche', p. 7.
55 Marcel Béalu, *Journal d'un mort* (1947) (Paris: Éditions Phébus, 1978), pp. 47–8.
56 Hugh Sykes Davies, *The Papers of Andrew Melmoth* (London: Methuen & Co., 1960), p. 166.
57 Henry Green, *Back* (1946) (London: The Harvill Press, 1998), p. 31.
58 Ibid. p. 51.
59 Rayner Heppenstall, *The Lesser Infortune* (London: Jonathan Cape, 1953), p. 262.
60 Jacques Yonnet, *Rue des maléfices* (1954) (Paris: Libretto, 1995), p. 181.
61 Ibid., p. 182.
62 Fisher, p. 97. This brings to mind the, now sensorially 'weird' when viewing repeats, uncommented on bombsites that make up the environments of popular TV shows like *Steptoe and Son* (1962–74) and even the later *Only Fools and Horses* (1981–96).
63 Fisher, p. 22.
64 Yonnet, *Rue des maléfices*, p. 183.
65 Jacques Derrida, 'Force de loi: le "fondement mystique de l'autorité"', pp. 990 and 992.
66 China Miéville (ed.), 'Editorial Introduction', *Historical Materialism* vol. 10, Issue 4 2002, p. 39–49. p. 42.
67 Yonnet, Rue des maléfices, p. 181.
68 Jacques Yonnet, *Le Cabaret des inconnus* (Paris: Lectures de France, 1945)
69 Frantz Vaillant, *Roland Topor ou le rire étranglé* (Paris: Buchet/Chastel, 2007), p. 41.
70 Topor in Jay, p. 20.
71 Vaillant, p. 32.
72 The chemical scrubbing of memory; the maxim glorification of past event of which the bodies still lie rotting in the fields.

73 Brian McHale and Randall Stevenson, *The Edinburgh Companion to Twentieth Century Literatures in English* (Edinburgh: Edinburgh University Press, 2006), p. 11.
74 Rayner Heppenstall, 'Introduction', in Guido de Ruggiero, *Existentialism: Disintegration of Man's Soul* trans. E.M. Cocks (London: Secker and Warburg, 1948), pp. 9–19. p. 18.
75 Robert Pinget, *Entre Fantoine et Agapa* (1951) (Paris: Les Éditions de Minuit, 1966), pp. 82–3.
76 Fisher, p. 74.
77 Marcel Béalu, Marcel Béalu and Marie-France Azar, 'Un Messager clandestin', *Le Regard oblique: entretiens avec Marie-France Azar* (Paris: J.M. Place, 1993), pp. 9–30. p. 17.
78 I here view humanity in terms of the faculty to experience, process and communicate, which stands at odds with what comes to be discussed as the ability to integrate with and adapt to environment and community.
79 As appears in a reading of Perec's *Je me souviens*.
80 Complained about in Perec's *Je me souviens*, and Heppenstall's *The Connecting Door*.
81 Philip Toynbee, 'Fiction Review', *Horizon* Jan 1947, pp. 73–82, pp. 74–5.
82 Ibid.
83 Rayner Heppenstall, *The Connecting Door* (London: Barrie and Rockliff, 1962), p. 67.
84 François Jost, 'Fragmented Representation', *Robbe-Grillet and the Fantastic: A Collection of Essays*, eds. Tony Chadwick and Virginia Harger-Grinling (Westport: Greenwood, 1994), pp. 125–38. p. 125.
85 John Ruskin, 'Modern Painters, I' (1846), *Selected Writing* (Oxford: Oxford World Classics, 2004), pp. 3–12. p. 3.
86 Ghose, p. 111.
87 Jacques Yonnet, 'Univers virgule cinq', *Bizarre II* October 1955, eds. Michel Laclos and Jean-Jacques Pauvert, pp. 26–36. p. 26.
88 Clement Rosset, p. 64.
89 Watts, p. 89.
90 Fisher, p. 122.
91 Yonnet, *Rue des maléfices*, p. 182.
92 Dubuffet, *Asphyxiante culture*, p. 15.
93 Nicholas Tredell, *Fighting Fictions: The novels of B. S. Johnson* (London: Paupers Press, 2010), p. 100.
94 B.S. Johnson, *House Mother Normal* (1971) (London: Picador, 2001), p. 7.
95 Gareth J. Buckell, *Rayner Heppenstall: A Critical Study* (Champagne: Dalkey Archive Press, 2007), p. 73.

96 Heppenstall, *The Connecting Door*, p. 118.
97 Ibid., p. 121.
98 Ibid., p. 150.
99 Kate Connolly, 'A Foucauldian Analysis of Disciplinary Power, Disease and Body Decay in *House Mother Normal*', *BSJ: The B.S. Johnson Journal*, Issue 1, Summer 2014, eds. Joseph Darlington, Hooper, Seddon, Tew, Zouaoui, pp. 47–68. p. 58.
100 Foucault, *Maladie mentale et psychologie* (Paris: PUF, 1954), p. 71.
101 Johnson, *House Mother Normal*, p. 17.
102 Ibid., p. 18.
103 Ibid., p. 17.
104 Ibid., p. 24.
105 Ibid., p. 22.
106 Watts, p. 70.
107 I here both agree and disagree with Georges Perec, who writes of the concentration camps 'we think we know the camps [...] because we think we know the numbers of dead. But statistics cannot speak. Thousands death, or hundreds of thousands, it makes no difference to us.': Perec, 'Robert Antelme, ou la verité de la littérature', p. 92. While facile reduction to statistics does represent a 'safe' mode of comprehension and discourse that distances, and removes the potency of the event, while for the First World War in that period these statistical quantifications were easily reconciled to a posteriori event comprehension, the statistics of the Second, as indicated in Perec's example, remain unknown; guessed and thus a traumatically incomplete reduction.
108 Heppenstall, *The Connecting Door*, p. 66.
109 Ibid.
110 Johnson, *House Mother Normal*, p. 82.
111 Catherine Belsey, 'English Studies in the Postmodern Condition: Towards a Place for the Signifier', *Post-Theory: New Directions in Criticism*, eds. Martin McQuillan, Graeme Macdonald, Robin Purves, Steven Thomson (Edinburgh: Edinburgh University Press, 1999), pp. 123–38. p. 134.
112 Coe, p. 24–5.
113 Connolly, p. 53.
114 Themerson, *Bayamus*, p. 55.
115 Ibid., p. 54.
116 Gérard Genette, *Figure II* (Paris: Seuil, 1988), p. 94.
117 Ibid.
118 See Jacques Derrida, *Glas* (Paris: Éditions Galilée, 1974), or Jacques Derrida, *Marges de la philosophie* (Paris: Éditions de Minuit, 1972).
119 See Rayner Heppenstall, *Two Moons* (London: Allison & Busby, 1977).

120 B.S. Johnson, *Albert Angelo* (1964) (London: Panther, 1967), pp. 64–97.
121 Roche, *Codex*, pp. 131–8.
122 Alan Burns, *Babel* (London: Calder & Boyars, 1969), pp. 150–2.
123 Ann Quin, *Passages* (London: Calder & Boyars, 1969), pp. 28–60, 84–112.
124 This implies the *pathway* taken is still ostensibly linear as a causal chain is very much active, however it has embraced a complexity and confusion beyond that what is laid out on the page. This brief conjecture will find grounding in partitions two and three.
125 Elements of 'reception theory' will prove interesting as both contrastive and grounding critical positions throughout the discussions of this study.
126 Terry Eagleton, *Literary Theory: An Introduction, 2nd Edition* (Oxford: Blackwell Publishing, 1996), p. 67.
127 Wolfgang Iser, *The Act of Reading: A Theory of Aesthetic Response* [Der Akt des Lesens. Theorie ästhetischer Wirkung, 1976] (Baltimore: John Hopkins University Press, 1978), p. 27.
128 Eagleton, p. 66.
129 Iser, *The Act of Reading*, p. 27.
130 Ibid., p. 28.
131 Be that friend, spouse, state censor, agent, editor, publisher, previous reader via marginalia, deletion or addition, or any number of social intrusions upon the framed 'text work' of both the writerly and readerly commitment.
132 Roche, *Codex*, p. 8.
133 Sollers, 'Préface', p. 11.
134 Eagleton, p. 68.
135 Wolfgang Iser, *The Implied Reader*, pp. 281–2.
136 Ibid.
137 Anthony Cheal Pugh (ed.), 'Introduction', in Robert Pinget, *Autour de mortin* (London: Methuen, 1971), pp. vii–xlii. p. xi.
138 Fisher, p. 83.
139 Bernard Stiegler, *De la misère symbolique* (Paris: Champs Essais, 2013), p.21.
140 Roland Topor, *Le Locataire chimérique* (1964), (Paris: Libretto, 2011), p. 96.
141 Freud, 'The Future of an Illusion', p. 3.
142 John Calder, 'Obituary: Roland Topor', *The Independent* 18 April 1997, http://www.independent.co.uk/news/people/obituary-roland-topor-1268000.html (accessed 3 May 1993).
143 Topor, *Le Locataire chimérique*, p. 167.
144 B.S. Johnson, *Christie Malry's Own Double-Entry* (1973) (New York: New Directions Publishing, 2009), p. 52.
145 Ibid.

146 Jonathan Raban, 'On Losing the Rabbit', *Encounter* May 1973, pp. 80–5. p. 82.
147 Sylvia Plath, 'The Shrike' (1956), *Collected Poems* (London: Faber & Faber, 2015), p. 26.
148 Christie's girlfriend then assumedly has a long, pointed nose.
149 Laing and Cooper, p. 175.
150 Deleuze and Guattari, *Kafka, pour une littérature mineure*, p. 57.
151 Patricia A. Struebig, *La Structure mythique de La Modification de Michel Butor* (Paris: Peter Lang, 1994), p. 75.
152 Michel Butor, *La Modification* (1957) (Paris: Club de la Femme, 1970), p. 181.
153 Butor, *La Modification*, p. 181.
154 In the implication that they are not written by any*one*, this information is forgotten, but exist as some mystical bubbling up of experiential ink on paper.
155 Butor, *La Modification*, pp. 181–2.
156 Greg Buchanan, 'Like loose leaves in the wind': Effacement and Characterisation in B.S. Johnson's *The Unfortunates* and Marc Saporta's *Composition no. 1*", *B.S. Johnson and the Postwar: Possibilities of the Avant-Garde*, eds. Martin Ryle and Julia Jordan (London: Palgrave Macmillan, 2014), pp. 54–70. p. 55.
157 Buchanan, p. 55.
158 Doesn't this, then, appear somewhat mimetic of dynamics discussed throughout this study?
159 Raban, p. 83.
160 Topor, *Le Locataire chimérique*, p. 98.
161 Marcel Béalu, *L'Expérience de la nuit* (Paris: Gallimard, 1945), p. 51.
162 Buchanan, p. 55.
163 Randall Stevenson, *The British Novel Since the Thirties: An Introduction* (London: B.T. Batsford Ltd: 1986), p. 212.
164 Christine Brooke-Rose, *Such* (1966), *The Christine Brooke-Rose Omnibus* (Manchester: Carcanet Press, 2006), pp. 199–390. p. 390.
165 Stevenson, p. 212.
166 Topor, *Le Locataire chimérique*, p. 78.
167 Ibid., p. 46.
168 Ibid., p. 95.
169 Roland Topor, *Joko fête son anniversaire* (Paris: Buchet/Chastel, 1969), pp. 16–17.
170 Ibid., p. 93.
171 Leonora Carrington, *The Hearing Trumpet* (1974) (London: Penguin, 2005), p. 44.
172 Ibid.
173 Ibid.
174 Raymond Queneau, *Le Vol d'Icare* (1968) (Paris: Folio, 2014)

175 Claude Debon, 'Récriture et identité dans le Vol d'Icare', *Doukipledonktan: etudes sur Raymond Queneau* (Paris: Presses de la Sorbonne Nouvelle, 1998), pp. 111–20. p. 112.
176 Dan Billany, *The Cage* (London: Longmans, Green & Co, 1949), p. 144.
177 Ibid., pp. 146–7.
178 Otto Gross, 'On the Problem of Insanity' [*Beitrag zum Problem des Wahnes*, 1920], *Otto Gross: Selected Works 1901–1920*, trans. Lois L. Madison (New York: Mindpiece Publishing, 2012), pp. 301–14. p. 312.
179 Valerie A. Reeves and Valerie Showan, *Dan Billany: Hull's Lost Hero* (Hull: Kingston Press, 1999), p. 84.
180 Ibid., p. 141.
181 Roland Jaccard, *L'Exil interieur : schzoïdie et civilisation* (1975) (Paris: Éditions de Seuil, 1978), pp. 135–136.
182 Dan Billany, *On George Bernard Shaw*, archival docs. 'A' and 'B', seen at the courtesy of Jodi Weston-Brake.
183 Otto Gross, 'Affective Capacity for Rejection' [*Die Affektlage der Ablehnung*, 1902], *Otto Gross: Selected Works 1901–1920*, trans. Lois L. Madison (New York: Mindpiece Publishing, 2012), pp. 23–34. p. 23.
184 Ibid.
185 Ibid.
186 Ibid.
187 Fisher, p. 84.
188 Burns, *Europe after the Rain*, p. 34.
189 Claude Simon, *La Route des Flandres* (Paris: Éditions des Minuit, 1960), p. 7.
190 Roland Topor, 'Petit mémento panique' (1965), *Panique: manifeste pour le troisième millénaire*, ed. Fernando Arrabal (Paris: Punctum Éditions, 2006), pp. 73–9. p. 74.
191 Freud, 'Mourning and Melancholy', p. 3.
192 Heppenstall, *The Connecting Door*, p. 121.
193 Roland Topor, *Erika* (Paris: Christian Bourgeois, 1969), p. 8.
194 Ibid.
195 B.S. Johnson in Coe, p. 185.
196 Hans Bellmer, *Petite anatomie de l'image* (*Petite anatomie de l'inconscient physique*, 1957) (Paris: Éditions Allia, 2012), p. 23.
197 Carrington, p. ix.
198 Gross, 'On the Problem of Insanity', p. 312.
199 Burns, *Europe after the Rain*, p. 87. Consider the use of holocaust victims' hair as pillow-stuffing, their bodies boiled down for soap, indeed their mouths searched and teeth pulled, for gold amongst other materials.
200 Topor, *Le Locataire chimérique*, p. 59.

201 Stefan Themerson, *Professor Mmaa's Lecture* (1953) (Woodstock: The Overlook Press, 1984), pp. 81–2.
202 Béalu, *Journal d'un mort*, pp. 151–2.
203 Quin, *Passages*, p. 111.
204 Béalu, *Journal d'un mort*, p. 152.
205 Burns, *Europe after the Rain*, p. 11.
206 Georges Perec, *Quel petit vélo à guidon chrome au fond de la cour?* (1966) (Paris: Folio Plus, 2011), p. 11.
207 Anne Clancier, *Raymond Queneau et la psychanalyse* (Paris: Éditions du Lion, 1994), p. 26.
208 Topor, *La Locataire Chimérique*, p. 92.
209 Ann Quin, *Tripticks* (1972), (Chicago: Dalkey Archive Press, 2002), p. 64.
210 Hélène Tuzet, 'Les Voies ouvertes par Gaston Bachelard a la critique littéraire', *Les Chemins actuels de la critique* (Paris: UGE, 1968), pp. 201–13. p. 208.
211 Quin, *Tripticks*, p. 17–18.
212 Boris Vian, 'Sartre et le merde', *Œuvres de Boris Vian* tome 4 (Poitiers: Éditions Fayard, 2000), pp. 237–9.
213 Billany, *The Trap*, p. 13.
214 Ibid.
215 An assault on the body, a loss of dignity, an assault on the self.
216 B.S. Johnson, *House Mother Normal*, p. 176.
217 Ibid., p. 67.
218 Jay, p. 95.
219 Jonathan Burt, *Rat* (London: Reaktion Books Ltd, 2006), p. 77.
220 Ibid., pp. 75–6.
221 Davies, p. 83.
222 Ibid.
223 Derrida, 'Force de loi: le "fondement mystique de l'autorité"', pp. 1008, 1010, 1012.
224 Ibid., p. 1010.
225 Billany, *The Cage*, p. 2.

Partition Three

1 Helen Palmer, *Deleuze and Futurism: A Manifesto for Nonsense* (London: Bloomsbury, 2014), p. 2.
2 Anne Lawton (ed.), *Russian Futurism Through its Manifestos: 1912–1928* (Ithaca: Cornell University Press, 1988), p. 68. (insertion of '[referential]': Craig Dworkin, 'To Destroy Language', *Textual Practice* 18 (2) 2004, pp. 185–97. p. 187.)

3   Dworkin, 'To Destroy Language', p. 187.
4   Ludwig Wittgenstein, *Philosophical Investigation* [*Philosophische Untersuchungen*, 1953], trans. G.E.M. Anscombe (Oxford: Basil Blackwell, 1986), p. 44.
5   Dworkin, 'To Destroy Language', p. 185.
6   Patricia Waugh, *Metafiction: The Theory and Practice of Self-Conscious Fiction* (London: Methuen, 1984), p. 63.
7   Louis-Ferdinand Céline, *Conversations with Professor Y* (*Entretiens avec le professeur Y*, 1955) (Champagne: Dalkey Archive Press, 1986), p. 4.
8   Topor, *Erika*, p. 8.
9   Wittgenstein, p. 48.
10 This is also discussed more broadly in Guignery.
11 Sebastian Jenner, 'B. S. Johnson and the Aleatoric Novel', *B.S. Johnson and the Postwar: Possibilities of the Avant-Garde*, eds. Martin Ryle and Julia Jordan (London: Palgrave Macmillan, 2014), pp. 71–86. p. 72.
12 Samuel Beckett, '9 July 1937, Kaun', *The Letters of Samuel Beckett Volume 1: 1929–1940*, eds. Martha Dow Fehsenfeld and Lois More Overbeck (Cambridge: Cambridge University Press, 2009), pp. 512–21. p. 518.
13 Fabian principles themselves appear locked within that which they attempt to alter.
14 Topor, *Erika*, p. 10.
15 Ibid., p. 11.
16 Ferdinand de Saussure, *Cours de linguistique générale* (1916), eds. Charles Bally and Albert Sechehaye (Paris: Éditions Pabot & Rivages, 1995), p. 53.
17 Ibid., p. 51–2.
18 Wittgenstein, p 82.
19 Georges Charbonnier, Georges Charbonnier and Raymond Queneau, *Entretiens avec Georges Charbonnier* (Paris: Gallimard, 1962), p. 13.
20 Topor, *Erika*, p. 8.
21 Aram Saroyan, *Untitled* (New York: Kulcher Press, 1968).
22 Topor, *Erika*, p. 8.
23 Espen J. Aarseth, *Cybertext: Perspectives on Ergodic Literature* (Baltimore: John Hopkins University Press, 1997), pp. 1–2.
24 Indeed, a concept itself invented in its contemporary form by Perec with his, *L'Art et la manière d'aborder son chef de service pour lui demander une augmentation* (1968).
25 B.S. Johnson, 'First', *The Unfortunates* (1969) (New York: New Directions Publishing, 2008), p. 1.
26 Wittgenstein, p. 188.
27 John Cage, 'Composition in Process', *Silence: Lectures and Writings* (1961) (Middletown: Wesleyan University Press, 1973), pp. 18–56. p. 51.

28 John Cage, 'Experimental Music', *Silence: Lectures and Writings* (1961) (Middletown: Wesleyan University Press, 1973), pp. 7–12. p. 8.
29 Johnson, 'southwell, the chapter house...', *The Unfortunates*, p. 1.
30 Johnson, 'that short occasion in Brighton...', *The Unfortunates*, p. 1.
31 Jonathan Coe, 'Preface', in B.S. Johnson, *The Unfortunates*, p. ix.
32 Johnson, 'The pitch worn...', *The Unfortunates*, p. 1.
33 Johnson, 'Away from the ground...', *The Unfortunates*, p. 1.
34 Guignery, p. 242.
35 Ibid.
36 Frank Kermode, *The Sense of an Ending: Studies in the Theory of Fiction* (Oxford: University of Oxford Press, 1967), p. 132.
37 Saussure, pp. 191–2.
38 'E' is missing, or perhaps 'e (French pron. 'he').
39 Johnson, 'the pitch was worn...', *The Unfortunates*, p. 12.
40 Billany, *The Trap*, p. 149.
41 Raymond Queneau, *Exercises de style* (Paris: Gallimard, 1947), p. 95.
42 Jean-François Bory, *Post-scriptum* (Paris: Eric Losfield Editeur, 1970), p. 158.
43 Wittgenstein, p. 45.
44 Raphael Rubinstein, 'Gathered, Not Made: A Brief History of Appropriative Writing', *Ubuweb* www.ubu.com/papers/Rubinstein.html (accessed 4 September 2013).
45 Queneau, 'La Littérature définitionnelle', p. 119.
46 Ibid.
47 Stefan Themerson, in Rubinstein, p. 1.
48 Rubinstein, p. 1.
49 Billany, *The Cage*, p. 34.
50 Raymond Queneau, *Zazie dans le métro* (Paris: Gallimard, 1959), p. 9.
51 Albert Doppagne, 'Le Néologisme chez Raymond Queneau', *Cahiers de l'Association Internationale des études francaises*, 1973, no 25. pp. 91–107. p. 93.
52 Ibid.
53 Billany, *The Cage*, p. 78.
54 Ibid., p. 79.
55 Jacques Derrida, 'Signature événement contexte', p. 368.
56 'those on the margins must use resistant reading practices, secondary discursivity and lateral communication to reinforce always frail constellated communities': Altman, p. 205.
57 Umberto Eco, *From the Tree to the Labyrinth: Historical Studies on the Sign and Interpretation* [*Dall'albero al labirinto. Studi storici sul segno e l'interpretazione*, 2007] trans. Anthony Oldcorn (London: Harvard University Press, 2014), p. 237.

58 This argument will be returned to below.
59 Johnson, *House Mother Normal*, p. 163.
60 Tredell, p. 105.
61 Ibid.
62 Ibid.
63 Wittgenstein, p. 64.
64 Doppagne, p. 104.
65 Michel de Certeau, 'Utopies vocales: glossalalies', *Traverses 20 : la voix, l'écoute* November 1980, pp. 26–37.
66 Ibid., p. 29.
67 Allen S. Weiss, *Shattered Forms: Art Brut, Phantasms, Modernism* (New York: SUNY Press, 1992), p. 81
68 Certeau, p. 33.
69 Ibid., p. 36.
70 Ibid., p. 26.
71 Gilles Deleuze, *Logique du sens* (Paris: Éditions de Minuit, 1969), p. 94.
72 Jean Dubuffet, letter to Jacques Berne (16 December 1946), *Lettres à J.B.: 1946–1985* (Paris: Hermann, 1991), p. 1.
73 Michel Thévoz, 'Introduction', *Écrits bruts*, ed. Michel Thévoz (Paris: PUF, 1979), pp. 5–13. p. 6.
74 Jean Dubuffet, *l'Art brut préféré aux valeurs culturelles*, preface to the catalogue of the exhibition organized in 1949 at the Galerie Drouin, Paris.
75 Thévoz, p. 5.
76 Ibid., p. 6.
77 Weiss, p. 86.
78 Octave Mannoni, 'Writing and Madness: Schreber als Schreiber', *Psychosis and Sexual Identity: Towards a Post-Analytic View of the Schreber Case*, eds. David B. Allison, Prado de Oliveira, Mark S. Roberts, Allen S. Weiss (Albany: SUNY Press, 1988), pp. 43–60. p. 58.
79 Annette, 'Le Feuilleton de la Qonestsans' (1942), in *Écrits bruts*, ed. Michel Thévoz (Paris: PUF, 1979), pp. 41–54. p. 42.
80 Anne Beyer, in Annette, 'Le Feuilleton de la Qonestsans', p. 42.
81 Georges Perec, *Les Revenentes* (1972) (Paris: Julliard, 1991).
82 Ibid., p. 7.
83 Michel Thévoz, in Annette, 'Le Feuilleton de la Qonestsans', pp. 41–2.
84 Weiss, p. 83.
85 Ibid., pp. 82–3.
86 Danièle André-Carraz, *L'Expérience intérieure d'Antonin Artaud* (Paris: Editions Saint-Germain-de-Prés, 1973), p. 139.

87 Antonin Artaud, 'Le Mômo', Œuvres complètes (Paris: Gallimard, 1976), p. 1139.
88 André-Carraz, p. 138.
89 Antonin Artaud, 'Le Mômo' galley margin fragment, Œuvres complètes (Paris: Gallimard, 1976), p. 1141.
90 Weiss, p. 84.
91 Ibid.
92 J. M. G. Le Clézio, La Guerre (1970) (Paris: Gallimard, 2008), p. 87.
93 Roland Topor, 'La Politique de l'archipel', Mutations: Zigzag Poésie. Formes et mouvements: l'effervescence, eds. Frank Smith and Christophe Fauchon, no. 203, 2001, p. 284.
94 David Toop, 'Language & Paralanguage of the Sacred' (1973), Notes from the Cosmic Typewriter: The Life and Work of Dom Sylvester Houédard, ed. Nicola Simpson (London: Occasional Papers, 2012) pp. 11–18. p. 13.
95 Gustav Metzger, 'Auto-Destructive Art' (1995), Damaged Nature, Auto-Destructive Art (Nottingham: Coracle, 1996), pp. 25–63. p. 27.
96 This problematic of utter dissolution of quotidian meaning does not appear present, or perhaps possible, in the scale of written communication in the novel as approached here – Artaud's readers as described below, approach his texts as those of a 'visionary' or 'mystic' which a priori codifies his writing as a genrefied literature.
97 Antonin Artaud, 'Position de la chair', Œuvres complètes (Paris: Gallimard, 1976), p. 51.
98 Toop, p. 15.
99 Beckett, '9 July 1937, Kaun', footnote 8, p. 521.
100 Félix Guattari, 'Notes on Power and Meaning' (1975), Schizo-Culture: The Event, eds. Sylvère Lotringer and David Morris (Los Angeles: Semiotext(e), 2013), pp. 182–3. p. 182.
101 Jean Baudrillard, L'Échange symbolique et la mort (Paris: Gallimard, 1976), p. 296.
102 Guattari, 'Notes on Power and Meaning', p. 182.
103 Gilbert Adair, 'Introduction', in Raymond Queneau, Zazie in the Metro (Zazie dans le métro, 1959), trans. Barbara Wright (London: Penguin, 2000), pp. vii–xiii. p. ix.
104 Johnson, Albert Angelo, p. 158.
105 Ibid., p. 160.
106 Céline, p. 64.
107 Ibid., p. 16.
108 Céline appears here to forget he too would come under the umbrella of 'the public'.
109 Ibid., p. 46.

110 Michel Bigot, *Michel Bigot présente Zazie dans le métro par Raymond Queneau* (Paris: Gallimard, 1994), p. 20.
111 Doppagne, p. 91.
112 However, we might wish, can the human be said to be the emotive element in this context? Or must this now be classified as pre-post-human? Or not-yet-post-human?
113 Jean Charles Chabanne, 'Queneau et la linguistique', *Raymond Queneau et les langages : colloque de Thionville 1992* eds. André Blavier and Claude Debon (Paris: Temps Mêlés, 1993), pp 23–55. p. 26.
114 Weiss, p. 4.
115 Ibid., p. 95.
116 Daniel Delbreil, 'Quenomatopées', *Raymond Queneau et les langages: colloque de Thionville 1992*, eds. André Blavier and Claude Debon (Paris: Temps Mêlés, 1993), pp. 135–56. p. 140.
117 Ibid.
118 Beckett, '9 July 1937, Kaun', p. 519.
119 Craig Dworkin and Kenneth Goldsmith, 'Brion Gysin: First Cut-Ups', *Against Expression: An Anthology of Conceptual Writing*, eds. Craig Dworkin and Kenneth Goldsmith (Evanston: Northwestern University Press, 2011), pp. 295–6. p. 295.
120 Dworkin and Goldsmith, p. 295.
121 Alan Burns, in Sugnet and Burns, 'Alan Burns', p. 166.
122 Raymond Queneau, 'Mode d'emploi', *Cent mille milliards de poèmes* (Paris: Gallimard, 1961), p. i.
123 Ibid.
124 Carl Darryl Malmgren, *Fictional Space in the Modernist and Postmodernist American Novel* (Lewisburg: Bucknell University Press, 1985), p. 153.
125 Ibid.
126 Ibid.
127 Ibid.
128 Ibid.
129 William Burroughs and Brion Gysin, *The Exterminator* (1960) (San Francisco: Dave Haselwood Books, 1967), p. 41.
130 Ibid., p. 11.
131 Brion Gysin, 'Brion Gysin: First Cut-Ups', *Against Expression: An Anthology of Conceptual Writing*, eds. Craig Dworkin and Kenneth Goldsmith (Evanston: Northwestern University Press, 2011), pp.295–6. p. 296.
132 Dworkin and Goldsmith, p. 295.
133 Burns, *Babel*, p. 141.

134 Ibid., back cover.
135 Madden, 'Alan Burns: An Introduction', p. 113.
136 Ibid.
137 Gustav Metzger, Gustav Metzger and Hans Ulrich Obrist, *Gustav Metzger* (Köln: Verlag der Buchhandlung Walther König, 2008), p. 26.
138 Ibid., p. 27.
139 Johnson, *Albert Angelo*, pp. 147–9.
140 Alan Burns, *The Angry Brigade: A Documentary Novel* (London: Quartet, 1973).
141 Ibid., p. 2.
142 Burns, Sugnet and Burns, p. 164.
143 Burns, in Madden and Burns, 'In Conversation with Alan Burns'.
144 Metzger, in Metzger and Obrist, p. 34.
145 Obrist, in Metzger and Obrist, p. 36.
146 Metzger, in Metzger and Obrist, p. 29.
147 Ibid., p. 11.
148 Perec, in Venaille and Perec, p. 100.
149 Ibid., p. 99.
150 Sigmund Freud, *The Interpretation of Dreams* [*Die Traumdeutung*, 1899], trans. A.A. Brill (London: Wordsworth Editions, 1997), p. 58.
151 Ibid.
152 Perec, in Venaille and Perec, p. 97.
153 William S. Burroughs, Conrad Knickerbocker and William S. Burroughs, 'William S. Burroughs, The Art of Fiction No. 36', *The Paris Review*, http://www.theparisreview.org/interviews/4424/the-art-of-fiction-no-36-william-s-burroughs (accessed 9 June 2015).
154 Conrad Knickerbocker and William S. Burroughs, 'William S. Burroughs, The Art of Fiction No. 36', p. 1.
155 Robin Lydenberg, *Word Cultures: Radical Theory and Practice in William S. Burroughs' Fiction* (Urbana: University of Illinois Press, 1987), p. 73.
156 Sigmund Freud, *The Interpretation of Dreams*, p. 170.
157 Ibid.
158 Lydenberg, p. 73.
159 Malmgren, p. 154.
160 Thus, potentially, the result of the process of reading 'will vary from individual to individual', but indeed 'only within the limits imposed by the written as opposed to the unwritten text' (Iser, *The Implied Reader*, p. 282), that is the outfolding frame of the novel, which implies both limitation, but too an opening up. The schema I feel most fitting to describe this is the *fata morgana*, which akin to a mirage, is a manifest vision of an object that does not exist. Looking out to sea,

above the horizon in the sky is witnessed a huge, magnified and disintegrated object, fluid and changeable, from one witness' point of view the object appears different to the next witness standing next to them, if the witness was to leave and return later the object would appear different. In this the visual object is the same viewed presence, and yet appears different to different observers at different footings, and to the same observer at a different time. Like communicated meaning, it synchronises with a different position within the reader depending on the fluid dynamic of that interiority. What is singular to the *fata morgana* phenomenon is that, though too far away to notice the originating source, it is an oblique reflection of a singular and concrete object. Below the disintegrated and magnified reflection is the miniscule and indiscernible singular, concrete object from which these huge and fluid projections are created. For example, a ship, or a rock. And yet to the viewer is presented a huge demonic ghost ship, or magic shifting mountain. These images can appear more or less as simulacra of their base object, they can be flipped or maintained, appear backwards, jumbled, broken up. To some degree this aligns with the readerly schema of stargazing laid down by Wolfgang Iser in *The Implied Reader*: 'two people gazing at the night sky may both be looking at the same collection of stars, but one will see the image of a plough, and the other will make out a dipper. The "stars" in a literary text are fixed; the lines that join them are variable' (ibid.). While this maintains the variable of connection of (a) 'fixed point(s)', Iser's analogy implies the ability to utterly recreate another's derivation of meaning, which this partition indicates is difficult, if not, as a totality, impossible. The *fata morgana* mutation of that image then accounts for this variation.

161 Ibid., p. 155.
162 Ibid.
163 William S. Burroughs, 'The Cut-Up Method of Brion Gysin', *The Third Mind* (New York: The Viking Press, 1978), pp. 31–5. pp. 33–4.
164 Burns, *Babel*, p. 150.
165 Malmgren, p. 155.
166 Lydenberg, p. 73.
167 Ibid., p. 73.
168 Johnson, 'that short occasion in Brighton', *The Unfortunates*, p. 2.
169 Coe, in ibid., p. xiv.
170 Buchanan, p. 55.
171 Tom Uglow, 'Introduction', Marc Saporta, *Composition no. 1* (1962, trans. Richard Howard (London: Visual Éditions, 2011), p. 1.
172 Marc Saporta, 'le lecteur est prié de battre ces pages', *Composition no. 1* (Paris: Éditions du Seuil, 1962), p. 1.

173 Kaye Mitchell, 'The Unfortunates: Hypertext, Linearity and the Act of Reading', Re-Reading B.S. Johnson, eds. Philip Tew et al. (London: Palgrave, 2007), pp. 51–64. pp. 51–2.
174 Johnson, 'So he came to his parents at Brighton. . .', The Unfortunates, p. 4.
175 Locked in referentiality, it is again, a result of a dice throw.
176 Johnson, 'So he came to his parents at Brighton. . .', The Unfortunates, p. 5.
177 Saporta, 'Les sentinelles ont été placées. . .', Composition no. 1, p. 1.
178 This critique appears present in the 'otherness' of the 'uncivilized' Moroccan soldiers as other, assured to the reader 'prone to barbarism', yet that separation is essentially a shallow vanity, that slips away as the brutality of the scene takes hold.
179 Justin Huggler, 'Allied soldiers "raped hundreds of thousands of German women" after WW2', The Telegraph 6 March 2015, http://www.telegraph.co.uk/news/worldnews/europe/germany/11455664/Allied-soldiers-raped-hundreds-of-thousands-of-German-women-after-WW2.html (accessed 7 March 2015).
180 Saporta, 'Helga commence à flamber. . .', Composition no. 1, p. 1.
181 Saporta, 'Helga n'oppose plus aucune résistance', Composition no. 1, p. 1.
182 Saporta, 'Helga bat dans la main comme un bengali prisonnier', Composition no. 1, p. 1.
183 Johanna Drucker, Sweet Dreams: Contemporary Art and Complicity (Chicago: University of Chicago Press, 2005), p. 2.
184 Billany, The Cage, pp. 1–2.
185 Craig Dworkin, Reading the Illegible (Evanston: Northwestern University Press, 2003), pp. 74–5.
186 Drucker, p. 2.
187 Perec, 'Robert Antelme, ou la verité de la littérature', p. 91.
188 Ibid.
189 Ibid., p. 95.
190 Again, in the sense of realizing there is something horrifically wrong.
191 Perec, 'Robert Antelme, ou la verité de la littérature', p. 91.
192 Ibid., p. 94.
193 Ibid., p. 94.
194 To reiterate this point, it is this suffering, this perpetation of suffering, that is effaced by 'Les Trentes Glorieuses'. In which it is a cultural veil that falsely imposes a discontinuity in human experience, despite the humans themselves continuing – where the experience of victim and perpetrator is given little representation in cultural representation. Both in the moment recently passed, and the continuation of those humans in the new 'peaceful' post-war world of flower power. It is an obscured experiential violence at the heart of post-war

societal continuation that the experimental novel therefore perhaps here indicates despite that effacement.
195 Jean-Yves Pouilloux, 'Trompe-l'œil', *Critique*, no. 503 April 1989, pp. 265 and 268.
196 Uglow, 'Introduction', p. 1.
197 Viz. the separation of the shared writerly-readerly genesis of the textual void partition one.
198 His readerly input is that of 'dead hands', rather than the 'living hands' that shuffle the deck elsewhere.
199 Joanna Gavins, *Text World Theory 21.03.13: An Event as Part of 'Suppose I Call a Man a Horse, or a Horse a Man?' Anna Barham's Residency at Site Gallery, Sheffield, 09.02–23.03.13* [text accompanying exhibition], p. 2.
200 Perec, *Je me souviens*, pp. 147–9.
201 Green, in Green and Southern, 'Paris Review Interview', p. 244.
202 Beckett, '9 July 1937, Kaun', p. 519.

Index

Aarseth, Espen 130
   Ergodic literature 130–1
Adorno, Theodor 13, 67, 69–70, 97
Altman, Rick 138
Amis, Kingsley 35, 37
Annette 143, 144, 145, 148, 149, 150, 151–2, 154
Apollinaire, Guillaume 27
Arnaud, Noël 40, 41–2, 43
   Paralittérature 40, 41
Arrabal, Fernando 15
Arrested Development 170–1
Artaud, Antonin 145, 146, 148, 149
avant-garde realism 7, 18, 21, 26, 64, 71, 83

Badiou, Alain 5, 47–8, 54
Balzac, Honoré de 24, 26, 27, 39, 47, 67
Barth, John 4, 27
Barthes, Roland 38
Bassil-Morozow, Helena 6, 11
Baudelaire, Charles 2, 12
Baudrillard, Jean 149
Béalu, Marcel 78, 85, 99, 104, 117–18, 120, 122
   Journal d'un mort 78–9, 99, 117–18
   L'Experiénce de la nuit 104
Beauvoir, Simone de 21
Beckett, Samuel 2, 128, 140, 148, 154, 159–60, 172
   Logoclasts' League 148, 154, 159, 172
Benjamin, Walter 64, 65, 122
Berman, Marshall 6–7, 11
Bernard, Claude x
Billany, Dan 16, 29, 35–6, 109–12, 119, 122, 123, 134–5, 136–7, 139, 145–6, 148, 167–8, 171, 172
   The Cage 16, 109, 110–11, 112, 123, 136–7, 167–8, 172
   The Trap 29, 35–6, 111, 134
Blanchot, Maurice 25, 163
Bory, Jean-François 134

Bourdieu, Pierre 35, 59, 140, 151
Bowen, John 35
Breton, André 27, 30, 47
Brooke-Rose, Christine 10, 12, 15, 18, 43, 44, 60, 105–6
   A Rhetoric of the Unreal 44, 60
   Invisible Author: Last Essays 10
   Such 105–6
Brophy, Brigid 15, 22, 25, 35, 52, 56, 60–1, 84, 89, 101
   Black Ship to Hell 52, 60–1
   In Transit 25, 56, 101
   'the perpetual cinema show' 60–1, 89
Burns, Alan 37, 72–4, 74–5, 77–8, 113, 116, 118, 154–5, 156–7, 158–9, 163, 164
   Babel 95, 156–7, 163
   Cut-up 154–5
   Europe After the Rain 72–3, 113, 116, 118
   The Angry Brigade: A Documentary Novel 158–9
Burroughs, William Seward (S.) 32–3, 43, 154–6, 160–1, 162
   Cut-up 154–6, 160–1, 162
Burt, Jonathan 121
Bury, Pol 15, 63
Butor, Michel 18, 22, 24, 39, 46, 67, 99, 102–3, 142
   La Modification 99, 102–3

Cage, John 131
Calder, John 33, 43, 99, 157
Carrington, Leonora 99, 108–9, 115, 145
   The Hearing Trumpet 99, 108–9
Céline, Louis-Ferdinand 42, 127, 131, 150, 151
   Entretiens avec le Professeur Y 127, 131, 150, 151
Certeau, Michel de 139–40, 148, 151
   Glossolalia 139–40
Charbonnier, Georges 130

Chekhov, Anton 158
  's Gun 158
Chesterton, Gilbert Keith (G. K.) 58
Cixous, Hélène 37
Cluedo 164
Coe, Jonathan 94, 132, 164
Cooper, David Graham (D. G.) 74, 101
Cooper, William 34

Dada 3, 33
Davies, Hugh Sykes 15, 79, 121–2
  The Papers of Andrew Melmoth 79, 121–2
Defoe, Daniel 130
Deleuze, Gilles 63, 140
Derrida, Jacques 82, 84, 122, 137
Descartes, René 105, 114
Drucker, Johanna 167, 168
Dubuffet, Jean 11, 19, 36–7, 56, 141–2, 149
Duvignaud, Jean 62
Dworkin, Craig 126

Eagleton, Terry 95–6, 161
Écrits bruts 127, 141–3, 151–2
electroshock therapy (ECT) 115, 146
Eliot, George 47
Eliot, Thomas Stearns (T. S.) 15, 150
Ernst, Max 72
experimental 23–6, 34, 63, 74, 163
  experimental novel ix, 7, 8, 13, 15–16, 17–18, 19–20, 21, 22, 24, 27–8, 34, 39, 43, 44–6, 63–4, 83, 94–7, 160–2
  experimental romantics 18, 19–20, 27–30, 97, 137

Fantastic, the 19, 59, 61, 70, 72, 79, 81, 82, 83, 85, 87–8, 119, 142
Fata morgana 162
Figes, Eva 15, 16, 37, 66, 75–6, 101
  B 75–6
  Nelly's Version 101
Fisher, Mark 45, 46, 51, 57, 59, 85, 97
Flaubert, Gustav 47
Foucault, Michel 63, 91
Freud, Sigmund 9, 36, 58, 71, 98, 114, 160, 161
  the rebus house 161–2
Frye, Northrop 95

Genette, Gérard 3–4, 5, 94, 129
Ghose, Zulfikar 15, 20, 61, 87
  The Contradictions 20, 61, 87
Gollancz, Victor 48–9, 50, 52, 67
Green, Henry 37, 39, 47, 79–81, 82, 84, 86, 88, 109, 112, 172
  Back 79–80, 84, 112
Gross, Otto 111, 112–13, 115–16
  thanatophilia 113, 125, 146
Guattari, Félix 63, 149
Gysin, Brion 154–6
  cut-up 154–6, 161–2

Hains, Raymond & Villeglé, Jacques 154
Harris, Wilson 15, 25, 95, 161
Harvey, David 2–3, 48
Hassan, Ihab 3
Heppenstall, Rayner 14, 16, 29, 31–2, 33, 38, 80, 84, 86, 90, 91, 93, 94, 96–7, 114, 142
  Sorge 84–5, 86, 98, 111, 170
  The Connecting Door 86, 90, 91, 93, 94, 97, 114
  The Lesser Infortune 80
  Two Moons 94
Horkheimer, Max 50–1, 55, 57–8, 85
Hull 134

Iser, Wolfgang 12–13, 20, 95–6
Isou, Isidore 130

Jabès, Edmond 71
Jaccard, Roland 111–12
Jameson, Fredric 2, 9, 12, 14, 59
Johnson, Bryan Stanley (B. S.) 4–5, 16, 22, 29, 31, 32, 35, 37, 41, 42, 43, 45, 56, 75, 77–8, 89, 90, 91–2, 93, 94, 96–7, 99, 100–1, 103–4, 114, 115, 120, 128, 131–3, 135, 138, 142, 149–50, 158, 159, 163–5, 170, 171, 172
  Albert Angelo 95, 149–50, 154, 158, 159
  Christie Malry's Own Double-Entry 99, 100–1, 103–4
  House Mother Normal 75, 89–90, 91, 92–3, 94, 97, 99–100, 103, 120, 138–9, 170
  The Unfortunates 75, 103–4, 128, 131–3, 134, 138, 163–5

Travelling People 138
Trawl 75
You're Human Like the Rest of Them 56
Johnson, Samuel (Dr.) 34
Joyce, James 12, 27, 31, 47, 48

Kafka, Franz 10, 12, 14, 47, 48, 101
Kavan, Anna 52, 57, 60
   Ice 52, 57, 60
Kermode, Frank 2, 132
Kierkegaard, Søren 14

Laing, Ronald David (R. D.) 74, 101
Le Clézio, Jean-Marie Gustave (J. M. G.) 147
Le Lionnais, François 16, 40
Lovecraft, Howard Phillips (H. P.) 146

MacDiarmid, Hugh 32, 43,
Mackay, Marina 8–10, 35, 53, 54, 62
McHale, Brian 2
Malevich, Kazimir 125–6, 128
Mannoni, Octave 142–3
Marlowe, Christopher (Kit) 158
Metzger, Gustav 15, 148, 157–8, 159–60
   auto-destructive art 148, 157–8, 159–60
Miéville, China 83
modernism-postmodernism 2–11, 27, 30, 44–5, 48, 54, 58
   intermodernism 8–10
   midmodernism 8–10
   permamodernism 8–10
myopic-amnesia x, 6, 17, 51, 64, 65, 66, 72, 75, 80, 84, 85, 86, 88, 89, 90, 92, 97, 101–2, 122, 131

Noys, Benjamin 54–5, 56, 58–9

Paz, Octavio 71
Perec, Georges 14–15, 16, 17, 20, 25, 28, 29, 37, 38, 55, 61, 62, 67, 68–9, 76–7, 78, 86, 118, 126, 133, 143–4, 160–1, 168–9, 171–2
   La Disparition 133, 144
   Cut-up 160, 171–2
   Je me souviens 76, 160, 171–2
   La Vie mode d'emploi 160
   Les Choses 55
   Les Revenentes 143–4

Quel petit vélo à guidon chrome au fond de la cour? 118
W ou le souvenir d'enfance 76–7, 160
Pinget, Robert 70, 77, 85, 97
   Cette voix 77
   Entre Fantoine et Agapa 85
   Passacaille 70
Powell, Michael 102
   Peeping Tom 102
Proust, Marcel 12

Queneau, Raymond 17, 29, 32, 39, 40, 55–6, 63, 69, 109–10, 118, 126, 130, 134–5, 136, 139, 143, 148, 149, 151–2, 153, 154–5
   Cent mille milliards de poèmes (1961) 154–5
   Exercices de style (1947) 134–5
   Le Vol d'Icare (1968) 55–6, 109–10, 126
   Littérature Définitionelle (Definitional Literature) 32, 135–6
   Une Histoire modèle 63
   Zazie dans le métro (1959) 118–19, 136, 139, 149, 151, 153, 154
Quin, Ann 37, 95, 118, 119, 172
   Passages 95, 118
   Tripticks 119, 172

Rancière, Jacques 11–12, 54
   Les Temps modernes 11–12
Ray, Man 168
   Lautgedicht 168
Rimbaud, Arthur 161
Robbe-Grillet, Alain 2, 4, 20, 21–2, 23, 32, 33, 38, 40, 41, 142
Roche, Maurice 27, 40, 77, 95, 96
   Codex 95, 96
   Compact 40, 96
Ruskin, John 86
Russell, Bertrand 32

Sansom, William 66–7, 68, 69
Saporta, Marc 164, 166–7, 168, 169, 170, 172,
   Composition no. 1 164, 166–7, 168, 170, 172
Saroyan, Aram 130
Sarraute, Nathalie 4–5, 15, 20, 21, 22, 39, 125

Sartre, Jean-Paul 21, 22, 27, 38, 41, 48–9, 52, 59, 69, 90
Saussure, Ferdinand de 129, 133, 134–5, 140, 149, 151
Simon, Claude 113
Smith, Hélène 140, 144, 148
social realism 18–19, 31, 34–5, 37–8, 40, 44–6, 55, 58, 73, 78, 97
Sollers, Philippe 13, 26–7, 29, 40, 45, 52–3, 96
Spark, Muriel 40
Sterne, Laurence 27, 33–4
Stevenson, Randall 105
Stiegler, Bernard 98
Storey, David 35
Sugnet, Charles 46, 158
surrealism 27, 48

Tacitus 59–60
Tardieu, Jean 75
Themerson, Stefan 15, 31–2, 43, 51, 58, 70, 74, 94, 117, 135, 137, 143, 172
   Bayamus 31–2, 51, 74, 135
   Professor Mmaa's Lecture 117, 172
   Semantic Poetry Translation (SPT) 32, 94, 135–6
   Special Branch 58
Thévoz, Michel 149
Todorov, Tzvetan 10, 14
Tolstoy, Leo 47
Toop, David 148
Topor, Roland 14–15, 16–17, 28, 33, 42, 43, 57, 63, 77, 84, 98, 99, 100, 102, 105, 106–8, 109, 113, 127, 128–30, 131, 137, 147, 148, 164, 165, 168, 172
   Erika 114–15, 127–9, 130, 137, 165, 168
   Joko fête son anniversaire 107–8, 109
   Le Locataire chimérique 98, 99, 100, 105, 106–7, 109, 113, 115, 116, 120–1
   Psychotopor 164
   Souvenir 77, 168
Toynbee, Arnold 2
Trocchi, Alexander 32–3
Turing, Alan 155

Vian, Boris 41, 42, 119
Virilio, Paul 56, 62

Wain, John 35, 37
Waterhouse, Keith 35
Waugh, Patricia 126
Weiss, Allen S. 140, 144, 146–7, 148, 152
White, Hayden 126
Wilhelm II, Kaiser 142
Williams, Raymond 8–9, 20, 24, 26
Wittgenstein, Ludwig 126, 128, 129, 131, 135, 139, 152
Woolf, Virginia 31

Yonnet, Jacques 81–2, 83–4, 87, 88, 89
   Enchantements sur Paris (Rue des Maléfices) 81–2, 88, 89
   Le Cabaret des inconnus 83

Žižek, Slavoj 70, 73
Zaum 125–6, 127–8
Zola, Émile x, 21–2, 23, 27, 29, 46, 65, 96
   Le Roman expérimental x, 21–3

www.ingramcontent.com/pod-product-compliance
Lightning Source LLC
Chambersburg PA
CBHW052041300426
44117CB00012B/1926